D0905331

Table of Contents

Acknowledgements

With a project of this magnitude, there are inevitably many people one must thank for their help and encouragement throughout the journey, which began in 1995. The first is Devra Hall, daughter of guitar legend Jim Hall, who was essential in helping me put the many pages of random ideas into a cohesive format that allowed me to proceed with clarity after a year or so of being idle. Peter Levinson generously offered his time and expertise as an author, agent, and friend; his enthusiasm for my work gave me hope on those days when I thought I was getting nothing done. Peter put me in touch with my agent Rich Barber, whose hard work is partly responsible for this book and to whom I offer my sincere gratitude.

I have many wonderful friends and colleagues who generously gave their thoughts, advice, ideas, encouragement, and whose presence at many of my gigs inspired me more than they know: Florence Manos, Cary Fonseca, Melinda Gardner, Ree Case, author Linda Laucella, Nora Tribys, trumpeters Craig du Plessis and Hagai Izraeli, Iris Falk, Nancy McFarland, jazz vocalist and historian Pam Laws, Sarah Booth, Kenny Burrell (jazz guitar legend and director of jazz studies at UCLA) and my former teacher, Professor Lindsey B. Sarjeant.

Beth Klein assisted me in organizing my sources, including my bibliography and discography, and many of the bios, as well as introducing me to Powell's Books in Portland, Oregon, which has the greatest collection of books on jazz I have seen so far. My best friends, Roy Parham and Allen Halliman III, have always been there to give me a laugh when I needed it, as well as being a sounding board for all things positive. Lily Beth Auycud organized and helped to catalog my vast CD collection. Dr. Kevin Eisensmith and the International Trumpet Guild gave me opportunity to present my work in a lecture during its developmental process. Thank you to Michael Cogswell and the staff at the Louis Armstrong Archives at Queens College for the opportunity to come into contact with all things Louis Armstrong; Bruce Raeburn and the entire staff at the Hogan Jazz Archives of Tulane University in New Orleans; Lorraine Gordon of the Village Vanguard for the Jabbo Smith photo; Doug Lawrence for the Buck Clayton photo.

Dave Monette continues to make me the best trumpets I could ever hope to play. He makes it easier for me to make music and his initial feedback on my work was very helpful. Thank you to Tom Raney for his help with finding and sending important photos, and the rest of the staff of the Monette Corporation for their hard work. I am deeply fortunate to work with the terrific students and faculty at Florida State University College of Music and the Department of Jazz Studies. A special thank you to my department chair, Professor Leon Anderson; Dean Don Gibson, Dean Jon Piersol, Dean Clifford Madsen, Dee Beggarly; and several of my students, Matt Postle, Thomas Warner, Corey Jay, and David Bell for their research assistance.

Many thanks to my publisher, John Cerullo, for understanding the importance of this work; my production editor, Belinda Yong, whose professionalism and patience were essential to the completion of this project; and my publicity manager, Jenna Young, for her enthusiasm and boundless energy. I am grateful to Nicole Julius, Doug Lady, Brad Smith, Larry Morton, and the rest of the staff at Hal Leonard for their support. And thank you to my editors, Leslie Kriesel and Mike Edison. Debbie Happy Cohen gave me great advice and counseling as author, businesswoman, and a dear friend, and her energy inspires me to work harder. My attorney, Steven Soden, puts my mind at ease with his expertise in law. I am especially grateful to Jack Bradley of Cape Cod, Massachusetts, a close friend of Louis Armstrong's: thank you to you and your wife, Nancy, for opening your home and incredible collection of never-before-seen photos and materials of Louis Armstrong, Miles Davis, and many other jazz legends to me. Allowing me to play yet another of Louis Armstrong's trumpets and insisting that I try on one of his suit coats are experiences I'll never forget. I am still astounded at what you have amassed and I thank you from the bottom of my heart for your generosity. This book is a tribute to you as well.

Heather Taylor, my web-site designer, book cover designer, and dear friend, was a partner during the most crucial steps of shaping this book over the last four or five years. She e-mailed me designs based on my ideas within hours of them. Her quick response resulted in several designs and redesigns that culminated to the product in your hands. She is an exceptionally talented graphic artist and I am deeply grateful for all of her exceptional hard work with the photos, designing the maps and illustrations, other research, great ideas, but, most of all, her enthusiasm. Any design studio would be privileged to have Heather's incredible talents.

Further, I would like to thank my family for always supporting me and my career. My mother, Shirley Ann Showers Barnhart, bestowed to me her talents of music and writing; my father, Johnny E. Barnhart, Jr., instilled in me the desire to work hard and not complain about it; my brother, Johnny E. "Kippy" Barnhart III, has always been supportive and taught me my first song on the trumpet; my sister, Sherry Ann Barnhart, allowed me use her bedroom to practice while we were in high school; and my uncle, Faterrell Showers, bought me a new trumpet when I needed one back in 1980. And to my late granduncle and namesake, William Terrell, whose friendship and love of jazz continues to be a major source of inspiration for me nearly twenty years since his passing. Thanks for playing my first Clifford Brown recording, leaving me your jazz collection, and also buying me a new trumpet in 1985. I'll never forget and promise to do the same for someone else one day soon.

Andrew Reiss provided me with a first-class jazz club that allowed me to work on my craft for all of those years (Andrew's Upstairs). Thank you to Ron Blessing, Steve Turre, Alvin Spencer

Walker II, Endre Rice, James Houston Leary III, Jose Bevia, Fiona Bloom, Melissa Walker, Frank Capp, Michelle Martinez, Dr. Lee Anne Martinez, Marvin E. Lewis, the rest of the Barnhart family, the Showers family, Ebenezer Baptist Church, Dr. Joseph L. Roberts Jr., Mrs. Christine King Farris, and the entire King family. Of course, a very special thank you to the Count Basie Orchestra.

I would like to acknowledge the men and women for whom this book is written. Some I only know through their legend and their music, some are my friends of many years, and others have since become friends while I worked on this book. Sonny Cohn was one of my first mentors. Freddie Hubbard showed me what was possible on the trumpet. Wynton Marsalis has inspired me for more than twenty years to be the best trumpeter and musician I could ever be and has always been generous with his time and efforts to see that others had what they needed to play this music we call jazz. Thank you for your contribution to the world of jazz and jazz education. My thanks to Frank Driggs, Dan Morgenstern, Tad Hershorn, and the Institute of Jazz Studies at Rutgers University, Bennie and Barbara Maupin, Kenneth Garrett and Patty Healy for the photo of the trumpets of King Tutankhamun, Rosemary Cord at Chuck Mangione's office, and Cynthia Sesso at CTSImages.com.

Finally, a very heartfelt thank you to Clark Terry, Snooky Young, Harry "Sweets" Edison, Nat Adderley, Freddie Hubbard, Clora Bryant, Joe Wilder, Humphrey Lyttleton, Jimmy Owens, Warren Vache, Sonny Cohn, Arvell Shaw, Maynard Ferguson, Joe Williams and Frank Sinatra, Randy Brecker, Stjepko Gut, bassist Laymon Jackson, Gunhild Carling, Charles Tolliver, Valery Ponomarev, Bobby Bradford, Ted Curson, Jack and Diane Sheldon, Barrie Lee Hall, Wendell Brunious, Gerald Wilson, Chuck Mangione, and Tony Bennett—who all gave generously of their time and experiences to help make this work possible. Your profound wisdom along with the million laughs will always be appreciated and never forgotten.

Scotty Barnhart
September 2005

Foreword

It is our pleasure to write the foreword to this book. This book is the first of its kind, a book about the world of jazz trumpet, *by a jazz trumpeter*.

You have in your hands a valuable document. *The World of Jazz Trumpet* is written with an authoritative, scholarly, and pleasingly interesting flare. Scotty has connected the dots from our African roots to our African-American experience with rare and refreshing personal insight. The two of us helped to create the world of jazz trumpet, and we understand better than anyone the importance of passing this art form on to future generations. This book will go a very long way in making sure it is done correctly.

We've both had the pleasure of playing with Scotty, one of the very best of a new generation of jazz musicians. He has a complete understanding of the work of the musicians who preceded him—it is obvious to anyone who has heard him that he has been diligent in studying this music—and he is sincere in his effort to see that it continues.

Through Scotty's thoughtful interviews, the personal stories of jazz trumpet pioneers are revealed in startling detail, and we were proud to contribute inside information that has not been printed anywhere else before. Scotty discusses the recorded work of the most influential trumpeters from every era of jazz, and places them in the proper context, establishing each trumpeter's unique contribution to the art. The practical philosophy section is also enlightening, offering valuable insight into the tribulations of playing that all jazz trumpeters face.

The World of Jazz Trumpet by Scotty Barnhart is a most welcome addition to our history as jazz musicians in the United States. Finally someone has taken the time to put together a volume that encompasses the full range of what we have given, and continue to give. It could not have been written any better than this, and we know. After all, we were there.

Clark Terry and Freddie Hubbard
October 2005

Introduction

When I was nine years old, I asked my parents for a violin. At that age, of course, I had no idea that I had asked a trick question. That became apparent when my mother returned home from the music store all smiles and opened the trunk of our green 1973 Plymouth Fury III. What lay inside was as far from a violin as you can get. I was fully expecting a violin and thought nothing else as I rushed to open the case. The fact that "Yamaha" was printed on it should have alerted me to that it might not be what I had asked for, but I was only nine. When I opened the case, expecting to see a finely crafted piece of wood, I got the surprise of my life. The sun hit the silver Yamaha trumpet and nearly blinded me. It was a sight that I can still see in my mind today, some thirty-one years later. My life has not been the same since.

As a child, I was very fortunate to be in a household in which music was a part of the daily fabric of my life. This included, and most especially, listening to my mother sing around the house and attending church every week at Ebenezer Baptist, and hearing the wonderful choirs, organists, and pianists that Daddy King (Dr. Martin Luther King Sr.) brought to our congregation. I also must mention that listening to the relaxed but deliberate delivery of Daddy

King's sermons each Sunday, complete with the perfect accompaniment of the church pianist/organist, would later give me a natural feel for how to improvise and accompany a vocalist. Along with the Church Choir, in which my mother sang and still sings today, we had a different choir featured each Sunday: the M. L. King Choir, which was named for Dr. Martin Luther King Jr.; the Male Chorus; and the Children's Choir, in which I eventually sang bass. The M. L. King Choir didn't use the huge pipe organ like the other choirs, but rather the smaller Hammond B-3 type of organ that Jimmy Smith, Wild Bill Davis, and Jack McDuff made famous in jazz. I was mesmerized and thrilled by the walking bass lines that the organist would play while the choir literally rocked the foundation of the church. Although I didn't realize it at the time, this would help to make the walking bass lines of Count Basie Orchestra bassists Eddie Jones and later John Clayton and Cleve Eaton easy for me to follow once I began to listen to jazz because they were so close in their harmony and rhythm. It was no wonder that Dr. King had this choir named in his honor, those very same sounds that would inspire and uplift his words and thoughts. The rich harmonies and unbelievable rhythms of the

Photo by author

Ebenezer Baptist Church Sanctuary, where I was first exposed to music.

choirs I heard each week permeated my very being in such a way as to lay a foundation of musical appreciation and understanding that allowed me to grasp fully the music of Count Basie, Louis Armstrong, and others. In fact, when I heard the Count Basie Orchestra for the first time, I understood what they were doing immediately because to me it was simply a sophisticated extension of the gospel choirs I heard at church every Sunday. When I look back at my life now from the age of forty, it is clear to see that the mysterious gift of organized musical tone became a part of me.

To say that I love music is an incredible understatement. My life is music. I love the trumpet. Jazz music is my life's passion and hobby. As a result, I consider myself to be one of the luckiest people alive because I get to make my living traveling the vast majority of God's planet Earth as a jazz musician—a jazz trumpeter. Also, anyone else who plays the trumpet, and especially jazz, I consider to be family. Therefore, this book is a celebration of the men and women who have created, assimilated, extended, and continue to refine the vocabulary of jazz trumpet in its many forms.

The trumpet has enriched my life with countless hours of music through practicing it, playing it, cleaning it, holding it, carrying it, and studying it closely. When Mr. Stanley Gosier, my very first trumpet teacher at Terry Mill Elementary School (aside from my older brother, Johnny E. Barnhart III, who actually taught me to play my first song, "Mary Had a Little Lamb") gave me the foundation of a good embouchure and made it fun for me to play and learn, I could feel the trumpet become an extension of myself. That confidence always made the instrument easy for me to play. In other words, whatever I heard someone else doing on the trumpet, I could always figure out his/her technique. I learned early on the necessity for strong lungs, quick fingers, supple but strong lips, and a flexible tongue. My progress continued as I entered high school and my band director, Mr. Gordon Boykin of Gordon High School in Decatur, Georgia (now named McNair Junior High), saw to it that I would begin to develop whatever talent I had. He insisted—actually threatened me if I didn't secure the services of a professional trumpeter. So I called upon Dr. Kevin Eisensmith, who at that time had just appeared in concert at my high school as first trumpeter with the U.S. Army Band at Fort McPherson, Georgia. We began private trumpet lessons when I was in tenth grade and from the very first lesson, he gave me information that made the trumpet even easier and more fun to play. I have never looked back. As a result, I have been able to play in nearly every major concert hall and important venue in the world, from Carnegie Hall in New York to the Hollywood Bowl in Los Angeles, to Suntory Hall in Tokyo, Japan, to the best halls in Vienna, Malaysia, Russia, South America, and elsewhere, but more important, with some of the world's greatest musicians from Clark Terry, Snooky

Young, Wynton Marsalis, Jon Faddis, Freddie Hubbard, and Nat Adderley to Rick Baptist, Bijon Watson, Bobby Shew, Tony Bennett, Joe Williams, Frank Sinatra, Nancy Wilson, and others.

Being a jazz musician was the furthest thing from my mind that September day in 1974 when I got my first trumpet, but this is where I find myself today—performing a kind of music that requires the highest level of concentration and skill, but simultaneously rewards me with an unparalleled feeling of camaraderie and spiritual elation. Once I began to listen to musicians like Count Basie, Duke Ellington, Freddie Hubbard, and particularly Miles Davis, not to mention trying to learn how to play (to improvise clearly and confidently), I understood immediately that jazz music is mature music. It takes years for a jazz musician to begin to make mature improvisatory statements; this is why we find no child prodigies in jazz. Unlike the numerous and celebrated five- to ten-year-olds in classical music who can perform the works of Mozart, Chopin, and others flawlessly, there are no children so young, or people in their teens and early twenties, who can consistently improvise on a level commensurate with being a seasoned jazz professional like Charlie Parker, Louis Armstrong, Thelonious Monk, or John Coltrane. The necessary adult experiences cannot be realized by a child. This is not to say that a child cannot be taught to improvise—they surely can be; being able to improvise is one thing, but being intellectually and spiritually aware of how to transmit the totality of one's life experiences into a coherent and clear musical statement that also shows a complete understanding of the *improvisational* tradition of the art is quite another proposition.

Being a professional jazz trumpeter is a most honorable and humbling profession. Each time I place my trumpet to my lips to improvise a solo or watch another trumpeter do the same, I am reminded at once that we are the inheritors of more than one hundred years of specific and infinitely varied instrumental techniques that always find their way into what we play. We are not simply standing there playing; we are completely aware and focused on all aspects of the music and the instrument itself—trumpet sound, intonation, posture, embouchure, breathing, melody, harmony, rhythm, attack, release, and continuity, all within the assimilation and structural function of improvised ideas. In other words, what we do as improvising jazz trumpeters is more than just put a horn to our face and blow. The mind of a jazz trumpeter or any other improvising jazz musician, regardless of instrument, is filled with the history of the music, which allows for two distinct possibilities: either pay attention and use the incredible vast canvas provided by the pioneers of one's particular instrument, and in doing so become an integral part of that lineage; or conversely, ignore those historical contributions and remain completely unconnected to a grand art, never to fully realize the spiritual connections and the special camaraderie it affords.

A great jazz trumpet solo has brought tears to my eyes many times, just as has a good swinging big band or trio. There is something in this music we call jazz that touches me like no other music. To be a part of the select thousand or so men and women who created and continue to extend the art form we call jazz trumpet is as humbling as it gets. This book has become a way for me to honor those great trumpeters who paved the way for me and countless others and to in some small way explain what they did and continue to do. These men and women, from Louis Armstrong to Miss Clora Bryant to Freddie Hubbard to

Wynton Marsalis and beyond, were and are also among the great thinkers of the twentieth and twenty-first centuries and understanding their work can be useful. The best music of Louis Armstrong, Dizzy Gillespie, Miles Davis, and Thad Jones, as well as Bessie Smith, Duke Ellington, Thelonious Monk, Charlie Parker, and John Coltrane, is, to me, no different from the timeless contributions of people like Socrates, Michelangelo, Bach, Beethoven, Phillis Wheatley, Frederick Douglass, Sojourner Truth, Ralph Ellison, and Albert Einstein. Through the medium of recorded sound, historians in decades and centuries to come will be able bring forth their work to the world.

As you will find from reading this book, the world of jazz trumpet is fraught with aesthetic and social contradictions. My experiences range from incredibly profound to intensely trivial by some standards. Being part of that world has allowed me to witness a naked and cold child being peddled for money in Macedonia, to watch the president of the United States become all smiles while he listens to our orchestra (Basie) play for him, to see an audience in Russia so moved by our music that they began to throw gifts of jewelry on the stage, to be pushed out of the way and told that I didn't have a first-class ticket—when I actually did—by a gate agent of a major U.S. airline, to watch a city in South America nearly destroy itself celebrating its victory in a soccer match, to having "Happy Birthday" sung to me in Japanese for two consecutive years, to nearly be killed by a drunk taxicab driver in London driving at a high speed on the sidewalk en route back to the hotel after a concert, and to watch the wife of one of the men in the orchestra fix a Greyhound bus with her bare hands. Whether I'm having a few laughs with Oprah Winfrey and Prince Albert of Monaco at a

party in the south of France, staring for hours at the wonder of Stonehenge or ancient Mayan ruins in Mexico, watching an artist copy major works of art in the Louvre in Paris just as jazz musicians copy their masters in order to learn how to play, or simply walking onto a bandstand in any part of the world with my trumpet and not having to say anything other than hello to be able to join in and make music that swings—the world that I experience as a jazz trumpeter is unique.

It will help to keep in mind that trumpet players are human beings first, just like everyone else. This along with a careful examination of the work of players from each era or style will give you a better appreciation for those listed here. I also hope that their work and that of trumpeters practicing today will stimulate the minds of those who might want to travel this path. I can promise one thing for certain: once you truly give yourself to the serious study of this art form of jazz (trumpet) improvisation, and learn as much as you can about its origins, evolutionary history, and musicians, your life will be better for doing so.

Briefly, as these next statements will be discussed in greater detail, trumpeters have always been at the forefront of every new era in jazz. The first era was right at the start of the twentieth century (1896–1902), when immigrants from Europe were arriving en masse at Ellis Island, New York as well as other major port cities like New Orleans and in various East Coast states, such as Georgia and the Carolinas. Jazz was in its infancy and ragtime was becoming the dominant new style of the day. Cornet soloists E. W. Gravitt, of Sedalia, Missouri, and Charles "Buddy" Bolden of New Orleans, Louisiana, along with pianist Jelly Roll Morton, were beginning to establish new ways of playing within and on top of ragtime. Their method, mainly improvising ovcr a very danceable ragtime rhythm for Gravitt and a New Orleans groove mixed with ragtime for Bolden, eventually came to be known as "jass" or "jig" music. As it had been for Bolden in New Orleans, this groove was mainly derived from existing marching/brass bands consisting of cornet, clarinet, trombone, bass drum, and tuba, and this would give way to the instrumentation more commonly used today in a jazz setting—acoustic bass, piano, drums, trumpet, trombone, and saxophones. What set Bolden and the New Orleans style apart from the others was the definitive rhythms of the bass and drums, which is the basis of how every soloist plays. For example, the bass and drums in a John Philip Sousa march like "The Stars and Stripes" would be a steady *ONE-two-ONE-two-ONE-two* at about 120 beats per minute. In a typical New Orleans composition, the two instruments have the freedom to interpret the rhythms *individually* but still remain loyal to the rhythmic integrity of the piece. An example would be each instrument playing a variation of *ONE-two-one-AND-two-AND-one-TWO-one-two-one-TWO*; the latter is much more interesting rhythmically, since it is never the same for each consecutive bar.

The next era was the Jazz Age, beginning circa 1922, when the great Louis Armstrong emerged from the shadow of his idol and employer, trumpeter Joseph "King" Oliver, as well as trumpeter Freddie Keppard. Upon the institutionalization of Buddy Bolden for mental deterioration in 1907, and following the brief reign of trumpeter Manuel Perez as the King of New Orleans trumpeters after that, Keppard ascended to the throne as the new "King" until Oliver earned the title around 1916. Jazz, from its beginnings up through Armstrong's arrival in Chicago in 1922, had remained an ensemble art exemplified by collective improvisation. Armstrong, however, completely redefined the music and took it to a new and much higher level. He was the first musician to make jazz into a soloist's art rather than strictly an ensemble art. Due in no small part to his prowess, the swing era emerged, when along with clarinetist Benny Goodman stood many trumpeters such as Charlie Shavers, Harry James, Billy Butterfield, and Roy Eldridge. Next was the modern jazz era also known as the bebop era, with Dizzy Gillespie and alto saxophone genius Charlie Parker ushering in a new and profoundly advanced way of expression.

Other trumpeters in the bebop era were Fats Navarro, Miles Davis, Kenny Dorham, Joe Guy, Howard McGhee, Clifford Brown, and Chet Baker; then came Lee Morgan, Nat Adderley, Donald Byrd, and Freddie Hubbard, and countless others in the hard bop period; then Don Cherry, Bill Dixon, and Barbara Donald with the avant garde and both Davis and Freddie Hubbard at the start of fusion in the early 1970s. Hubbard's commercially and artistically successful albums *Red Clay* and *First Light* (Grammy winner), and albums by other artists up through Chuck Mangione's two-million-selling *Feels So Good*, were all a direct (or indirect) result of Miles's various fusion albums, beginning with the pivotal *Bitches Brew* in 1970. The Davis, Hubbard, and Byrd recordings also helped to fuel further explorations of jazz fusion by other musicians, such as the late saxophonist Grover Washington and the group Weather Report.

For trumpeters, the next major hit in the world of jazz fusion other than guitarist George Benson's multimillion-selling *Breezin'* was by the former Jazz Messenger, Chuck Mangione. His chart-topping album *Feels So Good* was the talk of the day and his group filled arenas around the country. I remember hearing the title song on the radio constantly and playing it while in high school, just like all other kids my age. The album went platinum and sent sales of flugelhorns through the roof, and the song was played by every local jazz band and high school marching band.

Another trumpeter who made his mark in the world of jazz pop-rock was A&M Records founder Herb Alpert. His group, the Tijuana Brass, enjoyed million-selling hits in the 1960s, and Jerry Moss—Alpert's business partner and the second half of A&M, which stands for Alpert and Moss—was responsible for signing Chuck Mangione to a recording contract on their label. Alpert's 1980 hit album *Rise* had major airplay, and I remember learning some of his solos from this album, although it is not considered to be a jazz recording. I was being influenced by the radio just as many trumpeters had been years earlier. In fact, I learned to flutter tongue from learning Alpert's solo on the tune "Street Life." I didn't realize it at the time, but along with learning other solos by Freddie Hubbard (from the album *Bundle of Joy*) and from records by Ellington and Basie, I was in the midst of serious ear training and instrumental articulation that would provide a foundation upon which I would begin to build.

With the success of Mangione and Alpert being celebrated all over the airwaves, Miles Davis began to emerge from a self-imposed five-year retirement and proceeded to record the same type of material for the remainder of his career, until his death in 1991. Around this same period, about 1980, a young trumpeter from New Orleans had been listening to *Giant Steps* by John Coltrane and other significant jazz recordings by Charlie Parker, Dizzy Gillespie, Freddie Hubbard, Duke Ellington, and Thelonious Monk. With nearly unprecedented trumpet technique, jazz and classical great Wynton Marsalis, according to

Newsweek magazine, "stood on stage at the 1979 New Orleans Jazz and Heritage Festival and blew the roof off of the jazz tent and set the jazz world on its ear." Again, a trumpeter was at the fore-front of a new movement or renaissance in jazz.

All of the trumpeters listed herein cover a wide variety of styles and conceptions, all of which I consider valid and, most important, connected, due to the fact that all of these styles sprang from the same root planted by E. W. Gravitt, Buddy Bolden, and others around the turn of the twentieth century. As for the particular importance (in a hierarchal sense) of each individual, I will let this research and discography help you to reach your own conclusions.

One of the most wonderful things about doing the research for this book is that it allowed me to discover and rediscover hundreds of trumpet players and their music. Having the largest jazz recording collection possible has been my goal ever since that first time I felt swing go through my body. What I have amassed so far has enabled me to complete the majority of the research and listening needed, and the search for more is always in progress. During my early development as a musician and jazz trumpeter in particular, I studied and committed to memory untold hours of recordings. This effort continues, along with constant practical experience in various jazz settings, and has given me the foundation to become a trumpeter proficient enough to be called upon by the Count Basie Orchestra, Marcus Roberts, Delfeayo Marsalis, Nat Adderley, Jon Hendricks, Natalie Cole, Clark Terry, the Clayton-Hamilton Orchestra, James Newton, and others for gigs and recordings. My experience as a jazz musician has provided additional insight on the trumpet as well as a head start on this history project, as I happen to be in a position of practicing what I preach and preaching what I practice.

I have learned to appreciate each trumpeter's gift, regardless of category: Pete Minger playing the living heck out of the jazz classic standard "But Beautiful" from his first solo recording *Straight to the Source/Minger Painting* (Concord, 1980); Louis Armstrong revolutionizing not only the possibilities of the trumpet itself but music in general; Johnny Dunn, Buddy Anderson, Sydney DeParis, Bill Coleman, and Jabbo Smith playing with incredible technique and ease alongside Armstrong; Bix Beiderbeck finding the prettiest of notes; Sweets Edison and Clark Terry mastering the blues on any recording while swinging you into bad health; Cootie Williams making his trumpet sound like the oratorical majestic declarations of a king from antiquity; Nat Gonella, Gosta Torner, Valery Ponomarev, Warren Vache, Donald Byrd, and Harry James performing with such bravura and ease; Wynton Marsalis at age nineteen playing so much trumpet on "How Deep Is the Ocean" and rewriting the book with his performances on "Cherokee" years later; Miles Davis constantly searching and refining with perhaps the most unmistakable sound; Dizzy Gillespie playing with so much swing and intricacy that it nearly defies logic; Chet Baker, Clora Bryant, and Valaida Snow singing just as beautifully as they all play; Booker Little, Woody Shaw, Maynard Ferguson, Arturo Sandoval, and Freddie Hubbard doing unbelievable things on a trumpet; Lee Morgan making trumpet technique funky; Nat Adderley quietly adding a level of technique that only a handful of others possess; Doc Severinsen, Rex Stewart, Jimmy Owens, Ruby Braff, Charlie Shavers, and Bunny Berigan making you smile; Thad Jones being the Bartók of the trumpet; Blue Mitchell, Kenny Dorham, Al Aarons, Sam Noto, Joe Newman, Stjepko Gut, Joe Wilder, Bob Ojeda, Taft Jordan, and Rolf Ericson swinging ever so soulfully; Bobby Hackett, Muggsy Spanier, Bill Berry, Stu Williamson, and Billy Butterfield having a blast; Japan's Katsuji Sharai, Tomonao Hara, and Teramasu Hino playing with just as much soul and fire than anyone; Chuck Mangione, Herb Alpert, Leslie Drayton, Chris Botti, Michael "Patches" Stewart, and Mark Isham playing relaxed and beautiful melodies; Charles Tolliver, Louis Smith, Longineau Parsons, Nicholas Payton, Bill Dixon, Barrie Lee Hall, Kenny Wheeler, Ryan Kisor, and Carl Saunders each playing his own unique style; Snooky Young, Byron Stripling, Liesel Whitaker, Lew Soloff, Frank Green, Bijon Watson, Frank Szabo, Arnie Chykoski, and Jon Faddis swinging an entire orchestra; myself and Marcus Printup trading twos on a Marcus Roberts arrangement of Gershwin's "Rhapsody in Blue" from his Sony recording *Portraits in Blue*...it all comes down to us being musicians who happen to play the trumpet.

When giving lecture-demonstrations on the history of jazz trumpet and improvisation to students and musicians of all levels, I am always asked, "Where can we find the information you just presented to us in an organized and concise format for each instrument?" The answer I have always had to give is, "It does not exist." I have tried to solve this dilemma, for trumpeters at least, with this book and I hope I have answered the most commonly asked questions and provided insight into the world I am a part of. To the invaluable information collected in the interviews, I have added personal photos and other anecdotal information that I feel will be helpful in understanding and developing a deeper appreciation for the talents of the trumpeters listed here.

This book took shape as I began a serious quest to understand the work of the jazz musicians who came before me. It was and still is a simple proposition of trying to get better as a musician—as a jazz trumpeter. I wanted to be a part of those musicians who use swing as the basis for their creativity. Not swing in the sense of the swing era, but in the sense of the distinct and broad particulars of the eighth-note triplet.

EIGHTH NOTE TRIPLET EXAMPLE

This book also is a result of helping to guide several students on a path of learning how to become a successful jazz musician on any instrument. By "successful," I mean in the sense of art and not payment, although the two types of achievement have been proven to coexist. The path to arrive at where I am today as a trumpet soloist with the Count Basie Orchestra and leader of my own group included stops along the way that may have been different from those made by others, but it has afforded me opportunities to receive information directly from jazz trumpet pioneers Harry "Sweets" Edison, Snooky Young, Clark Terry, Dizzy Gillespie, Freddie Hubbard, Sonny Cohn, Nat Adderley, Willie Cook, Red Rodney, and Pete Minger, to name a few.

I have been lucky to also receive information from other jazz masters such as pianists Oscar Peterson, Marcus Roberts, and Kenny Kirkland; Professor Lindsey B. Sarjeant, my former college instructor at Florida A&M University in Tallahassee; saxophonists Frank Foster, Kenny Hing, Emmanuel Boyd, Frank Wess, Wes Anderson, and Branford Marsalis; guitarist George Benson; trombonists Grover Mitchell, Bill Hughes, Clarence Banks, Wycliffe Gordon, and Al Grey; drummers Jackie Mills (Dothan, AL), Elvin Jones, Billy Kilson, Tony Williams, and Jeff Watts; and vocalists Tony Bennett, Rosemary Clooney, Jon Hendricks, Pam Laws, Frank Sinatra, and Joe Williams.

The information and lessons I received sometimes didn't have anything to do with music—or so I thought. Sometimes, with Nat Adderley or Clark Terry, for example, not talking about specific musical ideas at all was a lesson in itself. One of the most valuable things I learned from these artists was to *think* while practicing, performing, and listening. This is the only thing that will ultimately set a musician apart from all others. As Tony Bennett once said to Basie baritone saxophonist John Williams, "If you want to be different, be yourself." I quote him to emphasize that my intentions here are not to pass judgment on any individual style or to point out who may sound better than whom. Rather, this book is meant to celebrate each trumpeter's contribution not only to jazz music but, also as important, to the whole of humanity. Of course, like anyone, I have my opinions about and favorites among those I believe to be the true pioneers of improvisational jazz trumpet, those who took the music and the vocabulary of jazz trumpet in new and different directions followed by many. But instead of focusing on my personal preferences, I would rather you do your own research with the guide I have tried to provide.

The most rewarding thing this project has led me to do, and its importance cannot be stressed enough, was to sit down and patiently listen and re-listen to all those trumpeters and various orchestras and bands that I normally would not have really cared to check out more than once.

This practice has opened my ears and eyes in several areas, with the most profound being the realization that we are all human beings with love to give. And whether a musician is swinging like mad for the love of the art or simply trying to put food on the table, both approaches are impor-

MILES DAVIS SOLO EXCERPT ON "STRAIGHT NO CHASER"

LOUIS ARMSTRONG'S SOLO ON "BLUES IN THE SOUTH"

tant, as they inform us of where the individual trumpeter stands in the long line behind Bolden, Armstrong, Gillespie, Terry, Brown, Davis, Hubbard, and Shaw. This is what I wanted establish with a particular degree of certainty.

My knowledge has been gained through mentally and physically learning numerous solos and through over twenty years of professional experience that is still in progress. Learning solos and recordings by ear and not from any book will help one to understand how the lineage of jazz trumpeters really unfolds because it can and must be *felt*. Once I had learned Louis Armstrong's solo on "Blues in the South" from 1952 and Miles Davis's solo on "Freddie Freeloader" from the classic 1959 recording *Kind of Blue*, I could *feel* the history flow through my trumpet, because with this Miles solo I felt him reach back to Armstrong in order to create a new way to express himself through his trumpet. But, even more so was when I learned Miles's solo on "Straight, No Chaser" from the album *Milestones*. On the third beat of the ninth bar of Armstrong's solo on the concert F blues, the G-minor chord, he plays a concert D-flat that turns the chord into a G-minor-seventh with the flatted fifth. Miles does the exact same thing on his solo on "Straight, No Chaser," but he plays the D-flat on the back half of beat four of eighth measure of the blues form and holds it over into the ninth measure for three beats, which changes the quality of the chord just as Pops (Armstrong) had done years earlier. Understandably, this intrigued me like never before and led me to learn many more solos by Freddie Hubbard, Clifford Brown, Dizzy, Sweets Edison, Blue Mitchell, and a host of others.

Historically, the trumpet has been used for nearly every kind of event from calls to war to celebrations of all sorts. The earliest known trum-

pets were made from the horns of animals such as the ram, or even perhaps the teeth of a shark or other large mammal. When the tomb of the Egyptian Pharaoh Tutankhamun (ca. 1336–1327 B.C.) was opened after 3,249 years in 1922, archaeologists found two trumpets buried with him that are amongst the earliest known. Could King Tut have been a trumpeter as well? We will never really know, but the fact that two trumpets were buried along with his other prized possessions is very provocative. We know that trumpets were used primarily for military and civil occasions, but there is nothing to indicate that the young Tutankhamun could not have played them for his own enjoyment. Thinking about how a young child (Tutankhamun was just nine years old when he became pharaoh) might love to play things that make noise makes it seem all the more likely that he did play at some time, whether the occasion was military or otherwise.

I had the great honor of seeing the trumpets of Tutankhamun up close and personal at the Los Angeles County Museum of Art on July 27, 2005. Being only a foot away from the oldest known trumpets on the planet, and those of an Egyptian pharaoh to boot, was an experience that I will never forget. There was only one real trumpet, the other being a wooden core that would fit perfectly inside the instrument to protect it from damage when stored. There were actually two or three trumpets originally found, but in 1939, during a BBC broadcast in London, a trumpeter with the last name of Tappern decided to put a modern trumpet mouthpiece in one of them and play it. Within seconds, the fragile trumpet that once belonged to King Tutankhamun shattered! The main trumpet I saw at LACMA was in perfect condition and is of beaten silver, with a rolled mouthpiece of gold with its radius about the size

Photo courtesy of Kenneth Garrett

This is one of the earliest known trumpets along with its wooden core protector. They were found in the tomb of Egyptian King Tutankhamun and date to around 3250 B.C.

of a U.S. nickel or a modern size Bach 7C trumpet mouthpiece. The trumpet is approximately thirty inches in length, with the bell rim trimmed in gold. The radius of the bell is approximately three and a half inches. Unlike modern trumpets, those found in Tut's tomb have no valves.

Before the invention of valves (circa 1814) and by the mid- to late sixteenth century, classical composers began writing music for this instrument that challenged its very design. Bach wrote his famous Brandenburg Concertos for the trumpeter Gottfried Reich. Maybe even then composers could hear the endless possibilities of this member of the brass family and began composing exclusively for it in an attempt to stretch both its technical and its musical capabili-

Photo by author

Above: Trumpeter Hagai Izraeli demonstrates the Yemenite shofar, an early trumpet (circa 500 B.C.) from Israel. According to the Holy Bible (Book of Joshua, Chapter 6), such instruments were used to bring down the walls of Jericho.

Photo by author

Right: Hagai demonstrates another early straight trumpet (circa 500 B.C.).

ties. Valves, which constituted the single most important advancement in trumpet design, were invented by Heinrich Stölzel of Saxony in about 1814 and patented in 1818. Valves allow the instrument to produce all twelve tones in Western harmony and free it from the limitations of only five or six notes of its particular overtone series. As a result, many different brands of valved

cornets, horns, and trumpets were designed and continue to be available.

This book is an acknowledgment and celebration of the work of those who, beginning in the early twentieth century, through improvised solos, began to give the trumpet a much more profound and distinct vocabulary that is continued even today by their creative heirs. This new way of musical expression on the trumpet was the result of a music genre we now call jazz. Before jazz began, there was a distinguished musician by the name of Francis Johnson (1792–1844), an African-American and a celebrated keyed bugler, composer, and band leader from Philadelphia, Pennsylvania. Johnson is important to the evolutionary prehistory of jazz trumpet; he was known for having the top society band in the city circa 1840 and played music that ranged from marches to two-steps. Since improvisation was common among musicians playing all types of music, whether it was for public consumption or not, I would offer that Johnson's playing on the keyed bugle, had it been recorded during his peak,

From left to right: German or Austrian postal coach horn made about 1860; English pattern bugle (modern version of bugles in use since about 1850); Graves B-flat seven-keyed bugle made in Winchester, New Hampshire, about 1840; Cornopean in B-flat made by Wood and Ivy, Manchester, England, about 1845.

All instruments courtesy of Robb Stewart, Arcadia, California. Photos by author

From left to right: copy of Courtois B-flat cornet made about 1880 in Europe; Buescher large-bore B-flat cornet made in Elkhart, Indiana, in 1917; Buescher 10-22 B-flat trumpet made in 1928, very similar to the one played by Louis Armstrong a year or two earlier; Conn 58B trumpet like the one Armstrong played in 1928.

From left to right: Martin Imperial trumpet made in 1938; Selmer 20 trumpet made in 1954; Couesnon flugelhorn made about 1975; Bach 37 trumpet made in 1971; the author's AJNA II B-flat, made in 2001 by David Monette of Portland, Oregon.

might have exemplified the earliest fusion of military marches, two-steps, classics, waltzes, slave work songs, folk songs, spirituals, and the earliest forms of the blues.

There are thousands of men and women who play the trumpet today, and for those of us who make a living at it, especially in jazz, the founding father of jazz trumpet seems to be Charles "Buddy" Bolden (1877–1931) from New Orleans, Louisiana. However, after researching Bolden and early music from New Orleans, as well as the origins of ragtime, one of the six major fusions of jazz (the other five being African rhythms, blues, folk music, classical music, and spirituals), I have come to the conclusion that there had to have been someone who influenced even him, such as Professor Jim Humphrey (1859–1937) who was a trumpet teacher in New Orleans during the period of Bolden's early childhood. However, we have to recognize that without ragtime, jazz as we know it might not have developed the way it did. And ragtime did not originate in New Orleans, but rather in such places as Sedalia, Missouri, which is where I came across the name and photo of a ragtime cornet soloist named of E. W. Gravitt. When I realized that Gravitt was a ragtime soloist, I thought about the implications: if he was soloing over ragtime music, which means that he was ragging the melody, then he was perhaps the true father of jazz trumpet, because "ragging" is simply another way of saying "improvising" or "improving," and this was done a few years before the evidence suggests Bolden began playing in New Orleans. When we recall that Louis Armstrong wrote, "Bolden was playin' ragtime," it becomes clear that at the creation of jazz trumpet, there was a broader-based phenomenon and that cities other than New Orleans warrant further study. Also, whoever influenced

Bolden may or may not have been a trumpeter. Many musicians have had major influences other than players on their particular instrument. After all, there were not too many bands that consisted solely of trumpets or bass drums or pianos. There was always a mixture of various instruments to provide a greater balance of rhythm and harmony and a more sophisticated level of counterpoint and possible nuances.

Bolden's significance, versus that of E. W. Gravitt, lies in the fact that Bolden lived and worked in New Orleans. This city was home to a myriad of musical styles and tastes and was literally a melting pot of numerous ethnicities, as it still is today. Primarily through the vast and important Mississippi River, the music of the blues (Memphis, Tennessee) and ragtime (Sedalia, Missouri) made its way to New Orleans, just as the music of New Orleans made its way as far north as Minnesota via the riverboats. Inevitably, in New Orleans, the music mixed with the local rhythms of Africans, Mexicans, Europeans, and Caribbean islanders to create the basis of New Orleans music, which eventually began to be called jazz.

Unfortunately, there are no recordings of Bolden known to exist, although my research leads me to conclude that Bolden did make a cylinder recording around 1904 that has since been lost. That lost recording would give us an idea of the majesty of sound for which he was legendary, but through his descendants, such as Bunk Johnson, who often played with Bolden as his second trumpet from 1905 through June 4, 1907 (Bolden's career ended when he went insane on June 5, 1907, during a funeral and parade), and up through Manuel Perez, Freddie Keppard, King Oliver, and later Louis Armstrong, we at least have an idea what he may have

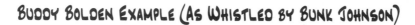

sounded like. There are two known recordings explored later in this book that seem to come as close as we may ever get to the true nature of what Bolton may have played, rather than how he actually sounded, since there are conflicting opinions about the nature of his tone. From all that has been written and said about Bolden, I am sure his tone was all at once powerful, sweet, bold, beautiful, and provocative.

The first recording I am referring to is a whistled example by trumpeter Bunk Johnson demonstrating precisely one of melodies he said that Buddy Bolden used to play. Bunk was rediscovered in the rice fields of Louisiana in the early 1940s by two men researching early New Orleans jazz. They helped to buy him a new trumpet and a set of false teeth and were instrumental in booking him gigs and concerts as far away as San Francisco and Boston. At one point, they interviewed Bunk and asked him to give an example of what Buddy Bolden sounded like. Bunk heartily agreed and this is the melody he whistled. I have transcribed it here.

The second recording is *The Legend of Buddy Bolden* (Village Vanguard Sessions, Sony) by Wynton Marsalis. I have heard him play this original composition in person a few times and on the recording and I even learned to play it myself. After listening to Marsalis play this many times and thinking about what he might have been after, it struck me as the most current statement, if you will, of the type of ideas Bolden may have expressed in his music, complete with whole-tone harmonic devices, unique staccato tongue attacks, and elements of grandeur and surprise. Of course, the work of trumpeters Bunk Johnson, King Oliver, Armstrong, and Freddie Keppard would still be the closest to Bolden's.

Another goal of this book is to give the layman as well as other musicians a better understanding of what it is that we jazz trumpeters/musicians do, and what is required not only from a musical standpoint but also from a physical one. Each time that I give a clinic on jazz improvisation, on a university campus or even someplace in a law firm's conference room for Black History Month, the first question I ask is: "Is there anyone here who does not have a clue as to what it is that jazz musicians are doing while they are performing?" There are always at least several hands raised. Much of what I explain in those situations will be covered here as thoroughly as possible. If I can get my father, who didn't seem to have any level of pitch recognition, to recognize certain things by ear when he watches me onstage, and then make comments like, "The saxophonist really played better this time than last night," or "You sounded happy tonight," then I know the information to follow will be helpful to many.

For those of you who are jazz trumpeters, I hope that this information will give you a broader understanding of the history of our instrument as well as the good feeling of knowing the group of musicians with whom you will forever be associated, but most important, a sense of where you stand among them. Some of the trumpeters here you may not have heard of before, and I am sure that I may have missed someone that you feel should be here and some that I haven't heard of either. I have exhausted every avenue I could think of to find most of the trumpeters included here. Any name that I found, I put on the list, because I wanted to make sure that those who never got the big break will at least have their names mentioned. I consider this book the first edition and I can add those not yet listed or fully researched in a revised edition. This book is the initial effort, to gather all those who have contributed to the lineage and vocabulary of jazz trumpet, whether we have heard of them or not. For obvious reasons, those who have recorded improvised solos will undoubtedly receive the greater attention to detail, as it is this facet of musicianship that ultimately determines the direction of the music.

Further, I know that being a musician is a gift from God, and to be a jazz musician, well, those of us who know the feeling understand. Most, if not all jazz soloists have experienced, at least once, that ultimate feeling of being in that zone of mastery that leaves behind the technical, but opens the gate for pure spiritual creativity. It is an indescribable passion and joy when we hear someone swinging with spiritual intensity on the trumpet or any other instrument, and I don't mean this in the strict sense of 4/4 time. Further, when we come to realize that we can be ourselves, we know that we have joined that long line of incredible jazz musicians who, over the last one hundred years, have made a difference in the lives of millions of human beings.

I am a jazz musician, a jazz trumpeter. Contained within these pages are the results of my experiences on the bandstand practicing the art of the improvised solo within a jazz context and more than thirty years of listening to as many musicians and recordings as I could. I have done my best to convey those experiences, which are ongoing, in the most clear and concise manner possible. While understanding the need to be grammatically correct, which my mother taught me to do at an early age, I am also keenly aware that our world of jazz trumpet is what it is. It is a world shaped by men whose ideals were and are as diverse as the stars, and it encompasses the full range of social, rhetorical, and political vernacular; it should not be sugarcoated to please any one particular taste. Of course, the exception to this would be the minds of the very young. They do not need to learn about specific adult behavior from me. So where necessary, I have cleaned up a word or phrase but still left the meaning obvious. The world of jazz trumpet is beautiful, made up of all manner of things, and my work here represents how I see it and experience it.

Finally, this book is dedicated to all jazz musicians in general and jazz trumpeters of the past, present, and future, but especially to that trumpet player whom I thought was a vagrant wandering through a shopping mall in Tallahassee, Florida around 1987. I had just finished a Sunday afternoon performance with my college sextet (which included the great trombonist Wycliffe Gordon) when he seemed to materialize out of thin air and asked to play my trumpet. I was alarmed at his presence but reluctantly agreed to lend him my horn. In turn, he proceeded to play some of the hippest and most swinging jazz trumpet I have ever heard in my life. To this day, I have no idea who he was or where he came from. All I remember is that he looked homeless and deranged, but he swung the hell out of something in the key of F minor concert with technique to spare, then simply gave me my horn back and walked off. I stood there absolutely stunned at what I had just heard. Wherever you are, and whoever you are, God bless you for that lesson.

PART I
FROM THE BEGINNING
A History of the Jazz Trumpet

From King Abubakari II to Buddy Bolden

The shores of the Atlantic Ocean, many miles of which kiss the continent of Africa just above the equator, are part of a vast body of water that is rich with the untold stories of human history and is the element by which men and women have journeyed to find new lands. This understanding makes it easier to visualize the great king of Mali, Abubakari II, who upon learning that hundreds of his faithful subjects had not returned after they set sail for the lands of the western Atlantic Ocean in 1310, rumored to contain human inhabitants, ordered even more boats and supplies; this time he would also make the journey himself. With a total of four hundred boats—two hundred master boats plus two hundred supply boats—Abubakari left the Sene-Gambian coast of Africa, never to set foot on his native land again. There is compelling evidence as to where he and his subjects before him landed.

As the research of Ivan Van Sertima—detailed in his groundbreaking book, *They Came Before Columbus: The African Presence in Ancient America*—shows, not only does the African presence in America predate the arrival of Christopher Columbus with the journey of Abubakari II, but recent archaeological evidence of the last seventy years has unearthed artifacts such as the giant Negroid heads at La Venta in Tabasco, Mexico, that date back to before 680 B.C.! Yes, over 2,700 years ago. This area is less than twenty miles from the Gulf of Mexico, which, of course, flows directly into the Atlantic Ocean. These Negroid statues, some of which are eight to nine feet high and twenty-two feet in circumference, "were all found to be facing East!; staring directly into the Atlantic Ocean." Understanding that politics and archaeology make for strange bedfellows, it is easy to understand Van Sertima's emphatic statement concerning the statues: "They expose the false, frail ground upon which the historical outlines of pre-Columbian American history had so far been built." Further, from the research of Gavin Menzies in his equally groundbreaking book *1421: The Year China Discovered America*, we learn that some one hundred years after Abubakari II, on March 8, 1421, the Chinese, by order of Emperor Zhu Di, and with the largest fleet the world had ever seen, sailed around the world in boats of teak wood that were up to five-hundred-feet long. Their journey lasted over two years and they circumnavigated the globe nearly sixty years before Ferdinand Magellan was even born. Magellan (1480–1521) has been credited as the first to circumnavigate the globe. Menzies proves

3

this to be clearly false. But evidence of the Chinese colonization of America, not to mention Antarctica and Australia, has been discovered in locations as far apart as the Mississippi River and the Amazon River toward the northern tip of South America.

After reading the earth shattering research of Mr. Van Sertima, including his discussion of basic facts of ocean currents and navigating by longitude and latitude, which was not fully understood by Europeans until the mid-eighteenth century, some three hundred years after Columbus's voyage to the already occupied Americas, I decided to study the currents that churn in the Pacific and Atlantic Oceans above the equator to better understand how they affect sailing on them. Once a boat or ship has left western Africa from the Sene-Gambian coast, due west of Mali, and has gone out into the Atlantic far enough, maybe two days' sailing, it will enter the Canary Current, which flows southwest and directly into the North Equatorial Current. The North Equatorial Current flows directly to the West Indies and the area that contains the present-day Bahamas and southern Florida. If the explorers from Africa set sail from farther south in Senegal, they could have begun their voyage with the Equatorial Counter Current, which flows both east and west; if it took them westward, it would put them into the South Equatorial Current that flows into the Caribbean Sea and between Jamaica to the north and Honduras to the south. Once in this area, it would have been only a matter of a few days or a week before they would be in the middle of the Gulf of Mexico and able to make landfall in what is now Cancun, Mexico; Corpus Christi or Houston, Texas; New Orleans, Louisiana; or Panama City or St. Petersburg, Florida. Even if they were lost and lacking the crucial knowledge of how to determine longitude and latitude, it would still be possible for them to land in any of those areas.

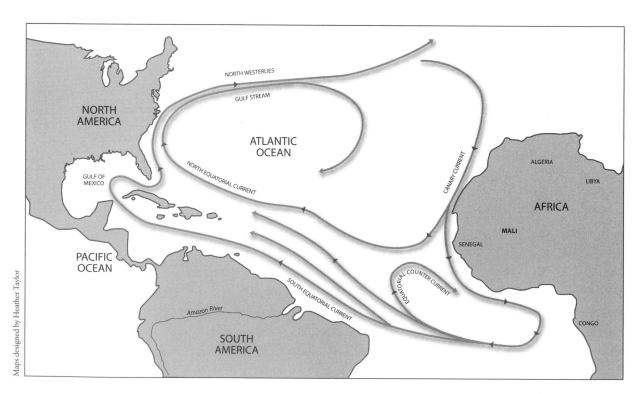

Maps designed by Heather Taylor

What does this have to do with jazz trumpet you may ask? I think it is necessary to show, which most accepted books on U.S. history do not, that the achievement of Africans, from as far back as 680 B.C., had a direct impact on the shaping of cultures in the Americas before the arrival of Columbus. More important, however, this influence continues today. This is an attempt to lay a foundation of understanding that may help the reader more fully grasp the profundity of the creations by the descendants of a truly ingenious and powerful people who were also—although they were not addressed as much during their time—fellow human beings. That jazz music is primarily African-American in origin and development is no accident. It would not exist if not for their presence on this continent and the work and the oppression of former slaves and their descendants. This music's improvisatorial exploration, daring, and confidence mirror the same in Abubakari II.

Setting the Stage for Innovation: Understanding the Conditions That Led to Ragtime and Jazz

To understand the evolution of any subject, whether it is the civil rights movement in twentieth-century America, ancient Greek or Roman art, the automobile, or especially any form of music, it is necessary to have a general grasp of the conditions under which it began. Among the African-Americans in the years following the Civil War, the conditions that eventually led to the creation of a new music called ragtime and eventually to jazz, were many.

The Civil War was one of two major conflicts in the early history of the United States that helped to liberate African-Americans. The first was the Revolutionary War, in which minority soldiers had already fought. Even several decades before, during the French and Indian War, the slave trumpeter (bugle) Nero Benson served under Captain Isaac Clark of Framingham, Massachusetts. Of course, jazz was not even thought of during Benson's time, but the life experiences he put into playing that bugle to signal men to battle could have only been full of emotional content and contradictions. An African-American named Francis Johnson (1792–1844), of Philadelphia, Pennsylvania, was a virtuoso on the keyed bugle as well as a composer and band leader of note. Throughout the 1820s and 1830s Johnson enjoyed an active career playing in many venues, including concerts, charity functions, church events, parades, balls, circuses, fire companies, canal openings, and military occasions. Some of his compositions are "Princeton Gallopade," "The New Bird Waltz," "Dirge," "Philadelphia Firemen's Cotillion," and "General Lafayette's Trumpet March and Quickstep."

The case of Mr. Johnson helps to show that among the many elements that went into shaping the eventual sound of jazz trumpet that at its core is the African-American experience. His music, as played by the Chestnut Brass Quintet with keyed bugle soloist Bruce Barrie (*Music of Francis Johnson and His Contemporaries: Early Nineteenth Century Black Composers*—Music Masters D-193198), contains those same syncopated rhythms that were crucial to the development of ragtime. If one listens closely to the music of Francis Johnson, Scott Joplin, Jelly Roll Morton, and Bunk Johnson, who in the early 1940s re-created some of the music of Buddy Bolden, the irresistible natural rhythmic shift away from the imposed European standard can be easily detected. Therefore, it is possible to hear traces of four hundred years of African-American history in jazz, the elements of oppression

Francis Johnson (1790–1844), celebrated keyed bugler and band leader in Philadelphia, Pennsylvania.

Photos courtesy of Robb Stewart

Unknown soldier with keyed bugle, circa 1850.

tempered by optimism. These elements can also be heard in the earliest work of King Oliver, Louis Armstrong, Roy Eldridge, Cootie Williams, Miles Davis, Sweets Edison, and Lester Bowie (in particular, Bowie's profound solo on "Hello, Dolly!" from the disc *Fast Last!*—Sony SRCS 9408), to name a few.

These types of influences would weave their way into the field work songs of the slaves, during the early to mid-1800s in particular; into their spiritual practices; and especially into expressions of their patriotism, even though they had to ask to fight alongside their white brethren.

Could jazz have been invented before the Civil War or the Emancipation Proclamation? Not likely unless other, similar circumstances had existed. The hold of slavery was so strong after the demise of indentured servitude in the early 1700s that the slave owners in conjunction with politicians and clergy, many of whom could claim two of those titles or all three, did not allow for any activity that they could not control. Jazz came about as a result of the realization that through music, basic human freedom was possible—as well as the optimism and confidence that would make it inevitable. Constrained by slavery and racial prejudices, forced to do hard labor, the only thing most African Americans could do to express themselves was to sing and chant to make their work go faster. And from this basic human reaction to suffering, they created the first strains of a sound that continues to develop today; a mixture of spirituals, folk songs, military marches, classics from Europe, minstrelsy tunes, blues, and African rhythms and harmonies that all went into the making of jazz.

The Emancipation Proclamation of 1863 would not completely end slavery. That would require the passage of the Thirteenth Amendment on December 18, 1865. The true reason behind Lincoln's document was to free the slaves so they could be recruited to join the military and fight with the Union against the Confederacy to win the Civil War. Again, the very people being oppressed and brutalized by slavery would be called upon to help their oppressors who, as their own behavior had shown, could not be fully trusted to grant freedom to anyone but themselves. Lincoln stated directly in the Emancipation Proclamation that this law was one of "military necessity," which clearly implied that liberating the slaves was the last thing on anyone's mind. Although he began his first draft of the proclamation in late June 1862, Lincoln first informed his cabinet of his idea for emancipating the slaves five days after the Battle of Antietam Creek in Sharpsburg, Maryland, on September 17, 1862, during which the Union lost approximately 12,500 soldiers.

Although free Africans began to arrive on the shores of the New World or, more properly, Native American territory, as early as 1311, nearly 200 years before Christopher Columbus, Spanish settlers brought the first indentured slaves to Sappalo Sound, Georgia in 1526. Indentured servitude, radically different from slavery, allowed for workers of many other ethnicities to work in exchange for passage, room and board, and possibly some of their wages. So from as early as the 1520s, free Africans came with explorers as indentured servants to the shores of what is now the United States. However, a Dutch ship from Africa carrying slaves arrived in Jamestown, Virginia, in 1619, and "officially" launched the beginning of slavery in America. Of the one hundred slaves shipped, only twenty survived. Slavery replaced indentured servitude and became a racially based institution.

When slaves were brought to the (eventual) United States, they had nothing tangible except their bodies. These men and women, however, possessed in their minds and souls thousands of years of customs, ancestral awareness, and traditions in agriculture, art, architecture, language, spirituality, dance, and especially music (harmony and rhythm), from which they drew the meaning of their lives. Whatever they were to face in terms of physical torture at the hands of the slave traders and their Euro-American owners, they would begin to retreat, secretly at first, back into their only comfort zone, that of their spirituality and their dance and musical expression.

Music, primarily in song form, allowed the slaves to begin to express their sorrow as well as hope for better days ahead. They began to invent various work hollers or field songs that helped them to cope with their backbreaking work. Singing together and with the same rhythm helped their work day go by faster. Interestingly and most hypocritically, in keeping with their Christian beliefs about Sundays being a day of rest, the slave owners allowed their slaves to rest and spend time with their families for a full day a week. Beginning around 1820, the slaves would generally use this time to reflect and revisit their own traditions of religious practices, music, and dance. This weekly "family reunion" meant the slaves never lost sight of their rich heritage. Unlike the Romans, who centuries earlier had practiced Bacchanalia and Saturnalia, festival days wherein slaves and their masters would exchange roles, the slave owners prior to 1865 continued the dehumanization of their "property." The racist effects of this type of thinking carried over well into the twentieth- and even the twenty-first-century society. But jazz musicians have offered hope and given shining examples of how that legacy can overcome. Listen to the music of Louis Armstrong, Duke Ellington, John

Coltrane, and Count Basie, among others, and this becomes readily apparent.

Slaves were not allowed to have any rest or any type of musical instruments other than drums, except on Sundays, as their "drum talk" or "wild beating" was unintelligible to their white owners and made them fearful and paranoid. During this time in the 1820s, the slaves began to gather in places such as Congo Square in New Orleans, now known as Louis Armstrong Park, to practice their religious rituals, including voodoo, and demonstrate their exotic dances and percussive genius, much to the amusement of the city's

Photo by author

Congo Square as it appears today. It has been renamed Louis Armstrong Park in honor of our most important jazz musician. The statue of Armstrong, with New Orleans trumpeters Endre Rice, left, and Wendell Brunious, right, honorably welcomes visitors to this important place in African and American history.

various ethnic groups. In the mid-1840s, however, slaves were forbidden to dance in Congo Square.

Access to such instruments as the bugle, keyed bugle, cornet, trumpet, piano, trombone, or violin was not to happen on a broader scale until the mid-nineteenth century. However, perhaps the most native of instruments to the African, now transplanted to America, was the drum in its many forms; some were reconstructed from memory as the slaves brought very few or none with them. They were also aware that they had to remake themselves; or, as Edmund Barry Gaither notes in his essay *Heritage Reclaimed: An Historical Perspective and Chronology*: "They had to change from being Africans in America to being Afro-Americans."

Most jazz historians have written—and many musicians, including jazz musicians—assert that jazz in its most primitive and basic form is a mixture of European harmonies and African rhythms. This is not the complete story—it implies that the African-American did not contribute harmonically during the embryonic stages of jazz's development, which is completely false. Various percussion instruments used and built by Africans such as drum chimes, kori drums, gullu drums, and water drums all have discernible pitches and can be tuned, and therefore, harmony as well as form and structure has long existed and been used in African music.

Musical creativity in Africa involves an abundance of other instruments such as the harp, the lyre, the flute, bells, and various types of horns. All African music is not simply "drumming" as most Westerners, historically, have thought. It is crucial to understand that as important as rhythm is there are essential harmonic and melodic aspects of African music. African-Americans were well aware of melody and harmony when they began to create blues, ragtime, and later improvised jazz. This fully explains their innate and natural use of "blue notes" and other daring harmonic constructions found in all music pioneered by African-Americans that went against the "rules" of Western harmony.

Only when African rhythms merged with the nineteenth-century harmonic ideals prevalent in European-based brass bands did the former's harmony in percussion begin to take a back seat. This was somewhat normal because most people can remember an instrumental melody much more easily than a percussive rhythm; rhythms, especially those found in jazz, tend to be complex and not readily heard. However, ignoring the harmonic presence in percussion was simply also a way to minimize any contribution made by a group of people who were not looked upon as equal human beings, let alone practitioners of a most brilliant art form.

To help explain the creation of a new musical language, let us take a look at the relationship of the origin of the human spoken language: how it began and evolved, and compare it to that of jazz trumpet. The comparison will allow us to perhaps determine with greater clarity and maybe even a degree of certainty what the earliest ragtime and jazz cornetists, such as E. W. Gravitt and Buddy Bolden, sounded like and what the state of jazz trumpet will be in the future.

According to Merritt Ruhlen, author of *The Origin of Language*, it is generally accepted that humans used simple gestures to communicate before they began to speak. The study of chimpanzees reveals that they use hand gestures to communicate, as we still do use them when we speak today. He also notes that the origin of language is taken to mean the evolution of the *capacity* for speech in our biological ancestors/cousins such as Neanderthal Man, *Homo erectus*,

Homo habilis, and the celebrated Lucy, a human female discovered in Africa and thought to have lived three million years ago. These early gestures eventually evolved into spoken sounds, such as a grunt or moan, to express a wide range of emotions. These grunts and moans did not further evolve into clearly spoken words, perhaps hundreds, thousands, or even millions of years.

As prehistoric humans observed and learned more about their immediate environment as well as the sky and stars above them, this information amounted to sort of a data bank of memories and stored information that could be used to find solutions to a myriad of questions, situations, or problems.

The first jazz musicians acted in a similar fashion in that they were forced to create something completely new, original, without precedent, and lasting. This new medium was necessary for their own self-expression and later proved to be instrumental in their overall adaptation to the dominant culture. In others words, the creation by African-Americans of the highest form of musical improvisation—jazz music—was, I believe, a necessary and inevitable part of their evolution and matriculation as citizens of the United States.

Now, we can begin to get closer to the actual situations that began to create ragtime (a parent or cousin of jazz) and then jazz itself. Because of Reconstruction after the Civil War and the introduction of the Black Codes, any new freedoms and privileges that African-Americans had gained were rescinded by denying them jury trials, forbidding travel without a pass, and most absurd, making it illegal to be unemployed. In spite of these and other hardships—or because of them—music became the first and perhaps most profound way these men and women would be able to rise above their deplorable conditions and progress toward what Dr. Martin Luther King Jr. would call nearly a century later his great American "dream."

The instinctive need for a new form of self-expression amid brutal oppression would soon find an opportunity to flourish. The former slave owners and politicians took back the promise of "forty acres and a mule" made by General Sherman after realizing that they still needed slaves to work the land. So slavery was replaced by sharecropping, which was another form of slavery—economic slavery. The arrangement kept generation after generation of black farmers in dire poverty. There are still effects of this system today.

Also because of the suffrage movement, the Fifteenth Amendment to the U.S. Constitution was ratified in 1870, guaranteeing African-Americans the right to vote. Although this would not be fully enforced until the mid-twentieth century, ex-slaves began to hold political office, purchase some land, and generally seek enjoyment of the artistic and finer things in life that their white fellow citizens had always been privileged to experience. Once the ex-slave had a small taste of freedom and access, the culture and society would never be the same again—especially in music.

From 1865 to 1877, when universal suffrage was legislated but not always enforced and the Black Codes were introduced, there was wider access to musical instruments, particularly brass instruments that had been primarily used by military bands during the Civil War. Bugles, cornets, trombones, alto horns, bass drums, cymbals, snare drums, and clarinets found their way into the hands of ex-slaves through antique stores, pawn shops, general stores, and simply being left behind on war-ravaged plantations and fields. With the slave's work hollers and chants and field

songs already established, the blues and the folk song slowly began to take shape.

The music of Bach, Beethoven, Haydn, Mozart, and other classical greats had been prevalent throughout the northern and southern U.S. for many decades, but the music of the brass bands was perhaps the most accessible to blacks in those years, so at least from a structural standpoint, it is natural that this was perhaps the main form of music that provided elements for the birth of ragtime. Ragtime, in general, is a heavily syncopated music with rhythmic patterns similar to those found in the playing of African percussion masters. Syncopation, the heartbeat of ragtime, by rough definition, is when rhythms of a duple nature, or with a "two-beat" feel, are juxtaposed with those that are not easily divided into two.

The unmistakable elements of the blues, field hollers, spiritual chants and songs, and rhythms of African origin were also omnipresent at the time and would be among the first notes to be played by an African American improvising or "ragging" the melody, perhaps on a piano or on a cornet within a brass band.

While researching the life of the king of ragtime, pianist and composer Scott Joplin, who was also the son of former slaves and played cornet, I came across a photo taken in 1897 of the Queen City Cornet Band. This band of about twelve musicians was formed in 1891 in Sedalia, Missouri, some 195 miles east of St. Louis and the Mississippi River. While looking at the photo, I was struck by the name of E. W. Gravitt, who was identified as a "cornet soloist." For the first time, it occurred to me that someone might have preceded pioneering cornetist Charles "Buddy" Bolden in improvising or ragging the melody in a musical context that was non-European in its essence. Could E. W. Gravitt be the first in the

Photo courtesy of Edward A. Berlin

The Queen City Cornet Band of Sedalia, Missouri, October 24, 1897. Arrow is pointing to cornet soloist E. W. Gravitt. Note: Dr. Edward A. Berlin told me that this photograph, which was noted in his book, *King of Ragtime—Scott Joplin and His Era* (Oxford University Press, 1994) as having been taken in 1895, was actually taken on October 24, 1897.

lineage of what would eventually be called jazz trumpet? We can also add the name of Francis Johnson to this question. And did Buddy Bolden and all of those other excellent cornet players in New Orleans follow their examples although no written or recorded evidence exists?

Before thoroughly addressing the influence of ragtime on what was to become jazz, we must examine a major factor that literally provided the path for this music to reach New Orleans: the Mississippi River. Created by the end of the Ice Age one million years ago, it is purported to have been given its width (in some areas it is more than a mile wide) by a massive earthquake. This 2,300-mile long stretch of water runs from Minneapolis in the north to New Orleans in the south, then empties into the Gulf of Mexico. The Mississippi separates or joins the eastern and western United States and at one time was the beginning of the western frontier. Biographer Lloyd Lewis calls it the "spinal column of America in the mid-nine-

teenth century"; my artist friend Michelle Martinez calls it "the Internet of its day."

By the start of the Civil War in 1861, this body of muddy brown water had become the principal avenue for commerce and travel in the U.S., and conquering or securing it would determine victory. Steamboats were the primary vehicles for trade and travel in the decades prior to the war, but after it ended, trains began to replace steamboats for hauling freight and steamboats began to be used for entertainment purposes. These boats carried a myriad of different types of acts, such as theater and variety shows, exotic animal shows, museums, and operas. The arrival of a steamboat was a major attraction in any town along the shores of the Mississippi circa 1870.

Steamboats originating in New Orleans, St. Louis, and Memphis would do one-nighters up and down the Mississippi River for small towns, but in larger places like New Orleans and St. Louis, they would stay longer. Such venues were where a host of black entertainers had their first large audiences. In 1879, despite the river being the new circuit of employment for Negro entertainers, local and state officials from Mississippi moved to shut down the parts of the river that were in their state and threatened to "sink any boats that carried Negroes." However, the river, without question, is one of the ways that the rhythms from New Orleans reached St. Louis, Sedalia, and other cities in the Midwest; it is also the same way that ragtime reached New Orleans, via the blues in Memphis.

Now, the question of whether E. W. Gravitt of the Queen City Cornet Band in Sedalia, Missouri was among the first—before Buddy Bolden of New Orleans—to improvise on a cornet in a band context can be discussed. If Gravitt, in the years 1891–1900, was "ragging" the melody, which

Map of the Mississippi River.

around 1895. Bolden played ragtime himself. Naturally, he began to improvise on it while incorporating elements of the blues and spirituals; thus he began to hear what was first called "jass." It is known that ragtime was the most popular music of the day when Bolden reached his peak of popularity and importance, around 1904–1905. The crucial difference between it and early jazz was that the variety of rhythms that would eventually define jazz were mainly in New Orleans, having arrived there from Africa and various parts of the Caribbean. However, the rhythms played by the African-American percussionists in the Queen City Cornet Band in Sedalia, Missouri, were being interpreted in an infinite variety of ways, like the rhythms easily found in New Orleans. Those rhythms had arrived in St. Louis and Sedalia as well as other parts of the Midwest and North, via the Mississippi River steamboats. This variety of interpretation supports my theory that the natural musical instinct of the African, especially the African percussionist, has never been one of monotony. This realization came to me while I was in high school. In marching band, our percussionists, all of whom were of African descent, never played the same drum cadence or arrangement the same way from week to week, or sometimes even from day to day. It changed and progressed constantly, and my band director used to marvel at what they would come up with next. It was actually hilarious because they not only did what seemingly came naturally to them but also defied authority in doing so. This will take on more significance later.

The job of a bass drummer in an American or European marching band is to basically keep a steady beat, or a consistent *boom-boom-boom-boom*. This way of playing is just not interesting enough for African-American rhythmic sensibili-

means he was improvising on it or improving it, then what he was doing can very well be considered what we today call jazz improvisation. And since Gravitt played the cornet, basically a short trumpet, he may have been one of the first jazz trumpeters.

It must be noted that musicians were playing ragtime in New Orleans before Buddy Bolden began to emerge as an important musician ties, I have found, so the drummer instinctively varies his patterns (such as *boom, BOOM, ba-boom-BOOM-boom, boom-BA-boom, BOOM-boom-boom-BA-boom,* etc.) to fit with certain phrases played by the group or soloist, especially those that are "ragged" and improvised. Since African-Americans were playing the rhythms underneath Gravitt's and Bolden's solo cornet, it stands to reason that such improvised rhythms, like the perpetual variations in accents and rhythmic displacement, gave jazz its essence.

The thing that set ragtime apart from all other music and made it so popular was its rhythm. What Scott Joplin and other composers of ragtime did was to basically place syncopated rhythms against the form and "two-beat" feel of the march. As Edward Berlin points out in *King of Ragtime: Scott Joplin and His Era*: "Combining these elements points to the dance origin of ragtime, because the march was also known as a popular dance form called the two-step." John Philip Sousa's "The Washington Post," a march written in 1889, was also used for dancing. I can remember playing the first cornet part to this march while in high school and watching my band director, Mr. Gordon Boykin, prance around the room to show us the emotion that this march was meant to arouse—the one that makes people dance, albeit squarely by today's standards.

Scott Joplin used the same twelve notes that Bach, Mozart, and Beethoven used, but he had a completely unique and different interpretation of rhythm, which Gravitt and the Queen City Cornet Band and others emulated. I learned very early in my development as a jazz musician that it is not *what* you play, but *how* you play it. Interpretation and specific inflections are what has allowed our music to progress from field hollers to blues to ragtime to jazz and what made Louis Armstrong,

Charlie Parker, Dizzy Gillespie, Duke Ellington, and especially Thelonious Monk all geniuses. It is also the reason why I can walk onto any jazz bandstand and improvise a solo using all twelve notes on any given chord. I can explain theoretically any of the notes I choose to play, especially if I am the only one who heard and felt those particular notes, but if I am not playing with a certain type of rhythmic intensity combined with a spiritual awareness most identified with what we now know as swing, then I am not in keeping with the style that defines jazz.

Because musicians such as E. W. Gravitt were most likely self-taught, the most natural way of learning an instrument such as the cornet, especially in the late nineteenth century, would have been for the musician to try to talk or sing through the instrument. With this realization, we have to take a look at how African-American spoken language and, more precisely, their dialects affected the sound that was eventually produced. This is key to understanding why jazz sounds the way it does on wind instruments particularly. How ex-slaves pronounced and enunciated words in imitation of white citizens in order to survive was a major factor in determining the sound of such players as E. W. Gravitt and Buddy Bolden. Whereas the "correct" way of speaking English in the United States was to pronounce words such as "that," "this," and "there" phonetically, the ex-slaves, with their completely different and relaxed inner rhythm and delivery of speech, and their still evolving native language, pronounced these same words with much different inflections and more syllables. "That" became "daht," "this" became "dis," and "there" became "dere." For example, a very famous composition written by jazz pianist Bobby Timmons, of the Cannonball and Nat Adderley Quintet of the 1960s, called "Dis Here," or as Cannonball Adderley pronounced it on the live recording of the *Cannonball Adderley Quintet Live in San Francisco* (Riverside OJCCD 035-2), "Dis Hii-uh."

So when the early ragtime and jazz musicians began to play, they brought to their instruments a broad sense of rhythm and harmony coupled with unique speech patterns. This new way of playing the cornet in particular was vastly different from the way classical musicians played the works written by composers such as Bach, Mozart, Haydn, Hummel, and cornetist J. B. Arban. Whereas the typical European cornetist would produce notes on his instrument by pronouncing through the mouthpiece the words "tah" or "tee" or "tu," the self-taught African-American in attempting to produce the same notes, naturally pronounced "tah" as "dah" or "tha," "tee" as "dee" or "thee," and "tu" as "du" or "thoo." They also found their own intonation, which is part of the reason that bent pitches or "blue" notes—the notes between the keys of the piano or those made when the valves of the cornet are pressed only halfway down—sounded good to them. These sounds were closer to the ones prevalent in the field hollers and work songs they were used to hearing. Ultimately, this provided for a vastly different sound on the cornet that affected the musician's creativity at his earliest stage of development.

Jazz trumpeters today who truly swing and do not play in a "square" or uptight fashion use the same articulation that came from Africans' native speech—"du," "dah," and "dee." When we scat-sing a solo, or improvise like a seasoned jazz instrumentalist, we are more apt to sing phrases that use the more relaxed words "du," "dee," "daht," "diht," and "dah," rather than the shorter and more square-sounding words of "tat," "tee," "tu," and "tit." It was simply a new language that at first

was rejected as being from a subclass of people with seemingly no artistic sensibility. But as with any art of consequence, this articulation would prove to be something that very few people could ever hope to do, regardless of the level of talent they might display in performing the best instrumental compositions in classical or any other styles. African-Americans proved with their creation of ragtime and jazz that the creation of high art is not the sole domain of the elite.

The work of ragtime and jazz musicians requires consideration in terms of four creative phases—Africa, Europe, the New World, and the artist's creative vision. Without understanding these elements in conjunction with one another, it may be difficult and in some cases impossible to fully comprehend and appreciate a particular instrumentalist, group, or style of the music.

Finally, having explored in a most basic form how the historical and cultural conditions, most particularly in the years following the Civil War, affected the early experimentation and discovery among the first ragtime and jazz musicians, we can now move on to that port city of New Orleans, Louisiana. It is a place that combines all facets of both Africans and Europeans—culture, politics, ethnicity, religion, cuisine, art, language, and of course, music—in a most unique fashion. This is where we can safely say that jazz—pure jazz—was born. This melting pot of a city had the necessary elements of European musical form, military marches, slave chants, African and Caribbean rhythms, blues, and ragtime, much like the various ingredients found in its best gumbo, to create the first legend of jazz. This legend from New Orleans, for a century credited as the primary source who combined all of the necessary elements to a new art called jazz, perhaps the Alpha of jazz trumpet, was Mr. Charles "Buddy" Bolden.

Charles "Buddy" Bolden to Joseph "King" Oliver: The Beginnings of Jazz Trumpet

New Orleans, Louisiana, in the year 1905. A handsome young man of African and Native American descent sits on the front porch of his home at 2309 First Street, only several minutes by streetcar from the French Quarter, playing his cornet. The neighborhood has many different ethnic groups, but is full of life and the many activities that would be associated with the essence of New Orleans—a strong reverence for simple fellowship with family and friends, with music as the central theme. The sounds emanating from his cornet, however, were much more than that. In keeping with a tradition of experimentation and improvisation in its purest sense from his African ancestors, Charles "Buddy" Bolden (1877–1931) produced a fusion of sounds derived from what he heard in his sanctified church, the blues, the military and John Philip Sousa marches he played in parades, the work songs and chants he heard on the banks of the Mississippi River, classic waltzes, original funeral dirges, the unique mixtures of African and Caribbean rhythms in the city, and most important, ragtime, which would form the nucleus of what would become the most important music of the twentieth century—jazz.

The legend of Buddy Bolden began as soon as he filled the New Orleans air with the powerful and unmistakable sound of his cornet. So much has been written about him that it is sometimes hard to discern where the legend ends and true facts begin. But one thing is for certain: Buddy Bolden was the first instrumentalist to fuse different styles of music, based on improvisation from an African-American perspective, in such a way as to create something that eventually became known as jazz. Before Bolden, no one dared to combine elements of sacred music with the secular sounds of the bawdy nightlife entertainment prevalent in bordellos, bars, and brothels all over the area of New Orleans called Storyville. But that daring was to become the

Photo by author

The home of Charles "Buddy" Bolden, a founding father of jazz: 2309 First Street, New Orleans.

17

Photo courtesy of Hogan Jazz Archives, Tulane University

The only known photograph of the Buddy Bolden Band, circa 1905. Bolden is in the back row, third from left, and next to the bassist. Valve trombonist Willie Cornish is to Bolden's right.

model for jazz, which set it apart from all other music because it is in itself a fusion.

Purportedly, there are no recordings in existence that would provide us with tangible proof of Bolden's talents, but my research has led me to conclude that the Bolden band made a cylinder recording around 1904 that has since been lost. According to Bolden's trombonist, Willie Cornish, who was interviewed in 1939 at his home on Perdido Street, the cylinder recording was made by a local New Orleans grocer. This would not have been unusual at the time, because Thomas Edison had introduced the cylinder recording in 1887, and by 1904, it was in wide use in the United States. And for a band as popular as Bolden's, a recording, however informal and experimental it may have seemed at the time, was very likely made.

So just what would that cylinder recording of Buddy Bolden have told us about his sound and talent? It is written that Bolden's cornet could be heard for miles across New Orleans when he would "call his chillun' home" to come and dance to his band at the legendary Funky Butt Hall. Given that New Orleans sits below sea level and

that at that time there were no loud noises of thousands of automobiles to clutter the night air, it is feasible indeed that Bolden could be easily heard for a few miles. The general nature of his tone or sound has to be derived principally from statements by the musicians who were with him or by the first generation after Bolden. Pops Foster, one of the fathers of the jazz bass, said, "I saw Buddy Bolden at Johnson's Park. He played very good. He played nothing but blues and he played it very loud." But the variety of music that Bolden played is most significant here, and the most concrete evidence of it is the whistled example provided by Bunk Johnson during a 1940s interview, transcribed in the introduction of this book.

From that example, what can we derive about Bolden? We can attempt to analyze rhythmically and perhaps harmonically the kind of things that Bolden liked to play, but not everything he played would have been like this one melody. This example is keeping with the gradual fusion of ragtime with the military march. The use of the blues would obviously be a part of Bolden's sound, but the choice of notes, upon first glance, might not indicate that he was playing the blues on this melody. The "blue" notes, so termed by historians in an attempt to name what they weren't used to hearing and therefore could not properly notate, do not necessarily have to be played each time a jazz musician plays the blues or plays with blues feeling. Any seasoned jazz soloist can play a blues using the pretty notes like the major thirds, sixths, and ninths and sound just as bluesy as anyone because they know what to with those notes. So this melody by Bunk, if played by any of us today, might not sound anything like Bolden, but it is concrete evidence of at least one melody he played.

Once of the major factors that would have contributed to the overall sound of Buddy Bolden would have been his spiritual upbringing, meaning the Catholic and/or the Baptist church, and the sacred music he heard there. Any musician who was raised in the church knows that it is impossible to completely eliminate traces of its musical influence in one's playing. His sound, as described by Dude Bottley to Danny Barker in *Buddy Bolden and the Last Days of Storyville*, was a powerful and even eerie mixture of spiritual hymns with the blues at its core. Another major factor would have been the method of playing the cornet as well as the instrument's sound in and of itself. Knowing something about Bolden's level of instrumental technique would provide another avenue for exploring what he was actually able to play. More detailed study needs to be done for that. However, I would venture there are reasons to believe that Bolden's technique, like that of many legendary clarinetists in New Orleans, such as Lorenz Tio Jr. and his students Sidney Bechet and Johnny Dodds, was formidable. In 1884–1885, New Orleans hosted the World's Industrial and Cotton Centennial Exposition, and the Mexican government sent the band of the Eighth Regiment of the Mexican Calvary to play concerts. The Mexican musicians, most of whom were trained in conservatories were renowned for world-class technique. After the exposition ended, dozens of them stayed in New Orleans, including the Tio family. They would soon become part of the music scene in New Orleans and would contribute significantly to the development of better technique among the natives of the city. On the cornet, for example, people whose native language requires more use of the *ka* sound and rolling of the tongue to produce the *r* sound tend to be able to execute tongued passages easier. And in my experience, it is the agility and strength of the tongue that allow the musician to control the cornet or trumpet to a degree commensurate with the highest levels of technique. Bolden undoubtedly came into contact with these musicians and was very likely influenced or inspired to achieve something similar himself. In the final analysis, I think that Bolden's legend, which has been seriously researched by only two or three people over the last fifty years, can safely be said to be real. He was no myth—no aberration of someone's mind. Mr. Bolden existed and he played the cornet like no one else on the planet during his time.

Beginning around 1904, Buddy Bolden was successful enough to be referred to as king of New Orleans jazz. This is why he was called "King Bolden." The term *king* began with him and subsequently was applied to trumpeters or cornetists Manuel Perez, Freddie Keppard, and Joseph "King" Oliver. But how that crown was transferred from Bolden to Perez, Keppard, and Oliver is a sad story. Bolden worked so much and was so popular that he eventually had several bands under his name working as many as four or five jobs at once. He would go to each job and play a little to honor the contract, but being stretched so thin began to take a toll on him physically and even more mentally. He eventually struck his mother in a fit of rage and was arrested and hospitalized. He recovered somewhat, but during a parade in 1907, he finally went insane. He was marching in the band of Henry Allen Sr. and simply dropped out of the line due to either extreme exhaustion or symptoms of heatstroke. Whatever it was, combined with being overworked physically and mentally, it was enough to cause a breakdown. That was the last time he ever played in public.

Once Bolden was taken out of the parade, he was taken home, and the medical authorities would eventually be called to take a look at him. But before that, as Dude Bottley reported to Barker, Dude went to Bolden's home to see if he was all right. Standing on the front steps, he saw and heard Bolden sitting in his darkened living room playing the blues mixed eerily with a spiritual.

It was decided that Bolden needed institutional care, and he was taken to a mental hospital in Jackson, Mississippi, where he remained for the rest of his life. He never fully regained his senses enough to play again or recognize where he was and why he was there. He died in 1931, seemingly forgotten. The musicians of New Orleans carried on and the crown of king of jazz trumpet went to Manuel Perez, then to Freddie Keppard. On one occasion around 1911, Keppard caused such a stir in the town square in New Orleans that the mayor reversed an ordinance against playing trumpets or loud instruments within the city. As noted in the brilliant research of Lawrence Gushee in his book *Pioneers of Jazz: the Story of the Creole Band* (Oxford University Press, 2005), Keppard was one of the stars of the Creole band that was the first band to "bring authentic jazz out of New Orleans to audiences around America," beginning around 1914. As Jelly Roll Morton states, "He had a beautiful tone and there was no end to his ideas. He could play one chorus eight or ten different ways." Morton also goes on to say that Keppard could make high notes as clear as a whistle and was "the first to start the high note business."

There were Keppard and other such cornetists as Manuel Perez, and Joe Howard (who would help mentor Louis Armstrong in the riverboat band of Fate Marable), Jim Humphrey, George McCullum, Joe Johnson, Willie Hightower, Kid Shots Madison, Kid Rena, and Frank Keely (who could make the trumpet sound like a chicken), Thornton Blue (who was playing so hard at a funeral one day that he dropped dead on the spot), Tig Chambers, Peter Bocage, Arnold Metoyer, Sugar Johnny, Dave Perkins, John Penerton, Johnny Lala, James Williams, Wild Ned (who, according to Louis Armstrong, was better than Buddy Bolden), Ed Clem (who used to substitute for Bolden), Harrison Goughe, Buddy Petit, and Nic La Rocca of the Original Dixieland Jazz Band.

These men would all take a back seat to the man who would be the last to be called of "king" of jazz trumpet—Joseph "King" Oliver, mentor and idol to Louis Armstrong. Not much is written about the early career of King Oliver except that he played with Kid Ory and was a major influence on the early development of Louis Armstrong. Oliver became an early master of mutes, and the natural tendency to find new sounds seemed to be strong in Oliver and his fellow New Orleans cornetist, Thomas "Papa" Mutt Carey. I was given information that suggests that when Oliver went to Chicago in 1918, he had developed and perfected a design for the Harmon mute. Oliver was playing at Paddy Harmon's Dreamland Ballroom in Chicago, and after he left for California, Harmon took the idea to a manufacturer. Oliver never got credit for the design, and to this day, nearly all trumpeters in the world use the Harmon mute at one point or another. As Jelly Roll Morton points out, "King Oliver was the one that caused mutes to come into existence."

King Oliver immediately established himself as Chicago's most talented trumpeter and the master of a new style that would soon be altered from its original conception ever so slightly. This was because Oliver arrived at a time in U.S.

history when the industrial age was requiring more manpower, especially in the city of Chicago. Thousands migrated north and brought along their tastes in music, art, fashion, cuisine, and politics. The music of New Orleans, which Oliver and his cohorts represented, would soon take on the urgency of the vibe of Chicago, and in doing so, the tempo became faster to reflect its new environment. The jazz musicians had to develop more instrumental agility and technique to play the faster tempos. As New Orleans guitarist Johnny St. Cyr said, "The Chicago bands played only fast tempos—the fastest numbers played by the New Orleans bands were slower than the Chicago tempo." This meant that the music, primarily due to environment, was beginning to undergo its first major transition, soon to be fueled by the arrival of Louis Armstrong in August 1922. This transition would confirm Chicago as the new center of jazz in the United States, although the music of James Reese Europe featuring cornetist Cricket Smith was helping to shape the sound of jazz in New York.

The reasons King Oliver sent for Louis Armstrong to join him in Chicago seem be clear. First, by 1918–1922, the music that Oliver brought up from New Orleans was undergoing a change that could be felt and heard nightly. Chicago demanded more sophisticated musical performers to match the caliber in its theaters, cuisine, fashion, and industry, and musicians found that they had to be as forward thinking in their craft as well as accommodating to the audience. The latter requirement, which would manifest itself fully some twenty years later in the swing era, would prove to be almost a death blow to musicians who were intent on making musical advancement rather than totally pleasing an audience.

King Oliver recorded a very important solo on "Dippermouth Blues" in 1923, during the same period that produced Armstrong's first recorded track with Oliver, "Chimes Blues." This cornet solo by Oliver is perhaps his most famous, because it demonstrates his mastery of the wa-wa effect and his natural and seasoned ability to play all up and inside of the blues. This solo would be learned by all serious trumpeters of the 1920s. But soon all the attention was focused on Louis. Beginning around 1924, Oliver had to shuffle from one gig to the next. When it became clear that New York was becoming the next new center of jazz, due largely to the success of Fletcher Henderson and to a 1927 Chicago city ordinance that closed most of the main ballrooms and other venues that jazz and nightlife thrived, Oliver left for New York. I have read that the management of the famous Cotton Club approached Oliver soon after he arrived about bringing in his band to provide music for the floor shows. Oliver thought that the money being offered was too little for someone of his stature, especially since he was in part responsible for the phenomenal success of Louis Armstrong, so he turned down the offer. The management of the Cotton Club made the same offer to Duke Ellington, and the rest is jazz history. Ellington came into his own at the Cotton Club. Maybe the legend of Oliver was always on Duke's mind, because from that very engagement throughout the remaining fifty years of his career and life, Ellington's band featured a trumpet plunger specialist in the style and manner of King Oliver, with the first being the great Bubber Miley.

Oliver had no truly significant and artistically pivotal engagements after missing out on the Cotton Club engagement. He did manage to have a successful run at New York's Savoy Ballroom for several months, beginning in May 1927, but when it ended, his band dispersed, leaving Oliver to do gigs with pick-up bands. Oliver toured from 1930 to 1936 in the Midwest and South with ten- to twelve-piece bands and eventually settled in Savannah, Georgia. He had terrible teeth and gum problems that eventually forced him to quit playing; he had to pawn his horn and some of his best clothes and began to do menial jobs, such as running a fruit stand and sweeping up in a pool hall to survive. Maybe because of pride, Oliver never asked for a helping hand from his protégé Louis Armstrong, now an internationally famous and wealthy musician, who could have helped him get on his feet. Finally, in April 1938 in Savannah, Joseph "King" Oliver—the New Orleans-born cornet master, inventor of the Harmon mute, and most important, the teacher and mentor to Louis Armstrong—died a poor and nearly forgotten man. However, his important contributions to the history of jazz trumpet are recognized and preserved in the accounts of musicians and historians.

Louis Armstrong:
The Most Important Jazz Trumpeter

Mr. Louis Armstrong. *Louis Armstrong. L-o-u-i-sssss*. If there was ever any doubt as to how to pronounce his name, listen to his self-introduction on his huge hit, *Hello Dolly!* in 1964. He sings emphatically, "This is *Louisssss.* Dolly." Arm*strong*. Pops. Satchmo. Dippermouth. The *father* of jazz trumpet sent from heaven to play for us. Mr. Armstrong. Son. Brother. Husband. Leader. Friend. World Citizen. Goodwill ambassador. *Musician*. Trumpet virtuoso. Vocalist, who sang through his trumpet. The epitome of swing. Rhythm. Sound. Gentle Giant. Genius. As Duke Ellington once said, "He was born poor, died rich, and never hurt anyone along the way."

I would not be writing this book if it were not for Mr. Louis Armstrong. More important, I am sure I would not be a jazz trumpeter. This holds true, I can safely say, for an untold number of my colleagues both past and present. Without the legacy of Armstrong preserved on recordings and film, none of us really would have an idea of what we would play today. Pops. He left us profound messages that are still being deciphered. For those of you who may not yet fully understand, go and get everything with Louis Armstrong's name on it; listen to him for several years—ah yes, years; really *listen*, then you might have an idea of what

a lot of us know. He was simply someone sent here by the Creator to revolutionize the basic fundamentals of music, and the trumpet, in a most personal way. In the course of doing so, he gave to his native land, one that had enslaved and brutalized his immediate ancestors and

Louis Armstrong, circa 1930.

23

continued to deny him basic human rights guaranteed in its own Constitution, an art form that has lifted millions of people around the world to a euphoric plane of intellectual stimulation that will never end. Louis Armstrong alone raised the worldwide understanding and acceptance of the artistic merit of African Americans to a new level. And he did so with a humble and gentle nature wrapped around and inside of his golden trumpet. As we go forward into the twenty-first century, his accomplishments, when weighed against the odds that were crippling the vast majority of his people, are even more startling in their profundity and timelessness.

Louis Armstrong was born in New Orleans, Louisiana, on August 4, 1901, to a poor family. The South had only been forced to free its slaves roughly thirty-five years earlier. There are numerous books that detail his life and work and, to my knowledge, all but one of them (*Louis*, by British trumpeter John Chilton) were written by people who are not jazz trumpeters or musicians. Although the biographical and some analytical information is generally correct and, of course, important, I have always felt that there could have been more written about what it really means to be able to create what he did on his trumpet. Unless one plays the trumpet and has attempted to perform Armstrong's music and trumpet solos, the true essence and magnitude of his gifts and efforts may not be heard on a particular level. It can only be theorized. When I put the trumpet to my lips and began to learn his solos and music, all theories were ushered out the door through a sobering realization of his genius based on practical application.

The trumpet is one of the most difficult, if not the most difficult of instruments to play, let alone master, and this process requires constant practice and performance, both mental and physical. For jazz trumpeters and pursuers of our correct history, the true pioneers are obvious, as they have added distinct and important vocabulary to the jazz language. At the top of the list is Charles "Buddy" Bolden, the first cornetist to fuse together elements of ragtime, blues, spirituals, and military marches with an inherent African approach to rhythm. That provided the foundation from which sprang forth unique individualists such as Bunk Johnson, Freddie Keppard, Manuel Perez, and eventually Joseph "King" Oliver, who was Armstrong's idol and teacher.

Mr. Armstrong, however, was the first jazz musician to synthesize all that came before him. The sacred music and varied elements of Bolden, the sweet tone of Bunk Johnson, the reckless abandon of Keppard, the quiet but competitive fire of Perez, and the complete soulfulness, generosity, and imagination of Oliver. He took all of those traits and added a level of instrumental virtuosity that was equal to and in many respects greater than that of the most celebrated cornet soloists of the period, such as Herbert L. Clarke and Jules Levy. The difference between Armstrong and those cornetists like Clarke, Levy—and even Haydn, Beethoven, and Bach—was that Armstrong was the first important musician to use his *bandstand* as his musical score. This idea will be discussed more later. Armstrong was also quite aware of the methods of composers Scott Joplin and Jelly Roll Morton, and developed a fresh and unique approach to jazz trumpet improvisation that is the foundation of what my colleagues and I play today.

Before I began to study Armstrong's work seriously, I listened to some of his records and saw him on old television specials from time to time and never really thought too much of it, although my parents would yell enthusiastically for me to run and catch him on TV. I was already learning Freddie Hubbard solos and solos from my Basie and Ellington records, which featured Ray Nance and a few others. I thought I had a pretty solid command of the trumpet from these solos along with my private classical studies from books by Sigmund Herring, J. B. Arban, Herbert L. Clarke, and Max Schlossberg. So years later when Wynton Marsalis suggested that I learn some Louis Armstrong solos, it went in one ear and out the other. I thought that he was old hat and not really playing too much. I could not get used to listening to the *sound* of the very early recordings of Armstrong's. I was used to listening to things in full stereo with good mixes and seemingly—but deceptively—greater levels of dynamics. The last thing I wanted was to sit down and listen closely to something that I could barely decipher from a sonic standpoint. One hot summer night around 1987, however, in my apartment in Tallahassee, Florida, I put on one of my Louis Armstrong records from a double album set (*July 4, 1900/July 6, 1971*–RCA) and made myself listen to it. My mind was relaxed and open to let this music in, really let it in. Suddenly, I began to feel as though the band from the record, the Louis Armstrong All-Stars, were in the room, playing just for me. I began to hear all of the instruments in the group clearly. The volume wasn't loud, but just right—enough to draw me in with much interest. Then it happened: the majestic, powerful, soulful, happy, imposing, advanced, big, pretty, rough, brilliant, full, brassy, earthy, and perfect sound of Mr. Louis Armstrong hit me like a freight train hitting a disabled golf cart. Then I began to understand. *This* was what all the fuss was about.

After coming down to earth, I began to re-listen to the album to see if there was a solo that I could learn. I found one on the last track of the album, a composition entitled "Blues in the South." Recorded in 1952, it seemed like a simple blues chorus that I could master within a half hour or so. I made a tape and then sat down with my trumpet to learn it. First, I listened to it about five times to make sure I could feel where the rhythm was. It was a blues in F concert and he only played one chorus or twelve bars in 4/4 time. I got the first phrase of seven consecutive notes (fourth space trumpet D) immediately, but the second phrase came down on me and my trumpet like a jackhammer smashing a fly! I thought, *What the hell is happening here? Unbelievable!* I was stunned at the profundity of Armstrong's seemingly simple, but actually complex and unique delivery of rhythm. About one week later, I finally had the solo. That was a major lesson in studying and understanding Armstrong's work. And after learning many more of his solos over the years, my humble study of this musical genius continues.

"Pops," as he was known most affectionately, was at his very core a singer. To understand his unique innovations melodically and rhythmically, this must be clear. He sang through his trumpet in a way that allowed him to transcend basic instrumental problems that face all trumpeters: consistent clarity, intonation, and ease of execution. Of course, he had to practice and learn the basic mechanics of the cornet/trumpet first. He began while living at the Colored Waifs' Home when he was twelve years old. He had been sent there after firing a loaded gun in the streets of New Orleans in the wee hours of New Year's morning in 1913. At the home, he was allowed to join the band on tambourine, but yearned for a chance to play the bugle. Mr. Peter Davis, the director of the band, allowed young Louis to play the tambourine, then the alto horn, and eventually the bugle. Armstrong would play in the morning and awaken the sleepyheads with the sound of his bugle. I can think of no better way than to be awakened than by the sound of Louis Armstrong playing.

Before being whisked off to the juvenile home, young Armstrong used to sing with his friends for money on the streets of New Orleans. They had a hot vocal quartet and would sing and harmonize various songs that provided Armstrong with a harmonic foundation and understanding that would guide him for the remainder of his life. Once Louis started playing the bugle at the home, he got really good at it quickly and Davis let him play the cornet after the main bugler at the home had been discharged.

Armstrong himself was discharged from the Waifs' Home after a year and a half. He went to live with his father, stepmother, and half-brother, but soon he yearned for his mother and sister. He returned to working to help support his family and became a frequent visitor to the part of New Orleans that featured the music of King Oliver, Kid Ory, and others. He would also hear Bunk Johnson, the direct disciple of Buddy Bolden, and even slept behind the piano until the band started to play. He describes in his earliest writings (*Louis Armstrong in His Own Words*) how he used to listen to Bunk's sweet tone with that port wine smell coming out of the bell. One day when King Oliver spotted Armstrong playing his beat-

Photo courtesy of Jack Bradley

Armstrong with Peter Davis (on stool in background) holding the cornet Armstrong had at the Waifs' home.

up old cornet, he gave the boy one of his own cornets. This made Oliver a hero to young Armstrong, who soaked up the lessons, formal and casual, Joseph "King" Oliver presented to him. The teenage Armstrong became a fixture at the Oliver household and even ran errands for Mrs. Oliver. The bond that was developing between the musician and his apprentice would serve them well several years later.

On November 12, 1917, Storyville, the center of musical nightlife in New Orleans where the main venues for the new music being called jazz were located, closed down due to a city ordinance. This event wiped out nearly all of the work for musicians, who began to migrate North. In June 1918, Joseph "King" Oliver left New Orleans for Chicago, which became the destination of many Americans during the so called "Great Migration." Chicago around this time was becoming the center of jazz, as most of the major practitioners of jazz were there. The teenaged Armstrong, however, continued to pay his dues by first taking over Oliver's spot in the band of trombonist Kid Ory. This was one of the first steady and important jazz jobs where he began to perfect his skills for improvisational counterpoint. His second major apprenticeship beginning in 1919 was with the riverboat band of Fate Marable on the *S.S. Sydney* (then the *S.S. Capitol*). The riverboats were among the first major avenues for black entertainment for sophisticated patrons, both black and white. The experience was extremely important for Armstrong as it taught him the disciplinary elements of professional musicianship: being on time, dressing accordingly, being prepared musically, and behaving in a sober and cordial manner. Armstrong almost didn't accept the offer, because he knew the musicians on the riverboat

Photo by author.

Armstrong played on riverboats like this one.

were superb sight-readers and he wasn't just yet. But he took the job after being assured that Marable's musicians would assist him with this. Dave Jones and first trumpeter Joe Howard helped Armstrong to perfect his sight-reading skills. This would prove crucial several years later when he would accept the invitation to join the great Fletcher Henderson Orchestra in 1924 in New York and then Erskine Tate in Chicago in late 1925.

Armstrong enjoyed the work on the riverboats for almost two years. He would go up and down the Mississippi River, one of the great "deliverers of jazz" to such towns as Memphis, Tennessee; St. Louis, Missouri; and Davenport, Iowa, where a promising young cornetist, Bix Beiderbeck, heard him in 1919. Also worth noting is the effect the riverboat atmosphere had on Armstrong's persona. With Marable, he learned the importance of pleasing an audience without having to sacrifice musical integrity. The varied audiences on those Streckfus Brothers boats helped him realize the importance of pleasing the audience, adding a smile and a laugh or two, and it was something that he would do for the rest of his life. Of course, his manager, Joe Glaser, also hammered home this reality, telling him to "Smile, Gotdammit! Give it to 'em."

Armstrong eventually left the riverboats because of exhaustion and not being paid what he thought he was worth. He went to New Orleans, with its seemingly endless supply of work for musicians, such as parties, funerals, dances, and parades. After one of those funeral parades, he received a telegram that would change his life. Joseph "King" Oliver, Armstrong's idol and mentor, who was in Chicago and leading one of the best bands there, saw a need for a second cornet to complement his lead. He thought of no one else but Armstrong and, in the summer of 1922, sent a telegram offering him the prestigious spot of second cornet in his band, the King Oliver Creole Jazz Band. Armstrong accepted immediately and was soon on his way to Chicago.

On August 8, 1922, as the train sped north from New Orleans, a twenty-one-year-old Louis Armstrong sat gazing out the window while eating the fish sandwiches his mother, Mayann, had prepared. This would be perhaps the single most important journey ever taken in the history of jazz music. His arrival in Chicago forever changed the way jazz music was practiced, performed, perceived, and understood. And because of Armstrong, Chicago became the center of the jazz world. In a few years, Armstrong would emerge from the shadow of Oliver and become the very first jazz musician to successfully combine the stylistic particulars of Buddy Bolden, Bunk Johnson, Manuel Perez, Freddie Keppard, and King Oliver himself.

Beginning with Armstrong's arrival in Chicago, and through the medium of recordings, it is possible to study his career in five distinct stages: with King Oliver, then Fletcher Henderson, his groundbreaking Hot Fives and Sevens recordings,

his big band years, and finally his years with the All-Stars, the band he would perform with until his death in 1971. Having paid his dues with Kid Ory and Fate Marable especially, we can see how he was already a professional when he arrived in Chicago to work with Oliver at the Lincoln Gardens. The close communication that Oliver and Armstrong shared enabled them to complement each other perfectly. As Armstrong played second cornet to Oliver's first, he gained a deeper understanding of how harmony and rhythm can function on a level other than the melody. His solos after his apprenticeship with Oliver hinted at implied countermelodies and alternate harmonies and rhythms that show how his music was also shaped by what he did *not* play.

The first recording to feature Armstrong after his arrival in Chicago is "Chimes Blues." It was recorded with King Oliver's band in 1923, and showcases for the first time on a recording the ease with which Oliver and Armstrong played together. According to most accounts, during the recording session, the studio engineers had to place Armstrong twenty feet behind all of the other musicians because his sound was so huge. This is another facet of his instrumental virtuosity: he was able to play the cornet/trumpet with so much power and volume, but at the same time with control.

The pianist in King Oliver's band, Lil Hardin, who had been classically trained at Fisk University, soon became enamored with the young Armstrong. She could see that he was already playing well beyond his peers and even the leader. She began to encourage him to sharpen all of his musical skills such as sight-reading and technique. Word was spreading all over Chicago, and even as far as New York, about the new cornet sensation and in 1924, Armstrong

Photo courtesy Hogan Jazz Archives, Tulane University

The King Oliver Creole Jazz Band in 1923. Armstrong is fourth from left and King Oliver is fifth from left, behind pianist Lil Hardin.

received and accepted an invitation to join perhaps the greatest jazz orchestra of the day, the Fletcher Henderson Orchestra. He had declined an offer to join Henderson in 1921. Henderson was a well-educated perfectionist who only hired the very best African-American musicians. His orchestra set the standard for which all others would soon follow. The members were well-rehearsed and attired in the finest tailor-made suits; and most important, they took liberties with the arrangements they played. Unlike other bands of the period, such as the popular Paul Whiteman orchestra, Henderson's musicians played the written music as if it were individual riffs based on the collective sound. This is the exact same thing that Count Basie refined to such a degree that his orchestra still performs to this day.

Armstrong arrived in New York in October 1924 to officially join the Fletcher Henderson

Orchestra. Within days, he was in the studio recording his first sides with the band. On the track "Go Long Mule" [disc 1, track 3, from *Fletcher Henderson: A Study in Frustration (Thesaurus of Classic Jazz)*–Columbia], Armstrong infuses the Henderson band with a confident and percussive quality to his playing that shifts the overall rhythmic conception of the group towards a freer and more loose feel. Armstrong's solo breaks in bars seven and eight of "Go Long Mule" show his lessons learned from his apprenticeship with Oliver. Especially worth noting is his eighth-note rhythm lead into bar three of the second chorus of the same tune. The way that he delivers those two simple eighth notes foretells his innovations on the *Hot Fives and Hot Sevens* recording, as well as the swing era, the complex medium of modern jazz—and even hard bop, to a point. This is but one example of how

Louis Armstrong began to change everything in jazz from the most obvious to the subtle.

Armstrong influenced several musicians in the orchestra, most notably Coleman Hawkins. This is significant because fifteen years later, in 1939, Hawkins would record his classic tenor saxophone solo on the standard composition "Body and Soul" that would seemingly revolutionize jazz and popular music. Hawkins would not have been able to do that had it not been for Louis Armstrong, whom he heard every night for a year. This is not to say that his solo wasn't a milestone and a masterpiece. But in 1935, four years earlier, Henry "Red" Allen, the second major link between Armstrong and Roy Eldridge with Jabbo Smith being the other, made a recording of "Body and Soul" (*Henry Allen: Original 1933–41 Recordings*–TAX S-3-2) that Hawkins could have very well copied in approach. Allen's version could have easily been recorded twenty years later when bebop was at its peak. In 1938, still another year before the Hawkins version, trumpet master Roy Eldridge, who always wanted to be better than Armstrong, along with another tenor saxophone giant, Chu Berry, recorded a version of "Body and Soul" (*Roy Eldridge: The Quintessence–Chicago to New York: 1936–1945* [FA 231, disc 1, track 15]) very similar to what Hawkins did a year later.

Armstrong decided to leave the Fletcher Henderson Orchestra in 1925, partly because he was not allowed to sing and felt that he was being held back. He went back to Chicago at the urging of his soon-to-be wife, Lil Hardin. She spoke with other club owners in Chicago and convinced them to book and bill him as the "World's Greatest Trumpeter." Armstrong's next pivotal move was to accept the invitation in late 1925 to join the Erskine Tate Orchestra at the Vendome Theater. This was when Armstrong switched from cornet to trumpet. The Tate orchestra played in the pit and were only feet away from the audience for their overture. As Armstrong told *Life* magazine in April 1966, "That's when I got a trumpet. Erskine's first chair man had a trumpet and he thought it looked funny, me with that stubby cornet." His sight-reading skills, honed to perfection with Fate Marable and Fletcher Henderson, began to pay off because Tate's orchestra routinely played compositions such as *Cavalleria Rusticana* that added to his experience and understanding of the work of great composers. These lessons soon helped Armstrong produce what are considered to be the most important recordings in the history of jazz music–the *Hot Fives and Hot Sevens*.

In November 1925, Louis Armstrong formed a group of five musicians to go into a Chicago studio to record original and popular pieces of the day for Okeh Records. With the combination of all of his years as a sideman and perfecting his skills as a unique world-class trumpeter, this

Louis Armstrong, left, watching and listening to Bunk Johnson, one of the pioneers of jazz trumpet, play. Circa 1945.

period in Armstrong's career was one in which all of the stars and planets were aligned in his favor. He revolutionized the world of jazz and popular music with his *Complete Hot Fives and Sevens* (Columbia Legacy, CK 6351) recordings.

With his timeless recording of the standard "I Can't Give You Anything But Love"; and his pioneering original compositions such as "Potato Head Blues," "Struttin' with Some Barbeque," and "Weary Blues"; and with the most important trumpet solo in jazz, the "West End Blues"—Armstrong began to define new standards. Whether you were a fellow trumpeter, a pianist, saxophonist, clarinetist, drummer, bassist, arranger, composer, dancer, lyricist, vocalist, band leader, comedian, or actor, his work affected the way you had thought about music up until that point. Every trumpeter then was trying to learn Armstrong's solos on "West End Blues," "Cornet Chop Suey," and "Potato Head Blues"—just as the smart ones are doing today. Others were trying to figure out what kind of trick cornet/trumpet he had that could allow him to improvise so brilliantly and flawlessly, while simultaneously extending the technical possibilities of the instrument. There was no special cornet/trumpet, just the gifts and dedication of a supreme musician pursuing excellence in his art.

The stylistic particulars of what Armstrong played on the *Hot Fives and Hot Sevens* would never even be given a thought of explanation by the man himself. Even today when student musicians and "scholars" want Freddie Hubbard, Wynton Marsalis, Clark Terry, Bobby Bradford, Maynard Ferguson, and others to explain their use of particular chords and notes, the response is bewilderment and a "you have missed the point entirely" look. I can analyze Armstrong's solos and come up with all kinds of explanations why he

played this and why he played that. But that is not the point of this book—to place example after example of his solos on paper so that they can be added to the growing list of visual aids that do nothing to help people to understand the complete picture. This music is aural and the best way to understand is to listen and listen and listen. Then listen some more. This is far more difficult than sitting down with a pencil over a transcribed solo and marking points of interest to try to further the understanding of an artist's style.

For the sake of those who do not have the time for intense listening, however, I will offer a brief analysis of what Louis Armstrong contributed through his *Hot Fives and Sevens*. First, there is the very basic nature of what he was doing as an instrumentalist. Until these recordings, there was no one on record who demonstrated such a complete command and control of the instrument from an improvisational standpoint. There were famous classical cornet soloists such as Herbert L. Clarke who had all manner of technique, but for the most part, they performed music that was already written down and committed to score. All they had to do (no easy feat either) was sit down and practice slowly each section of the piece they were to perform and memorize it, if possible. Practicing this consistently over a period of years enabled them to develop the level of technique needed to play such difficult pieces as J. B. Arban's interpretation of *Carnival in Venice*, *The Bride of the Waves*, *Flight of the Bumblebee*, and various other cornet classics. Then they could simply transfer their technique to other pieces to play them as well. But the real difference between classical music and jazz is in individual creativity. Louis Armstrong used his technique to create the unheard. This is what makes the *Hot Fives and*

Hot Sevens so monumental—no one had ever done that before on such a high level. Armstrong did not simply regurgitate the same solo ideas over and over, but rather began to use his instrument and the bandstand as his complete musical score. He was, just as all jazz soloists are, a composer, creating music using all of the necessary tools—melody, harmony, rhythm, form, and structure—and in various permutations together.

Armstrong also used major elements associated with the classic cornet solos, such as the break and especially the cadenza. Whereas the typical classical cornet cadenza would come at the end of a piece, Armstrong reversed this for his pivotal solo introduction on "West End Blues." Before he recorded that song, there had not been an introduction in recorded jazz history to compare it with. This cadenza is unique in several ways. First, it begins in what sounds like E-flat major concert. Then it goes up in triplets to a high C (trumpet D), which makes it sound like it is in the key of C concert. Then it goes through a combination of sounds that flirt with E-flat major concert again as well as B-flat major concert,

because it pauses on a low A-flat concert which implies B-flat major concert to me. Then it goes to a B-flat concert, which clearly sets up the piece in E-flat major concert. I say "major," but I actually mean the sound of the dominant, the flatted seventh of E-flat. Above all, and a point easily overlooked, Armstrong uses all twelve notes of Western harmony for this cadenza.

When I learned Louis Armstrong's solo on "West End Blues," at first I felt that Armstrong was playing the trumpet backwards. This was probably because the first four notes were in descending order. More than that, I was forced to realize that this man was powerful both compositionally and especially instrumentally. The breath control and technique required to play his music was on the highest of levels. It was not necessarily *what* he played but *how* he played it. Armstrong's solo on paper may look like an average grade one cornet solo, but when you are listening to it, clearly there is more there than just notes. Even the most proficient trumpeters cannot play this solo. They can play the notes and the rhythms, but the spirit with which Armstrong delivered this

LOUIS ARMSTRONG'S OPENING CADENZA TO "WEST END BLUES"

address carried over into the sound and feel that he was able to produce—a sound and feeling that belong to him alone. This piece is one man's individual thoughts, perceptions, and experiences based on years of learning a craft that there is no one way of perfecting.

Other solos from the *Hot Fives and Sevens* recordings that warrant serious listening and further study are "Weary Blues," where Armstrong shows his skill for maintaining an ongoing dialogue within the group and displays a deceptively high level of instrumental virtuosity; "Struttin' with Some Barbecue," with a lively and bouncing beat that reflects the positive spirit of life in New Orleans; and "Potato Head Blues," a masterpiece in rhythmic exploration. Undoubtedly, Henry "Red" Allen and Dizzy Gillespie knew this solo and Armstrong's style well enough to adapt it for their own methods, especially Gillespie who, along with Charlie Parker, was able to create an entirely new style of music, modern jazz.

Armstrong moved to New York in 1929, where the next phase of his career began, leading a big band until 1947. He made successful tours of Europe and also was signed to exclusive management by an astute man named Joe Glaser. They formed a partnership that lasted for the remainder of both of their lives. Armstrong's big band period allowed him the opportunity to really reinvent much of the popular material that he touched on with the Hot Fives, including "I Can't Give You Anything But Love." He would record nearly every major popular tune written for Broadway, thus transforming them into jazz standards. Critics of this period of his development often do not understand and hear that Armstrong was still developing as a musician, especially as a trumpet virtuoso. His breath control was startling, as witnessed by his perform-

ance on the composition "Jubilee." This piece can be found on the *Complete Decca Studio Master Takes*, disc 3, track 4. At 2:00 into the track, Armstrong begins to sail above the orchestra with a gleaming and powerfully sweet tone. To be able to play this way requires tremendous breath control and accuracy. What makes this example so amazing is that even though it was recorded on primitive equipment apparatus, the power of his sound comes through. If this had been recorded with today's technology, Armstrong would have certainly been put in a booth alone so as not to completely drown out the orchestra. Listen to the entire track but especially to the final 41 seconds. As if he hasn't already given other trumpeters something to cry about with this performance, Armstrong gives them another beautiful thorn in the side by ending on a high G and holding it for three seconds—*and* with vibrato!

Moreover, Armstrong was not lost on what was about to occur with the modern jazz musicians, as is clear from a recording of "I Double Dare You" from January 12, 1938. Louis Armstrong, on this 1938 date, played what can easily be called bebop. I immediately took out the liner notes and noticed where I had already marked the track with the word "Boppish." Specifically, after the tenor saxophone solo, he begins the first phrase, which seems to be a carbon copy of what "modern" jazz musicians would do. It starts at 2:13 of the track. The second and most telling phrase only lasts for a second or two, but its implications are clear. It occurs at precisely 2:31 in the track. He slurs and tongues in exactly the way the beboppers do. Different from his usual method of attacking or tonguing the majority of his notes, Armstrong combines the two, which makes a distinct difference compared to the rest of his solo. As Miles

Davis said, "You can't play anything on the horn that Pops hasn't already played—even modern."

During this period, Armstrong also began to do Hollywood movies, which for the most part basically demeaned him by having him portray characters like a field hand who plays cornet for a horse, a scared skeleton, and even the devil dressed in leopard skin. A good book about most of his movie appearances is Gary Giddins's *Satchmo*. But with the big band, there was an experiment in New York in 1947 that would change Armstrong's routine format. It was a concert of a type familiar to Armstrong, playing with a small group of five or six musicians to replicate his Hot Fives and Hot Sevens success. The audience gave such enthusiastic approval that Glaser saw all manner of commercial implications. Thus the Louis Armstrong All-Stars were formed. With few exceptions, Armstrong played in this small-group format exclusively for touring and recording for the remainder of his life.

When I interviewed bassist Arvell Shaw, who joined the All-Stars in its first year, 1947, he told me that night after night Armstrong, despite playing the same material, such as "When It's Sleepy Time Down South" and "Back Home in Indiana," he never played the same solo twice. This is an incredible feat—the subtleness of which can easily be missed by the untrained ear.

With the formation of the All-Stars, Louis Armstrong in a sense joined the modern jazz musicians in exploring a concept of rhythm section (bass, piano, drums) with three horns (trumpet, trombone, saxophone/clarinet). The possibilities for this type of instrumentation are endless, because it can sound like a small group, which it is, or a large ensemble. To stand in the middle of such instrumentation and play, as Armstrong did and I have done, fills one's ears

Photo courtesy of Jack Bradley

This never-before-seen or published photo of Louis Armstrong is my favorite. He is in the middle of a solo, his knees bent, using his body to make a point, and he is dressed in a fine tailor-made suit.

with a varied array of sounds and ideas. This constant input allowed Armstrong to continue to create and expand his ideas night after night and year after year.

By this time in the late 1940s and early 1950s, Armstrong's ability as a trumpeter in particular was reaching its zenith. He was touring incessantly under the management of Joe Glaser and was beginning to realize some of the fruits of his labor. He bought a modest home in Corona Queens, New York, and his wife of more than thirty years, Lucille, provided him with the stability of a home environment to balance his international road life. During the 1950s, he collaborated with high-caliber artists on a number of important albums, including *Porgy and Bess*, with Ella Fitzgerald; *Louis Armstrong Meets Oscar Peterson*, with pianist Oscar Peterson; and *Louis Armstrong Plays W. C. Handy*. The advent of stereophonic sound in the early 1950s allowed recordings to capture the full power of Armstrong's musicianship—the increased range, the advanced breath control, and the clarity and precision of his attack. On *Porgy and Bess*, for example, the power of Armstrong's entrance on "Summertime" has to be heard to be believed. No other trumpeter in the history of music could have such a startling effect on an entrance alone with just his sound, except maybe Cootie Williams on the plunger. (Williams was a direct Armstrong disciple and part of Duke Ellington's solution to not being able to actually hire Armstrong himself.) With Oscar Peterson on "Let's Fall in Love" from the *Louis Armstrong Meets Oscar Peterson* album, Armstrong's breath control is again amazing. This is a good solo to learn for any trumpeter wishing to develop the upper register.

Also worth noting are two particular solos by Armstrong. One is "St. Louis Blues," on *Louis Armstrong Plays W. C. Handy*. Armstrong nearly blows the bell off his trumpet. The power that he displays in addition to the flat-out, bluesy-as-hell solos is enough to make you slap somebody close. This recording is a milestone, so perfect that it brought tears to the blind eyes of the composer, W.C. Handy, who was in the studio during the session. The other solo is Armstrong's heavenly interpretation of "When You're Smiling," recorded on December 12, 1956 (*Louis Armstrong Sings Back Through the Years*—MCA; disc one, track 7). Armstrong's reading of this standard must be heard to be believed. He seems to transcend the instrument and get directly to the essence of the composition and lyrics by his natural and effortless

singing and gentle yet majestic trumpet playing. It is a textbook example of how to make the trumpet sound like it has echoes of the centuries of its development within it. Armstrong's ideas, coupled with his melodic and rhythmic inventiveness, are still what put him in a class all by himself. He was still refining his statements well into his fortieth year of performance. The luxury of having a full-time band and no real worries about keeping it together financially allowed this continued freedom of exploration for Armstrong, just as would later be the case for Duke Ellington, Miles Davis, and Wynton Marsalis.

As the 1950s drew to a close, and with the civil rights movement in full swing after the 1955 Montgomery Bus Boycott, Armstrong found that he could no longer simply be an entertainer and not voice his opinion on the some of the ills facing his people in the United States. After the governor of the State of Arkansas barred a little black girl from entering a white public school, the National Guard had to escort her in because President Dwight Eisenhower would not personally intervene. Armstrong was furious and said that Eisenhower had "no guts" and was "two-faced." This was a major statement that placed him under the watchful eye of the FBI for the rest of his life. Armstrong then refused to go to Russia on a U.S. State Department-sponsored tour that had been in the works. He said, "The way they are treating my people in the South, the government can go to hell." People who up to that point regarded him as a smiling Uncle Tom in show business finally began to see the real Louis Armstrong—someone who, when pushed far enough, would came out swinging just as he did with his music. He knew what was just and would not be silent any longer.

One of the most incredible and important photos ever taken. Louis Armstrong, out front, on the soil of his African ancestors in Ghana, being followed by a line of African trumpeters all playing along with him.

In the late 1950s, Armstrong and his All-Stars traveled to West Africa in a triumphant tour that Arvell Shaw described to me as "awesome." (See Shaw interview on p. 81.) This tour also encouraged a young South African trumpeter named Hugh Masekela. It is my understanding that Armstrong was responsible for sending a trumpet to Masekela. The injustices that the black people in South Africa were facing mirrored the problems of African-Americans in the United States, and Masekela was able to use his trumpet to send a message of optimism that exposed to many Americans the evils of apartheid.

As the 1960s began, Armstrong began to show the strain of countless one-nighters around the world in addition to endless television appearances. He would simply not complain and go on taking his music everywhere Joe Glaser sent him. Elvis Presley and rock 'n' roll were beginning to sweep the airwaves; soon a group of four musicians from Liverpool, England, arrived in the United States and changed the scale and focus of popular music performance and, in some respects, the awareness of the importance for jazz—at least to Americans. However, just a few months before the arrival of the Beatles, Armstrong went in to the studio and would be asked to record a tune that he didn't think too much of. It was called "Hello Dolly!" This was in December 1963.

The following year, in February 1964, the Beatles arrived in New York and turned the youth and most of the rest of mainstream America on its ear. Rock 'n' roll—which had its roots in jazz, blues, and rhythm and blues, music pioneered by African-Americans—became hugely popular and inspired all manner of good and mediocre imitators to spring up in hopes of making it as the Beatles had. Rock music seemed to seal the fate of many "old timers" in jazz who, in comparison to the massive commercial appeal of the Beatles, Elvis, and others, did not seem as "hip" as the younger bands. Jazz venues began to shift toward booking of rock 'n' roll, and a lot of jazz musicians who were already living week to week were forced to get day jobs wherever they could find them. A few jazz stalwarts like Miles Davis, Duke Ellington, Count Basie, and especially Louis Armstrong would be able to sustain their regular touring around the world, as their audiences were solid. No one thought that the Beatles, a group that represented the youth of the world, would be knocked into second place on the radio charts by anyone, let alone by a sixty-two-year-old jazz master.

As Arvell Shaw, bassist for Louis Armstrong for twenty-five years relayed the story to me, in

Photo courtesy of Jack Bradley

Jack Bradley with Louis Armstrong.

Photo courtesy of Jack Bradley

An important photo showing two of the most important musicians and trumpeters to ever live. Louis Armstrong, left, talking with one of his direct disciples in Miles Davis during the recording *Louis Armstrong and His Friends*.

mid-1964 the All-Stars were on the road somewhere in Iowa. They were in the middle of one of their standard numbers when suddenly the crowd began to yell, "Hello Dolly!" "Hello Dolly!" The band didn't understand what they meant until someone told Armstrong it was that song he had recorded back in December 1963. Each night thereafter, the crowd became more and more vocal, wanting to hear this tune. Finally, a call was placed to Joe Glaser to have the arrangement sent out on the road so the band could play it. When they played it that night, pandemonium broke out. The crowd went absolutely wild, as they had been hearing the song on the radio and it soon reached the number-one slot on the charts, passing the Beatles. This was a monumental achievement for Louis Armstrong, who at this point in his career seemed to be completely insignificant to many critics and musicians. That he was able to simply do what he normally did and have it sweep the nation and the world is testament to his never ending relevance in the realm of popular music and of course, jazz. His trumpet solo on "Hello Dolly!" is the culmination

of more than forty years of refinement in an art that he made his own.

For the remainder of the 1960s, Armstrong's health began to slow him down, but he still made international tours and one-nighters that would have ruined a younger man. In 1970, there were numerous seventieth-birthday tributes to the now frail Armstrong, who had all but given up playing the trumpet on doctor's orders. Not knowing the real date of Armstrong's birth—which was to be proven decades later to be August 4, 1901, instead of the usual accepted July 4, 1900—fans all over the world sent tributes. Armstrong still felt that he could take on the road to a degree and record some new material. For his birthday celebration, he recorded an album called *Louis Armstrong and His Friends*, which included a who's who of jazz royalty as his choir. That such a diverse group of musicians came to pay their respects to Armstrong shows once again that they knew who had truly helped to gave birth to this music. They were all his children.

Louis Armstrong's career can be defined in many different ways, but I like to think of this genius and humble man as, first and foremost, a human being, but a human being who had been given a unique talent. The music that he gave to the world expressed the love that he had in his heart for his fellow man. The two—the music and compassion—coupled together are what made him so powerful and this is why people will be listening to his music and writing about him for centuries to come.

Mr. Armstrong's health finally gave out around May 1971. His last official engagement was at New York's Waldorf Astoria Hotel. He tried to fulfill the obligation, but told his band one night that he could go on no longer. He was taken home and eventually to the hospital with several ailments related to lung cancer. He insisted on going home and tried to sneak in playing his trumpet once back home. Armstrong was looking forward to getting better and actually had plans for another tour, when he died peacefully in his sleep on July 6, 1971. The nation mourned and condolences poured in from around the world. The world seemed to be a colder place without his presence, but his spirit and his music brought light and hope for a better future.

Photo courtesy of Jack Bradley

Louis Armstrong, the most important jazz trumpeter, 1901–1971.

Dizzy Gillespie: The Father of Modern Jazz Trumpet and Bebop

It was a warm and lovely summer day in my hometown of Atlanta, Georgia, as I stood waiting for Dizzy Gillespie. I was beyond excited to meet one of my idols on the trumpet. Dizzy was about two hours late for his appearance at the 1990 Atlanta Jazz Festival with the group M-BOOM, led by the great drummer Max Roach. My friend was one of the festival organizers and had secured me an all-access pass for the day.

As the jazz fans eager for his arrival were content to eat their food, drink their wine, and mingle on the lawn of Atlanta's Grant Park, I decided to act as the lookout, not knowing if Dizzy would ever show up. It turned out that the organizers of the festival had forgotten to send someone to pick him up at the Atlanta airport, one of the largest and busiest in the world. As he was wandering the airport looking for his ride, a lady recognized him and thought he seemed lost. She asked what was wrong and discovered that he needed a ride to the festival that was featuring him that evening! She proceeded to load him into her van and they were on their way.

After some time just wandering around and talking to Max Roach about his association with the late great trumpeter Clifford Brown, I noticed a slow-moving van inching toward the backstage area, where we were all waiting. As the van, which looked like a soccer mom's van complete with wood paneling down its sides, pulled closer to where I was standing, I realized that it was Mr. Gillespie in the front seat, looking quite weary and tired. This was Dizzy Gillespie—jazz trumpet giant, distinguished, regal, a world traveler many times over, confidant and friend to Charlie Parker. His very presence commanded attention and respect all around the world. As the van slowed to a stop, I looked him over like a kid overjoyed when his long-lost puppy finds its way home. I noticed his green Oakland A's baseball cap; his wildly checkered red, white, blue, and green pants; the huge gold medallion around his neck; and finally his somewhat angry expression and droopy eyes, most likely from the confusion he'd endured the previous several hours. He then fixed his lips, looked up at me, and said in a comically annoyed tone, "Negroes! ...Got DAMMIT!"

Gillespie took his sweet time getting to the stage. He let me carry his case and accompany him backstage, where he proceeded to demand a meal. He sat down at the table provided along with Max Roach and me. Someone brought out a plate of barbecued chicken and collard greens, corn on the cob, and some cornbread. To make matters worse, while he as sitting there trying to eat his food and talk to Max Roach, a very persistent photographer approached and asked to take his picture. Without missing a bite, he said to the photographer, "You had better get the hell out of here before you get cut." However, when Gillespie noticed a young boy approaching, he opened up and began to play with him, much to the delight of us all. He even tried to teach the kid to play his trumpet!

Once he finished eating, Gillespie warmed up, then went onstage with his trumpet and proceeded to unleash the most haunting sounds over the exotic and pulsating rhythms of the percussion ensemble. The audience seemed to be in a collective trance. The flickering of candles accompanying their picnics could be observed for some two hundred yards around, and this provided for a most intoxicating evening of music with Gillespie at center stage.

John Birks "Dizzy" Gillespie (1917–1993) was born in Cheraw, South Carolina. His father, a local band leader, encouraged his musical training, and Gillespie taught himself to play the trombone and then the trumpet. His career spanned fifty years and he was one of a kind. He was a musician who seemed to defy the norm at every turn, but unlike most, with beautiful results. It is almost impossible to copy his solos perfectly, for he had a most imposing command of his trumpet. Behind the humor and puffed cheeks was a man who was in a league all by himself. For many, Dizzy Gillespie is the apex of jazz trumpet.

So what about those puffed-up cheeks? Generally speaking, for trumpeters who were formally trained, puffing one's cheeks to the extent Gillespie did is tantamount to playing the piano with your knuckles—it's simply not done. The vast majority of trumpeters are taught from the beginning that one should never puff out the cheeks. Many muscles and veins in the cheeks and face are used along with the teeth and jaw to control the air stream produced by proper breathing. If this air stream is not controlled, then the result will be a weak and uncentered sound.

So how could Dizzy Gillespie play this way for so long and not be looked upon as a freak of sorts? To answer this question, we must understand several things. First, when he began to play, Gillespie did not have puffed cheeks as early photos of his career will attest. However,

Photo by author

Dizzy Gillespie trying to get kid to play his trumpet while the kid's mother tries to show him how to puff his cheeks.

40

Photo by author

Photo courtesy of Jack Bradley

Right: Dizzy Gillespie warming up. Notice how his cheeks obscure the side view of his noise, his mouth, and the cup of the mouthpiece. Above: Herman Autrey, playing a pocket trumpet, also warming up. Autrey was trumpet soloist for Fats Waller.

around the time he and Charlie Parker and others began to play continuous all-night jam sessions while creating the new music called bebop, he was playing for hours and hours and in the heat of battle or cutting contests most of the time. He could not let fatigue set in and be blown off the bandstand, so he was compelled to continue playing even when the other trumpeters had stopped—and more important, when his muscles were tired. Playing alongside bebop saxophonists like Charlie Parker had to contribute to Gillespie's cheeks puffing, because saxophonists can play for five or more hours without the same level of fatigue as trumpeters. When trumpeters play, our lips vibrate against each other and the metal mouthpiece, whereas the saxophonists' lips only vibrate against a mostly soft and wooden reed. Thus, when a trumpeter's embouchure muscles get tired, normally after three or four hours of continuous playing, the cheeks will automatically begin to expand more than normal to compensate for the decreased muscle support. This is what happened with Gillespie.

The main reason he was not ridiculed or seen as odd for his puffed cheeks is that there was no one else on the planet that was playing as much trumpet as he was during the early 1940s and into the 1950s. Musicians, critics, and fans alike were compelled to concentrate on what he was playing, not what he looked like doing it. Further proof of Gillespie's resolve is the fact that he began to use his cheek muscles to supplement the air from his diaphragm! He puffed his cheeks, but he had complete control over the air stream.

In the early years of his career, beginning around 1937–1938, he left South Carolina for Philadelphia and eventually New York. While in school in South Carolina, he had an opportunity to hear the bands of Joseph "King" Oliver and others who traveled through his area. While in Philadelphia, Gillespie played in the bands of Frankie Fairfax and others. During this time, he picked up the moniker "Dizzy" because of his antics on stage. Soon, however, Dizzy was in New York and began making the rounds to various nightspots to sit in and play with the best musicians. He played with the orchestras of Tiny

41

Bradshaw, Earl Hines, Teddy Hill, Cab Calloway, and vocalist-trumpeter Billy Eckstine. The job in Cab Calloway's orchestra placed Dizzy alongside other trumpet masters, such as Jonah Jones.

During one concert, a band member shot spitballs at Calloway's back. Calloway accused Gillespie, who strongly denied the charge, and a fight broke out. Gillespie even cut Calloway with a knife he grabbed. According to *Groovin' High*, the most comprehensive book on Dizzy Gillespie, and a televised interview with his fellow trumpeter in Calloway's band, Jonah Jones, it was Jones who shot the spitballs. But as a result, Gillespie was fired. He joined the Billy Eckstine orchestra, whose trumpet section included Fats Navarro and later Miles Davis. It was with Eckstine that Gillespie, along with Charlie Parker, began to plant the seeds of modern jazz.

Dizzy Gillespie is perhaps best remembered as one of the creators of modern jazz, although it is purported that Johnny Anderson, a trumpeter from the band of Kansas City pianist Jay McShann, may have been one of the first to play in the different style. Could it stand to reason that fellow bebop genius Charlie "Yardbird" Parker, who was also with Anderson (as well as trumpeter Orville Minor) in McShann's band, heard and was influenced by Anderson? This is just food for thought, since Dizzy Gillespie himself said, "When I heard Charlie Parker, I said to myself that *that* is how our music is supposed to sound." Additionally, it is documented in Bird's own words that he discovered this new way of playing by his continuous work on the composition *Cherokee*. I have a 1942 recording of Parker playing this tune in a hotel room in Kansas City. It is evident that a new style was already in play.

So just what made Dizzy Gillespie such an innovative trumpeter and musician? The answer

Scotty Barnhart and Dizzy Gillespie at the Atlanta Jazz Festival, 1990.

could fill a book, but from my perspective as a jazz trumpeter, Gillespie developed a unique and personal style derived principally from the great trumpeter Roy Eldridge, that explored the unknown and, more important, the *unheard* that planted the seeds for all trumpet styles to come after bebop. Gillespie dared to play certain notes that others had not and *would not* up to that point—and twice as fast, with a much more expansive trumpet technique and groundbreaking rhythm. Simply, no other trumpeter was playing that way. Everybody started to listen, including those who didn't want to believe it and in some cases understand it—such as the most important of all jazz trumpeters, Louis Armstrong. How is that for irony?

The trumpeter Joe Guy was also very important to bebop's early development, since he was one of the leaders of the house band at the infamous Minton's Playhouse, where Gillespie and others jammed for hours in the early 1940s. Gillespie's work with pianists Bud Powell, Clyde Hart, Al Haig, and Thelonious Monk; saxophonist Charlie Parker; bassists Ray Brown and

Charles Mingus; and drummers Kenny Clarke and Max Roach are well documented and legendary. The collaboration with Gillespie and Charlie Parker produced some of the most advanced and revolutionary music ever heard during that period. Their jam sessions at the infamous Minton's and other clubs in New York would soon coalesce into the strongest movement in jazz and signal the end of the swing era. Gone were the somewhat short and "easy on the ear" phrases from the swing players; in their place were the longer and more complex rhythms and harmonies that seemed to defy not only space and time but logic as well. Gillespie and his cohorts began to stretch and reinvent the music in a way that seemed almost blasphemous to some of the older players such as Armstrong, who spoke out against bebop at its start.

As a trumpeter in general, Dizzy had a brilliant, brassy, and multicolored tone. He also had a great attack with a deeply rooted and hard swinging ability. As a jazz trumpeter, however, his improvisational exploits remain unmatched. With his unique use of harmony and rhythm combined, Gillespie had and has no equal on the trumpet. I am still amazed at the sheer velocity and intricacy of most of his solos, especially from the early 1950s and 1960s. A few recordings that stand out at this writing are *Diz and Getz* (Verve, 1953), *For Musicians Only* (Verve, 1956), *Jazz at Massey Hall* (Verve), *Have Trumpet, Will Excite* (Verve), *Roy and Diz* (Verve), and *Oscar Peterson and Dizzy Gillespie* (Pablo, 1975).

Dizzy Gillespie was one of the first musicians to fuse modern jazz with the exotic and percussive rhythms of Cuba. He formed his Afro-Cuban Orchestra in 1947. Perhaps his most famous composition, "A Night in Tunisia," has a most infectious Latin groove (it also shifts to straight 4/4 swing) that is immediately recognizable. Mario Bauza, the outstanding trumpeter from Cuba who was one of the leading exponents of Latin jazz, also played lead trumpet for Cab Calloway, and was greatly influential in bringing Gillespie to Calloway's orchestra. Gillespie in turn was also crucial in advancing the career of another brilliant trumpeter, Arturo Sandoval, originally from Havana, Cuba, but is now a U.S. citizen. Dizzy's love for the fusion of Latin music and jazz is just another example of his fifty year curiosity and love of experimentation.

Throughout the 1960s, '70s, and '80s, until his death in January 1993, Dizzy Gillespie kept up a pace of touring the world that would have exhausted those half his age. He made television appearances with the Boston Pops, performed a solo at a memorial for Dr. Martin Luther King Jr., recorded many times with the likes of Oscar Peterson and others, and generally began to be recognized as one of jazz's top ambassadors. Just a few months before he died, several trumpeters including Wynton Marsalis, Jon Faddis, Claudio Roditti, Doc Cheatham, and Wallace Roney recorded with Gillespie at New York's Blue Note in a seventy-five-birthday tribute. The recording is *To Diz with Love* (Telarc). Jon Faddis, with whom I've often played and as recently as in 2004, is the only trumpeter I know of who can approximate the complete style of Gillespie and play it an octave higher! It is no wonder that he was playing with Gillespie as a teenager. Faddis was also present when the master passed away and we all know that he was and still is Dizzy's number one musical son.

The last time I was in the presence of Dizzy Gillespie was at Carnegie Hall a couple of weeks after the episode in Atlanta. I was with the Marcus Roberts Septet, and we were the opening act for

Dizzy Gillespie's United Nations Orchestra. I found myself standing in a circle backstage at Carnegie with none other than the great trombonist Slide Hampton, saxophonists James Moody and Paquito D'Rivera, trumpeter Jon Faddis, and the master himself, Dizzy Gillespie. All of a sudden, I realized that I was in the midst of six of the greatest musicians in the world and I was working with them at Carnegie Hall! Then, I somehow brushed against Gillespie's arm and made him spill his hot cup of coffee all over his blue silk suit. As I was trying to help him clean it up, I hit his arm again and more coffee stained his suit! I couldn't find a hole big enough to run into, but he was nice and called me a few names, with love, as only Gillespie could. We all had a belly laugh at my expense, but it was well worth it.

Since his death in 1993, Dizzy Gillespie is considered by many to be the greatest of jazz trumpeters, and has started to receive the thorough study that his achievements have warranted, such as a two-hour television special about his life in 2001. His collaborations with Charlie Parker and other artists left an indelible mark on jazz music, and trumpet playing in particular, that will never be erased and in some respects never surpassed.

With the spectacular harmonic and rhythmic innovations of Dizzy Gillespie, the era of modern jazz trumpet, also known as bebop, was under way. Its stylistic particulars, unlike those of the swing era and of the Jazz Age, were so many that it was often written that this is when jazz trumpet became a "problem." Of course, for those who understood what was going on, it was not a "problem" at all but rather a period in which a significant number of instrumentalists began to take note of the examples set by Gillespie and Parker, who daringly explored the formerly taboo—rhythmic and harmonic improvisations that went against the sweet-sounding and generally consonant tones of jazz before 1940.

As for Gillespie, the way in which he studied the work of his idol, Roy Eldridge, is significant because Eldridge was already pushing the boundaries, playing higher and faster, and was not afraid to play the "wrong," based on Western examples of harmony, notes. Most notable is his use of the flat ninth in many of his solos. For the layman, this is about the "wrongest-sounding" note anyone could play. Intrigued by the implications of the flat ninth, Eldridge employed this strong harmonic device much in the way a bassist or pianist would delay the resolution of a chord. Obviously, this intrigued young Gillespie, who in his 1937 recordings with the Teddy Hill Orchestra, sounded nearly like a carbon copy of Eldridge. Gillespie eventually composed a blues, "Wheatleigh Hall," based on the flat ninth. Pablo Picasso's 1901 painting *Death of Casagemas* shows how he was influenced by the earlier work of Vincent van Gogh, and Gillespie's quarter-note and staccato-type phrasing, as demonstrated on "King Porter Stomp" from his recording with the Teddy Hill Orchestra on May 17, 1937 (*The Complete RCA Victor Recordings*—Bluebird 07863), is equally representative of his study of Eldridge. In the larger picture, that detailed study is required and it indicates the serious jazz soloist is thorough in his or her preparation. This is but one example that refutes the absurd myth that "you just play what you feel."

But like most solo artists who were trying to find new ways of expression, Gillespie began to build on Eldridge's work in a particular fashion by adding more complex rhythms, deeper harmonics (flat-sixths, sharp-ninths and sharp-elevenths), and a more flexible trumpet technique reminiscent of Jabbo Smith's some ten years earlier. As Clark Terry told me, "When everybody else was playing like Louis Armstrong in the '20s and '30s, Smith was already playing twice as fast with sixteenth and thirty-second notes and with more technique." Clark's statement is supported by Smith's recording of the introduction to "Jazz Battle" from 1929—just one example of Jabbo's influence on Gillespie.

At Minton's Playhouse in Harlem and other clubs, Dizzy Gillespie stood next to Charlie Parker and played with him every night. That Dizzy was able to do this—and to play with Thelonious Monk, Bud Powell, Kenny Clarke, and others, but especially Parker—in an experimental situation allowed all ideas that sounded good to be accepted. This gave him added confidence to try things on his trumpet that rivaled what could be done with relative ease on a saxophone or a piano. Remember that playing the trumpet requires a few distinct things physically not needed on other instruments. The lips must vibrate together to produce the tone that is then pushed through the mouthpiece (with the lungs) and into the tubing of the instrument. The air stream then must regulate and balance this air, because different levels of vibrations or speed are needed for the different registers (high and low) of the trumpet. For instance, pressing the first valve down can produce a low B-flat, an F in the first space of the staff, a B-flat on the third line of the staff, a D on the fourth line of the staff, an F on the top line of the staff, or still more notes above the staff. If the second valve, the third valve, and various combinations of valves are added, all notes can be played. With jazz trumpet, we are forced to be accurate and to know what we are going to play *before* we play it. There is no guessing involved in a great trumpet solo. This is what makes the contributions of Dizzy Gillespie so groundbreaking. He

was able to play incredibly intricate passages that were revolutionary both rhythmically and harmonically, to extend the bandstand score provided by Armstrong, and simultaneously to expand the vocabulary of the trumpet.

Much has been written and even more can be discussed about the work of the jazz trumpeter schooled in modern jazz or bebop. Gillespie had and has so many disciples, both direct and indirect, and was pivotal in the evolution of jazz in general that his work has had an effect similar to what fourteenth-century Medici scholarly advisor Cosimo Bartoli said about the excellent work of the new generation of sculptors inspired by Michelangelo Buonarroti (1475–1564). Bartoli believed that Michelangelo, in creating a style for his own time, had liberated his successors from futile envy of the antique. This captures the influence of Gillespie perfectly and explains to a great degree why the bebop style of improvisation he pioneered after Armstrong, Henry "Red" Allen, and Roy Eldridge demonstrated the possibilities of its endless array of rhythmic and harmonic variations. This style is by far the most widely used among jazz trumpeters everywhere nearly seventy years after its inception. A new breed of musician was being cultivated, and this new music was not a "problem" for anyone who dared to take up the rhythmic, harmonic, and instrumental challenge set forth by Gillespie, Parker, and others.

Because the work of Gillespie and Parker, as well as other significant social conditions prevalent in the United States, many other trumpeters also became immersed in the new style. Some of them might not have been as aware of Gillespie as those who had heard him live or on records were, but similar forms of art can develop geographically apart but artistically close together. This could be the case with why music began to change drastically among African-Americans following June, 1938, and during and immediately following World War II. I believe that the June 1938 defeat of German boxer Max Schmeling by African-American Joe Louis was but one watershed event that had a particular effect on jazz musicians who, it must be remembered, were the popular musicians of their time. The United States winning World War II simply added to an already simmering restlessness that would soon be voiced through the horns of those musicians in Harlem at Monroe's, Minton's Playhouse, and other venues.

Louis versus Schmeling: A Provocative Cultural Parallel

In 1936, when the German boxer Max Schmeling defeated Joe Louis, an African American and the grandson of slaves, Louis was regarded and referred to as a "black man" or a "negro." In June 1938, however, when Louis fought Schmeling in a rematch for the heavyweight championship of the world, he was simply referred to as an "American." This sudden shift in perception came from two primary sources. The first was when U.S. President Franklin D. Roosevelt invited Joe Louis to the White House, and upon feeling his biceps, remarked, "Joe, we need muscles like yours to beat Germany."

This contest would turn out to be perhaps the single most important sporting event in the twentieth century, because the United States and its allies were about to try to stop Adolph Hitler from advancing further in his conquests in Europe and eventually other parts of the world. So, in effect, Joe Louis was fighting for all of America, not just those oppressed in his own community. When he entered the ring on the night of June 22, 1938, in New York's Yankee Stadium to fight Max Schmeling, a representative of Hitler's ideal Aryan "master race," the announcer—who had previously introduced Louis as the "colored" opponent—this time called him the "American." This was significant because as legendary Grambling University football coach Eddie Robinson remarked, "I had never heard a black man being called an American." Louis knocked out Schmeling at 2:04 in the first round, and for the first time in America's history, its hero was a black man. And as former aide to Martin Luther King Jr. and U.S. Ambassador to the United Nations Andrew Young concluded, "In a way, with his defeat of Schmeling, Joe put an end to the notions of racial inferiority."

Joe Louis's decisive and humiliating defeat of the German champion Schmeling gave an immeasurable amount of pride to the African-American community in the United States. It would even inspire a twelve-year-old trumpeter in St. Louis named Miles Dewey Davis to take up boxing. Davis would even record an entire album in 1970, complete with his own liner notes, in tribute to the first black heavyweight champion, Jack Johnson. *A Tribute to Jack Johnson* contains some of Davis's most funky trumpet solos from his fusion period. Boxing was Davis's primary physical exercise and sport for the remainder of his life. More important, Joe Louis's victory over Schmeling gave African-Americans and no doubt other minorities further confidence and hope for the betterment of their lives. I do not think that it is a coincidence that in the year of 1938 Louis's victory, a singular moment which would greatly inspire his people, that there was a musical revolution brewing that would embody those very ideals of confidence, empowerment, and optimism. Those were the hallmarks of a new music called bebop. In fact, as mentioned in the previous chapter, with his January 12, 1938 recording "I Double Dare You," Louis Armstrong had already given notice of what was to come. Just as Joe Louis's victory can be seen as a direct affront to the "establishment," bebop bore the same to the swing era, which two years before had taken the country by storm with the trumpet of Bunny Berigan (in Benny Goodman's band) playing the "King Porter Stomp" at a dance that was broadcast over the radio waves.

The achievements of the musicians who created bebop—including saxophonist Charlie Parker, pianist Thelonious Monk, and trumpeter Dizzy Gillespie—would again prove that high achievement in art is not the sole domain of the elite.

Just as George Washington Carver had developed more than a hundred ways of using the peanut, the bebop musicians found even more ways to play on any particular chord or chord sequence. A succession of chords is improvised or composed on in a continuing or repeating cycle, in conjunction with the collective improvisation, assimilation, and resolution of rhythms; this places the music of the modern jazz musicians, the beboppers, on a plane that has had no equal before or since. For perhaps the first time in Western art, a type of music, in addition to challenging the musician like never before, also challenged the audience and transformed the bandstand into the musician's score, as pioneered by Louis Armstrong. Modern jazz contains elements of dance music, but its complexity raises it above the heads of all of those who do not listen closely and/or study for themselves. Moreover, the prevailing sentiment among most fans and even some musicians at the start of bebop was that this music could not be danced to. But as Grover Sales points out in his book, *Jazz: America's Classical Music*, the bebop musicians remarked, "*You* can't dance to it." Having played hundreds of gigs with my own band playing essentially bebop, as well as tunes with one chord, I know it can easily be danced to as long as it is swingin'. I have seen it done. As with any great work of art, it may not be easily understood at first.

The Women of Jazz Trumpet: Heroines in a Noble Endeavor

Throughout history, an untold number of courageous and brilliant women have contributed to the whole of humanity. Women are the givers and primary nurturers of life and they alone possess the necessary physical, psychological, and physiological qualities for these roles. Even this simple understanding seems to have been ignored and or conveniently forgotten by those whose thirst for power and control has engendered constant conflict and war around the world. Of course, women have always been capable of, and continue to accomplish, incredibly much more than those basic functions of running a household and supporting the children and spouse. This separate chapter is intended as hopefully another positive effort to oppose the usual direction of tacit admissions and glaring omissions of their importance.

Women were the first musicians. *In Music and Women*, author Sophie Drinker states, "There can be no doubt that women were creative musicians in the age which preceded written history." Further, archaeology tells us that the oldest illustrations of human achievement and daily life are found in cave paintings and carvings on rocks throughout Europe and Africa. Some date as far back as 9,000 to 10,000 B.C. Drinker surmises that these rock paintings and carvings suggest that "the act of music may have begun in the singing of magic by women and that women were the first musicians and maybe for some time the only ones."

Sappho of Lesbos, the great lyric poetess in the seventh century B.C., is credited with having evolved the mixolydian mode (in today's jazz nomenclature—this is the dominant chord, i.e., G7, C7, A7, etc.—and is the chord that can be altered successfully more than others) as well as creating a different style of music by dividing the meter to make for more varied rhythms. Other early female artists were Telesilla of Argos, the poet-musician and warrior, who led a village of women in battle against the Spartans, and Corinna, the poet-musician of Boetia. No doubt many other women artists, poets, and musicians have been neglected from history, but their spirits, I believe, still live among those young women of today who are working to develop their talents.

There is not enough space here, nor is this the proper medium to try to fully bring to light the thousands of years of artistic accomplishments of women such as Sappho, but more recent women musicians that can be found in history books are seventeenth-century vocal composer Barbara

Strozzi; Francesa Caccini (1587−1638), who was the first woman known to have composed opera; Amy Marcy Beach (1867−1944), a composer and pianist and perhaps the most celebrated woman composer of her time; and up to the brilliant twentieth-century African-American jazz pianists and composers Mary Lou Williams and Lil Hardin. Hardin was essential to the success of Louis Armstrong's *Hot Fives and Hot Sevens* landmark recordings, which changed the direction of popular music and particularly jazz in the mid-1920s.

Some scholars have theorized that God's archangel trumpeter was not a male, Gabriel, as it is written in the Bible, but a female, Gabri*elle*. Historians and scholars of religion acknowledge the authors of the Bible—all of whom were men, and under various influences from the major religious centers of their time—wrote but also continually *edited* so as to omit, emphasize, or alter numerous important events and people, to further their own beliefs, especially those that allowed the subjugation of women. Although today's society is patriarchal, roughly 3,000 to 5,000 years ago, most cultures were matriarchal. Women were respected and honored for their ability to give birth and sustain life.

Women have been and still are high priests, rulers of nations, commanders of military forces, groundbreaking scientists, physicians, poets, incredible artists and musicians, as well as mothers and managers of households. They have always been a vital part of every facet of human life and interaction. In the male dominated society of today's Western Hemisphere, particularly that of the United States, women artists and musicians, especially jazz musicians, of all hues and nationalities have been largely ignored or relegated to the back pages of most historical accounts of life in America. Here I attempt to bring to the forefront the timeless contributions of artists like Clora Bryant, Valaida Snow, Tiny Alexander, Billie Rodgers, and other jazz trumpeters and musicians.

Many women are a part of the lineage of jazz trumpeters that began in the late nineteenth century with E. W. Gravitt, Buddy Bolden, and others—from Tiny Davis, whom Louis Armstrong tried to get to join his band, to Los Angeles's own Clora Bryant, to Jean Starr, Betty O'Hara, Barbara Donald, the wonderfully swinging Edna Williams, and Norma Carson, to Saskia LaRoo, Ingrid Jensen, Stacy Rowles, and Tanya Darby. They too have practiced for untold hours; experienced life on the road on buses, trains, airplanes, and in cars; played in the greatest concert halls in the world, and hundreds of other venues, as well as those smoky dives masquerading as jazz clubs. They have made recordings and performed on television, and know what it is like to breathe life into a cold and heavy chunk of brass. They are among the important links in the chain that allows for the continuation of this grand profession.

In the early stages of jazz, from about 1900 through 1925, women could not even vote and were mostly confined to the role of domestic servant. There were exceptions to this rule, however, such as Madame C. J. Walker, an African-American who started her own hair care business and became the first negro millionaire in the United States. In entertainment, however, women thrived mostly as actresses on the vaudeville circuit, singers, and dancers; some instrumentalists played, for the most part, the piano and stringed instruments, such as the violin. In jazz, the most influential, famous, and accepted women were pianist Lil Hardin Armstrong and vocalists Bessie Smith, Ma Rainey, and Alberta Hunter. The "masculine" instruments—the trombone, acoustic bass, saxophone, and trumpet—were not the ones that most women gravitated toward when deciding to become professional musicians. Even recently, I've witnessed young women being ostracized and discouraged from playing those instruments. Who knows how many women trumpeters, trombonists, bassists, and saxophonists we would have enjoyed had the stereotypical chauvinistic male not stood in the way?

Women jazz trumpeters seemed to finally reach the mainstream with the emergence of Billie Rodgers of the Woody Herman band in the 1940s, the great Tiny Davis of the International Sweethearts of Rhythm, and perhaps the most important, Clora Bryant. The International Sweethearts of Rhythm was an all-woman orchestra that originated on the campus of Prairie View College in Mississippi in 1939; it featured Davis, as well as Bryant for a short time. The instrumentation consisted of five saxophones, four trombones, four trumpets, and a rhythm section that had acoustic bass, drums, piano, and guitar. This group was originally put together to perform at luncheons and other events to raise money for the school. But after several outstanding appearances, they were soon booked in theaters and halls as far away as Washington, D.C. They were a polished group that played arrangements by the likes of Don Redman and Jesse Stone, who had contributed to the libraries of Fletcher Henderson, Count Basie, and many other important jazz orchestras of the day.

There is a videotape of the International Sweethearts of Rhythm that showcases the explosive power of trumpeter Tiny Davis in her younger days as well as an eighty-year-old Davis playing just before she passed away. The Sweethearts disbanded after only a couple of years and were never able to take their rightful place in the lineage beginning with Henderson, Lunceford, Ellington, Basie, Miller, Herman, and others. But their work, of which some has been preserved, may one day be studied and truly appreciated for what they were able to give to society at large.

When Billie Rodgers joined the Woody Herman orchestra as a trumpet soloist, or when the great Valaida Snow performed as a soloist with the Count Basie Orchestra, I am certain that the thing paramount in everyone's mind was music. Whatever other reasons there may have been to have these professionals join the ranks of an established group , they pale in comparison to the task at hand—making music that sounded good and was swingin'. There were other women who played, such as Thelma Lewis, Maxine Fields, Lois Cronen, Bobbie Taliaferro, Florence Shefte, Dolores Gomez, Norma Carson, Fran Shirley, and Jean Ray Lee and Marie Johnson, who were soloist and lead trumpeter respectively for the Darlings of Rhythm. The opportunities for women instrumentalists were somewhat limited within the mainstream, so one option they had was to join the military as musicians. The U.S. military had all-women bands such as the African-American group WAC (Women's Army Corps) Band Number 2 at Fort Des Moines, Iowa, and bands that played for wounded troops. One such group that played jazz was Ada Leonard and Her All-American Girl Orchestra, featuring trumpet soloist Jane Sager. Sager, who could play several of the hot and popular solos of trumpet ace Harry James, recounts in Sherrie Tucker's book, *Swing Shift: "All-Girl" Bands of the 1940s*, how she was asked to play Bunny Berigan's famous trumpet solo on "I Can't Get Started" for a soldier with no limbs. That a soldier on the brink of death would

Photo courtesy of Jack Bradley

Trumpeter Billie Rodgers of the Woody Herman Orchestra, 1940s.

Photo courtesy of Clora Bryant

Clora Bryant, trumpet soloist extraordinaire in the 1950s.

ask for a jazz trumpet solo is another example of the depth of this art we call jazz.

With bebop taking the place of swing, a young woman from Texas, who had been a member of the International Sweethearts of Rhythm for only a short while, was already studying the music of the father of modern jazz trumpet, Dizzy Gillespie. This was no small feat for anyone, especially someone who was already a double or triple minority in the United States. None of this mattered to Clora Bryant, who in my opinion is the grand dame of jazz trumpet. When interviewed for this book, she told me how she had to "cut" many a male trumpet player in Los Angeles and wherever she might be playing. Gender didn't mean jack to her. If you couldn't play, you had better get off the stage or risk being embarrassed to a serious degree. Bryant, as her solo recording *...Gal with a Horn* demonstrates, possessed all

the necessary tools of being a professional jazz musician—flawless technique, a personal sound, daring, continuity of ideas, and inherent optimism that allows for endless creativity. At age seventy-eight and not able to play anymore due to doctors' orders, Clora Bryant has left a legacy that we are now discovering in its entirety. No less than Dizzy Gillespie and Clifford Brown praised her talents and she is also the only woman to ever play with jazz legend and genius Charlie Parker (at the High Seas Club in Hermosa Beach, California, in 1954) and with Clifford Brown shortly afterward. She even lived with Brown and his wife, LaRue, while she was in between residences.

In the work of Clora Bryant, the only recording by a woman jazz trumpeter of the period, we find a perfect example of a musician who, had she been given the proper media treatment and proper study by the jazz historians of the 1950s, would have no doubt produced some of the most important recordings. ...*Gal with a Horn* is definitely important and a must-have recording for any jazz musician and enthusiast. It set a precedent for trumpeters regardless of gender with the outstanding combination of Bryant's flawless and spirited vocals and her well-executed ideas on the trumpet. The only comparison I can truthfully make would be to Louis Armstrong, who also was able to combine his vocals with his trumpet playing like no one else. Clora's renditions of "Tea for Two" and "Sweet Georgia Brown" in particular are so rooted in the understanding of her idols Roy Eldridge, Charlie Shavers, Harry James, and Dizzy Gillespie that many a professional musician who listened to her without knowing who it was named all of her idols except her as the trumpeter!

I must also write a little about Valaida Snow—to me, simply the Josephine Baker of the trumpet. She was a beautiful woman who attracted everyone around her and had exquisite taste in clothes and a love of the finer things in life (she once had a wardrobe that matched her Mercedes, her chauffeur's clothes, and the suit on her monkey!). She also was an excellent trumpet soloist, as witnessed by her appearance with the Count Basie Orchestra and her own recordings. The photo of her soloing with the Count Basie Orchestra in 1945 is the type of thing that should have been in history books the very year it was taken. But of course, we all know why it was ignored and only used in the inside jacket of one of her reissued albums. Snow was so popular and so free to do as she pleased and in every way that while she was on tour in Europe, the Nazis placed her in a concentration camp for almost two years. She eventually escaped or was released, but at least she was able to record in her prime. These recordings from the 1930s and '40s showcase her full and rounded tone and her bouncy rhythmic attack. The beauty of her tone and its crystal clear and bell-like quality can be heard to the fullest, albeit for a few bars, on the standard "It Had to

Photos courtesy of Rosetta Records

Valaida Snow with Count Basie (back) and his orchestra in 1945, and a publicity photo of her taken around the same period.

Gunhild Carling.

Stacy Rowles.

Saskia Laroo.

Be You" from the album *Valaida Snow: Queen of Trumpet and Song* (DRG 8455).

I am only scratching the surface of a history that could fill a book in itself. There were no doubt other women who were jazz trumpet soloists and for one reason or another we do not have complete listing of their careers. Some of them, like Billie Rodgers, are not even listed in the *Grove Dictionary of Jazz* and other important books. Not everyone got the big break or was able to solo on every radio broadcast or record date, but this does not diminish in any way the fact that they were and are a part of a grand tradition. Many of the women in the International Sweethearts of Rhythm, for example, simply had to quit playing to raise a family and/or seek another profession that would allow them to make a living. The economics of the times dictated this. It was then and it still is today a man's world and we must not forget how this affects women everywhere.

The women of today who play jazz trumpet may not know about Billie Rodgers, Clora Bryant, Valaida Snow, and Tiny Davis, but at least they have some great musicians with whom they can immediately identify. I only wish that record producers and other historians would seek out those rare and forgotten recordings that give us further proof of the careers of such women. Today in the world of jazz trumpet, we have such esteemed performers as the incredibly versatile Gunhild Carling of Sweden who also plays trombone so well that she was a special guest with the Count Basie Orchestra, during a concert in Sweden in 2004 and 2005. She also has the unique talent of playing three trumpets at the same time and *in harmony*! Carling can tilt her head back, balance the trumpet vertically on her lips while playing it and the banjo at the same time. There is also the wonderfully lyrical Saskia LaRoo, who was amazing in the North Sea Jazz Festival jam session heard in July 2005 in Europe in the artist's hotel along with Roy Hargrove. Ingrid Jensen has always been a wonderfully consistent player; Stacy Rowles is a seasoned veteran on the Los Angeles scene and daughter of the great pianist Jimmy Rowles; Tanya Darby; Crystal Torres; San Francisco's Michelle Latimer, who is also a terrific singer; wonderful lead trumpeters Liesel Whitaker, Anne King, and Glenda Smith; and others that I have not even heard or met yet and they are all worthy of further listening and study. They continue the work of Louis Armstrong, Dizzy Gillespie, Miles Davis, and others, and I hope that someday their art may be carefully studied and appreciated on its merits alone.

Ingrid Jensen.

Crystal Torres.

Jazz Trumpet in the 1960s

"Jazz speaks of life. This is triumphant music. When life itself offers no order and meaning, the musician creates an order and meaning from the sound of the earth which flows through his instrument. Much of the power of our freedom movement in the United States has come from this music. It has strengthened us with its powerful rhythms when courage began to fail. It has calmed us with its rich harmonies when spirits were down. Everybody needs to clap hands and be happy. Everybody longs for faith. In music, especially this broad category called jazz, there is a stepping stone toward all of these."

—Dr. Martin Luther King Jr., opening speech from the 1964 Berlin Jazz Festival
(courtesy of Intellectual Properties Management)

Beginning with the recording of *Kind of Blue* by Miles Davis, Ornette Coleman's *The Shape of Jazz to Come* featuring trumpeter Don Cherry, the work of Booker Little with Eric Dolphy and Frank Strozier, Thad Jones, and the ever-present Dizzy Gillespie and Louis Armstrong, a measured level of refinement in jazz trumpet improvisation was taking place at the start of the 1960s. The work of trumpeters Freddie Hubbard, Lee Morgan, Nat Adderley, Don Ellis, Cat Anderson, Cootie Williams, Clark Terry, and Woody Shaw would add to this. The impact of the phenomenal Clifford Brown was still being felt and absorbed by many (Brown died in 1956 at his peak and was only twenty-five years old). The social and political tensions of the 1960s fueled in part by the civil rights movement, crystallized by the racially motivated 1963 bombing and murder of four innocent little black girls at their Sixteenth Street Baptist Church in Birmingham, Alabama, influenced the music as well. The very nature of accepted harmonies and rhythms of bebop and even hard bop were challenged, rebelled against, but ultimately extended through the work of the John Coltrane Quartet, Ornette Coleman with Don Cherry, and the Miles Davis Quintet in particular. Davis, Don Cherry, Freddie Hubbard, Don Ellis, and later Bill Dixon and Woody Shaw, defied most conventional and historical approaches to jazz improvisation on the trumpet. With the influence of pianists Cecil Taylor and Thelonious Monk, bassist Charles Mingus, and saxophonists

John Coltrane, Albert Ayler, Ornette Coleman, and Eric Dolphy being felt on bandstands everywhere, trumpeters like Miles Davis began to use standard material, such as the compositions "Stella By Starlight" and "My Funny Valentine" to redefine the harmonic and rhythmic possibilities that had developed for the previous twenty years with bebop. Using Davis, who was able to keep a steady working band together, with minimal if no personnel changes, and produce consistent recorded output, as an example—if we compare his 1958 recording of "Stella by Starlight" (*Stella by Starlight*—Columbia 47835) to his groundbreaking live version of the same song six years later in February 1964 on the recording the *Complete Concert, 1964* (Columbia C2K 48821), it is clear that the art of jazz trumpet improvisation was being boldly reinvented. Davis set a new precedent in terms of approach, execution, group sound with group accompaniment, and harmonic, rhythmic, and instrumental reflexes. He was one of the first to incorporate fully his band mates' accompaniment into his solos, and then add that to his repertoire. He trusted his band fully, and this placed him with Duke Ellington, Thelonious Monk, and John Coltrane, in terms of hearing and using all that was happening on the bandstand. On the 1964 recording, in particular the ballads "Stella by Starlight" and "My Funny Valentine," Davis plays as if he is alone with his thoughts but completely aware of his group—pianist Herbie Hancock, bassist Ron Carter, and drummer Tony Williams. They seem to redefine the most primitive form of improvisation by anticipating Davis's every note, phrase, and breath, and support him as he boldly and freely invents a new way of improvising as a jazz musician. Notice I used the term *musician* in the last sentence. This is because Davis joined Louis Armstrong in transcending the trumpet itself and allowed the spirit of the music to be the ultimate vehicle through which his thoughts would manifest.

My understanding of the above came not only from listening to these recordings of Miles Davis for years, but more important, from learning his solos on "Stella by Starlight" and "My Funny Valentine." I could feel clearly the historical and technical connections to the earlier solos of Davis himself, Freddie Hubbard, Clifford, Fats Navarro, Dizzy Gillespie, and Louis Armstrong. Davis was doing something new in 1964 that nobody else was doing on the trumpet, at least on recordings. That 1964 recording was done live with an audience. Every jazz soloist would tell you that their best performances are always live because there are no time restrictions and quests for perfection, allowing for the spirit of the music to be free, enhanced by the audience's enjoyment, and unconstrained by an engineer or producer. Moreover, the audience becomes part of the band, which adds to the collective vibe. The live atmosphere always lends itself more to unobstructed exploration, which many times can result in a new precedent for the art.

Also worth noting is the indirect influence of Don Cherry and Ornette Coleman. Cherry's recorded solos on Ornette Coleman's "The Shape of Jazz to Come" were unlike anything Davis had recorded up to 1959, with the closest example being Davis' solo *sans* piano on "Sid's Ahead" from the *Milestones* album recorded in 1958. Or was this track a major influence on Cherry? On *The Shape of Jazz to Come*, he created bold and very free but structured lines that were helped in part by the absence of the piano. Improvising without the piano forces the trumpeter to hear the harmonies and rhythms more clearly in his head and provides for greater—albeit a more difficult—freedom of expression. This fact led many of the elder statesmen in jazz, upon first hearing Coleman and Cherry, to blast their work as a joke. Whatever the pianist plays will give a certain and unmistakable sound that is only that sound and without it one can create and hear many more things to use. This is far more difficult and requires extra sensitive hearing and bolder improvisations.

Also in the early 1950s, Chet Baker along with baritone saxophonist Gerry Mulligan and tenor saxophonist Stan Getz, recorded without the piano. They were among the first to publicly front a group without a piano, at least to my knowledge. The difference, however, between their work of and that of Coleman/Cherry was the function of the bass and drums, the heart of rhythm section for any band. The bassists and drummers for Baker/Mulligan/Getz were playing standard bebop lines, rhythms, and patterns with standard material, including "All the Things You Are," "Move," and "The Way You Look Tonight." The overall group sound gives the impression that the pianist is sitting right there at the piano and simply not playing. With Coleman/Cherry, however, the sound is vastly different, despite having the identical instrumentation. The music written and performed by Coleman, Cherry, bassist Charlie Haden, and drummer Billy Higgins is on a different and more complex level than that of Baker/Mulligan/Getz, which would serve as the platform for most of the "free jazz" to follow in the 1960s. Pianists also learned from the piano-less group by having to invent a style that implied that the piano was a separate entity within the group but actively participating nonetheless. It was if the pianist had to play without really being there, to allow for maximum freedom for the soloists.

Ornette Coleman's group began to rehearse in Los Angeles in the early to mid-1950s, and took an entirely different approach toward improvisation and composition. Listening to, but most important, playing the type of music they pioneered reveals that although they were free to improvise, they also had the deep responsibility of resolving whatever harmonic and rhythmic ideas that surfaced individually and collectively. This still baffles critics of their music, which some listeners and musicians with untrained ears call "noise" or react to by asking, "Where is the melody?"

Understanding the conventional approaches to improvisation and composition, Coleman and his group were able to combine the two, which had been separated because musicians in the Jazz Age of the 1920s had to entertain an audience rather than explore the infinite possibilities of music itself. The recording *The Shape of Jazz to Come* served notice that musicians could return to the essence of what music means—which is to create and not regurgitate, within the more primitive realm of the group. The arrogant practice of imposing a preconceived and well-thought-out set of patterns and clichés on a piece of music, which was becoming more prevalent among the musicians who used the work of Coleman and Coltrane to avoid studying and practicing, was not a part of Coleman's and Cherry's beliefs. This basic sentiment helped to shape the sound of 1960s small group jazz, and it was simply a reflection of the times in the United States. The idea of continuing things as they had been—whether social, political, racial, or economic—was no longer accepted and listening closely to the work of Don Cherry, Miles Davis, Freddie Hubbard, and Charles Mingus demonstrates this.

Another factor that influenced the sound of 1960s jazz trumpet was the Beatles' arrival in the

Photo courtesy of Jack Bradley

Miles Davis, the jazz innovator who turned the world of jazz on its ears.

United States in 1964. Almost overnight, rock 'n' roll bands sprang up everywhere, and this would soon cause important venues for jazz to close their doors for good or to place a premium on booking rock bands. The serious economic effects led many jazz musicians to leave the U.S. for Europe in search of better artistic and financial opportunities, and led others to try and beat the rockers at their own game. Trumpeter Freddie Hubbard, for example, even recorded an album entitled *Backlash* (Atlantic—1967) that was clearly more than a rhetorical statement. It was a strong musical one as well, complete with its Motown influenced beats and sound on the title track. But Hubbard did something that almost

none of the rockers could do. He shifted gears musically and delivered an original composition entitled "Up Jumped Spring," which is still a major jazz standard some forty years later. It contains all the elements produced by a master musician intent on making music with substance, yet entertaining. There was never a need for jazz musicians like Hubbard, embarrassed by what rock 'n' roll seemed to represent—at least musically—to use a title other than their own name.

However, remaining true to the art of being a jazz musician in the traditional sense—e.g., taking elements of another form and incorporating them into a personal conception and sound without sacrifice in any respect—became more difficult because of the economic reality many of musicians were hit with: begin to play rock 'n' roll, which is what the masses wanted, and pay your bills or become homeless and starve. Some musicians like Louis Armstrong—who, in 1964, topped the Beatles on the record charts with "Hello, Dolly!"—could remain true to their vision without fear of going broke or having to do other work for the basic necessities. Other trumpeters, like Clark Terry and Dizzy Gillespie, whose unique abilities and sound always kept them in demand and busy could stay true to their vision (although Clark did TV work and soundtracks to movies). Art Farmer moved to Vienna, Austria, and some, like the great Kenny Dorham, who worked with Charlie Parker, had to find day jobs, which would rob them of a certain level of creative optimism. Gone were the days of practicing from sunup until sundown and making constant strides in one's particular conception.

Other trumpeters in the 1960s whose music began to reflect the times were Bill Dixon, who recorded with Archie Schepp (*Bill Dixon/Archie Schepp*—Savoy; *Bill Dixon Collection*—Cadence

Jazz), as well as haunting examples of solo trumpet that seemingly cry out for all manner of justice; Randy Brecker on *Score* (Atlantic); Bobby Bryant on *Ain't Doin' Too Bad* (Cadet 795); Alan Shorter's *Orgasm* (Verve); Bobby Bradford with Ornette Coleman on *The Complete Science Fiction Sessions* (Columbia); and Nat Adderley with Cannonball Adderley on *Mercy, Mercy, Mercy* (Capitol Jazz), which went even deeper in showing the origins of jazz and the influence of the Baptist church. One trumpeter in particular used this "dilemma" of the popularity of rock 'n' roll dwindling away audiences from jazz artists and accomplished the rarity in music: the combination of artistic and financial success. Of course, I am referring to Miles Davis. Fueled with the results of the 1960s that witnessed the assassinations of President John F. Kennedy, Malcolm X, Dr. Martin Luther King Jr., and their potential ideological successor in Senator Robert F. Kennedy, as well as the horrors of the Vietnam War, the work of modern visionary artists like Picasso, lifesaving medical breakthroughs, and landing a man on the moon—Davis, with three decades of experience behind him and his celebrated thirst for innovation, was set to change the world of jazz trumpet, which would affect the world of popular music itself. Louis Armstrong had done the same thing forty years earlier with his *Hot Fives and Hot Sevens* recordings.

Jazz Trumpet in the 1970s

Some critics have called the 1970s the most damaging decade for jazz. It can easily be viewed that way if you discount the notion that change is inevitable whether it is a natural occurrence or a forced or contrived one. There were great recordings made in the 1970s that stuck to the straight-ahead concept established with swing and bebop. Jazz legends Duke Ellington, Count Basie, Art Blakey, Buddy Rich, Benny Goodman, Dexter Gordon, Sonny Stitt, the Adderley Brothers, Ella Fitzgerald, Sarah Vaughan, Joe Williams, Charles Mingus, and others were still touring and recording regularly. The influence of rock 'n' roll was everywhere, even in the work of some artists mentioned earlier in the paragraph. But one musician, whom all others seemed to follow, made it his business to go toward it—that was Miles Davis. Rock 'n' roll seemed to reach its zenith with Woodstock. The performance of guitar legend Jimmy Hendrix might have inspired Miles Davis to look for new ways of expression. He said that he was also paying a lot of attention to James Brown, but "it was Hendrix that I first got into."

In the mid- to late 1960s, Davis had a new quintet, consisting of pianist Herbie Hancock, bassist Ron Carter, saxophonist Wayne Shorter, and drummer Tony Williams. Beginning with *The Complete Concert* and *Live at the Plugged Nickel* (both in 1964), continuing with *E.S.P.*, *Miles Smiles*, *Filles de Kilimanjaro*, *In a Silent Way*, and culminating with *Bitches Brew*, the influence of rock 'n' roll and rhythm and blues found its way into the group's work and the Davis conception. Just as with *Kind of Blue* ten years earlier, Davis let the musicians experiment with the musical canvas he provided, with the direction toward a specific goal being, to a large extent, unknown. *In a Silent Way* tipped the building, so to speak, and *Bitches Brew* knocked it off its foundation and turned the jazz world upside down. It is both scary and very provocative at first listening, if not approached with a historical perspective. My former roommate, saxophonist Herb Harris, said when he first heard it, it "made me want to go to church." Miles proved that it was acceptable to fuse more elements of pure jazz with the popular sounds of the period. It seemed as if everyone else was waiting for him to take the plunge first. He had done so earlier in his career and was doing so again. Also noteworthy is his rock 'n' roll—and R&B-influenced *A Tribute to Jack Johnson* (Columbia, CK 93599).

The 1970s, as far as jazz trumpet improvisation is concerned, included all of the previous styles, as well as those being pioneered by Davis and others musicians like Freddie Hubbard, Marvin Hannibal Peterson, Randy Brecker, Eddie Henderson (a disciple of Davis), and especially Woody Shaw. Freddie Hubbard in particular didn't sacrifice trumpet technique for innovation and continued to improve as a trumpeter, without resorting to electronic devices so much so that they obscured his beautiful sound. Dizzy Gillespie also continued his amazingly advanced harmonic approach, and his style became heavier and harder to decipher as the decade went on. His recording with piano virtuoso Oscar Peterson (*Oscar Peterson and Dizzy Gillespie*—Pablo 2310-740-2) is an example. There were also recordings by Roy Eldridge; a young Jon Faddis, who officially joined the ranks of trumpet royalty on his recording with Oscar Peterson entitled *Youngblood* (RCA); and perhaps the last true jazz trumpet innovator before 1980, the late and unique Woody Shaw (*Song of Songs* and *Rosewood*).

Woody Shaw is, after Freddie Hubbard, the last complete jazz trumpet innovator who could improvise consistently like no one else. Unlike most jazz trumpeters, with the exception of Dizzy Gillespie and to an extent Booker Little, Shaw developed a style that was more similar to what the saxophonists were playing—a logical extension of what he heard Hubbard play. Hubbard had studied directly with saxophone masters John Coltrane and Sonny Rollins. Shaw's style, which was developing in the late 1970s, is still rarely attempted to this day by the majority of jazz trumpeters because of its high level of difficulty. It was almost as if Shaw had to invent his own niche of trumpet technique, much like pianist Thelonious Monk and guitarist Wes Montgomery had to do. Trombonist Steve Turre, who was in Shaw's band for many years and made several recordings with

him, told me a story about going with Woody to a club in New York to hear Dizzy Gillespie. At that time, the late 1970s, Shaw had clearly established with his recordings *United*, *Woody III*, and *Rosewood* that he was playing in a way that was indeed not being done by anyone else—at least we thought. Shaw had his horn with him and Gillespie invited him to sit in. After Dizzy gave him a great introduction, Shaw proceeded to play in his own style, in the spirit of not competition, but rather of pure jazz trumpet improvisation as he felt it. Turre stated that Woody "played himself and was so unique and unbelievable." His use of oblique intervals and dissonant harmonies seemed to place him on a level that was his alone. That is, until Gillespie stepped to the microphone. When Dizzy Gillespie began to play, according to Turre, he unleashed a torrent of improvisatory statements that, not only matched Shaw's, but surpassed him in every respect. Turre reported, "Woody and I sat there with our mouths open and our jaws on the floor. And Woody had a smile on his face. It was like listening to a father speak to his son. Diz was playing so much shit that it was nearly indecipherable."

Miles Davis, for the first half of the 1970s, was fully entrenched in exploring fusing electronics with his own innovations. Despite the wild costumes and becoming famous for turning his back on the audience (he said he did this to better hear his band), Davis still had an unmistakable sound with the open horn and especially his Harmon mute. He would usher in younger musicians, like Keith Jarrett on piano and Jack DeJohnette on drums, to feed his creative expression the same way he had done with Hancock, Shorter, Carter, and Williams. Davis's late-1950s nurturing of John Coltrane—who earlier that decade had risen to the top of the list of musicians that weren't afraid to go where their vision led them, and was successful at it—is one example of his power over the thoughts and actions of musicians and record companies that were beginning to shift toward the type of music he played. Incidentally, Davis called Columbia Records executives and persuaded them to sign Woody Shaw, although Shaw's concept was vastly different from his own. Would this happen today?

Other recordings by Freddie Hubbard (*First Light*, *Keep Your Soul Together*, and especially *Red Clay* and *Super Blue*), in addition to Shaw's *Rosewood*, were perhaps the best examples of the highest levels of composition and instrumental advancement, outside of Davis. In particular, Hubbard attained such a level of improvisation, trumpet technique, and beauty of sound during the 1970s that it is hard to think of another trumpeter who had as many gifts in combination. Whatever he played and recorded, he always paid attention to his sound, and it got more expansive and more flexible. By the time he recorded *Bundle of Joy*, it was almost impossible to tell if he was playing a flugelhorn or a trumpet. His solos on *Bundle of Joy* exemplify that rare balance of extended instrumental technique that does not take away from the musical statement. This might be because, as Hubbard told me, he recorded parts of this album as a parallel statement to Marvin Gaye's antiwar album *What's Going On?*, which places the emphasis on music within a political statement, not money. Listening to the title track on *Bundle of Joy* makes clear and defeats any notions of this not being a period or an album in which anyone is "saying anything."

In 1974, when Miles Davis recorded *Get Up with It*, it was a culmination of the things he had done previous in the decade, and he simply quit playing and went into a five-year retirement. It

came as a shock to those musicians following him and looking to him for direction, but I believe it also allowed for others to not feel the pressure of emulating him. This hiatus also served an opportunity for Hubbard and Shaw to get signed to large recording contracts on Miles's label since the mid-1950s, Columbia Records. During this period, other great trumpeters released significant recordings; these artists included Clark Terry, Dizzy Gillespie, and Roy Eldridge, all with Oscar Peterson, Terumasa Hino of Japan, Blue Mitchell, Bobby Bradford, Bobby Shew, Nat Adderley, Bill Hardman, Randy Brecker, and Marvin Hannibal Peterson. Blue Mitchell made one of the greatest jazz trumpet albums ever, *The Last Dance*, with one of his last sessions before his death in 1979. It is a straight-ahead recording of standards and demonstrates that, regardless of what is going on in the world of jazz music, playing the basic standard repertoire is a timeless achievement.

As the 1970s drew to a close, Jimmy Carter was elected president, the United States was recovering from a fuel shortage, and fifty-two Americans held hostage in Iran tested the public's resolve. Against this political and social framework, a variety of trumpet stylists had made their mark in relation to the lineage that began at the start of the twentieth century. Freddie Hubbard added a level of technique and sound that stood alone; Clark Terry also added a refined dexterity coupled with circular breathing (listen to "Shaw-Nuff" from *Oscar Peterson and Clark Terry* [Pablo]) that had not been done before through jazz trumpet improvisation and would not be done again until Wynton Marsalis in the mid-1980s and early 1990s; Dizzy Gillespie added a weight of harmonic and rhythmic complexity *again*; Woody Shaw added a series of advanced intervallic concepts for trumpet that revealed his

Photo by Mitchell Seidel

Wynton Marsalis (left) getting extremely valuable information from jazz trumpet pioneer Woody Shaw (right), circa 1980.

cally although this is generally ignored by those who only see financial success as proof of advancement. Granted, the death of Louis Armstrong in 1971, Duke Ellington in 1974, the popularity of 1970s rock as personified by the Bee Gees, the arrival of disco, and the absence of one of jazz's major figureheads, Miles Davis, for five years dealt jazz a lethal blow financially and, to some extent, musically. At the close of the 1970s, Woody Shaw was leading the pack with his unique

connection to Sonny Rollins, Ornette Coleman, and Dizzy Gillespie; Jon Faddis joined Cat Anderson and Maynard Ferguson in developing a consistent level of upper-register playing at which Faddis has proven to be the more advanced; Sweets Edison and Blue Mitchell both arrived at a level of refinement of attack and swing; Hannibal Peterson figured out how to combine elements of Coltrane, Coleman, and Mingus, coupled with fantastic trumpet technique to produce electrifying musical performances as heard in his *Live in Berlin* (MPS 2554); and although Chuck Mangione was selling millions of records with the instrumental pop hit "Feels So Good," he still was an improvising jazz trumpeter, as his live version of that song from the *An Evening of Magic, Live at the Hollywood Bowl* concert proves. Thus, the world of jazz trumpet in the 1970s, although initially led by Miles Davis, developed into a extremely varied and personal set of standards that continued to push the genre forward musi-

intervallic and improvisational concepts: this is significant because Shaw was very serious about passing on what he had developed to the next generation of trumpeters. As if on cue, a young trumpeter would soon emerge and give a boost to the world of jazz, the likes of which the world had not seen since the arrival of Louis Armstrong in the 1920s. A native of New Orleans, the city where jazz truly began, this trumpet player would restore the respect and reverence for the pioneers of the music that had waned in the years following the arrival of the Beatles. Trumpet great Wynton Marsalis would soon provide the necessary spark that would return jazz to a place of public enthusiasm, high artistic achievement, and respect. He would seek out the lessons of the pioneers, such as Woody Shaw who said, "You have to earn the right to play this music." And Marsalis would soon find himself in the most prepared position to set a new precedent in the world of jazz trumpet.

Wynton Marsalis:
The 1980s Renaissance Begins

During the spring of 1982, I heard from a child-hood friend and marvelous saxophonist, Frederick King, about a new young trumpet player on the scene who possessed so much technique that he would double-tongue and triple-tongue in some of his solos. Double-tonguing is when we say *ta-ka-ta-ka* into the trumpet instead of the normal *ta-ta-ta-ta* to produce the notes. Triple-tonguing is when we say *ta-ta-ka-ta-ta-ka*. Double- and triple-tonguing allows us to play extremely fast and difficult passages that single-tonguing does not. I could already double-tongue and triple-tongue, so I really didn't think too much about this news until a month or so later. I had been a huge of fan of NBC's *Tonight Show star-ring Johnny Carson*, because his band leader, Doc Severinsen, was one of the best trumpet players in the world. I used to stay up late at every night hoping to hear him play during one of

the commercial breaks. I even wrote Johnny Carson a letter in 1980, complaining that he never let the band play long enough or often enough. I still have the reply. As for Doc, I had heard him perform live with the Atlanta Symphony Pops Orchestra a year or so earlier and he just blew me away.

I had settled into watching *The Tonight Show* that particular evening, and Carson's guest host was comedian and jazz lover Bill Cosby. All of a

Wynton Marsalis warming up in dressing room before a concert at Lincoln Center, May 5, 2005.

Photo by author

sudden, Cosby held up an album with a trumpet player on the cover. He then said, pointing to the cover, "I want this young man to marry my daughter." I saw that the name on the cover was Wynton Marsalis, the same musician I had heard concerning the double-tonguing. Cosby then introduced the Wynton Marsalis Quintet. I had never heard or seen so much trumpet being played so cleanly and with so much fire in my life. And he looked about my age. I will never forget that night as long as I live.

Wynton Marsalis's performance on *The Tonight Show* that evening, which was his national television debut, ignited the already simmering musical fire in me into a blazing inferno. I knew that becoming a jazz musician was my calling. I met Marsalis and his band—including his brother, Branford, drummer Jeff Watts, bassist Phil Bowler, and pianist Kenny Kirkland—two months later in July 1982 at Ronnie Scott's Club in London, England. I remember feeling instant camaraderie, but I had no idea that we would be recording together seven years later, on my Marcus Roberts debut.

Over the years, Marsalis and I would talk on the phone and I would see him at his concerts whenever he was in my area. He passed along invaluable information that he had been fortunate enough to receive from trumpet masters like Dizzy Gillespie and Clark Terry, things that may be written down in this book for the first time. Perhaps the most crucial advice he gave was to tape-record all my performances. Then I could compare myself to the masters and what they played on their recordings and analyze the gap between myself and the greats—such as Armstrong, Gillespie, Davis, etc. From this, I could focus on those particular facets of my playing. Now I have in my library hundreds of

recordings spanning some fifteen years of my development as a jazz musician, and I still record my small group performances. The other practical advice Marsalis gave me was to be sure to pack a lot of underwear and socks for touring!

In what still seems like a dream sometimes, my first recording with pianist Marcus Roberts, *Deep in the Shed* (RCA/Novus, 1989), featured only two trumpeters—yours truly and Wynton, who used the pseudonym E. Dankworth. We would also play together on another Roberts project, *As Serenity Approaches* (RCA/Novus, 1990).

Wynton Marsalis was born October 18, 1961 in New Orleans, Louisiana. He is arguably the most important jazz musician on any instrument since 1980. Since his arrival on the world jazz and classical scenes, he has received every kind of accolade a trumpeter could possibly garner. Among the most important is being the first musician to win the prestigious Grammy Award for both jazz and classical performance in the same year. This happened *twice*, in 1984 and 1985. I have a videotape of the 1984 Grammy telecast, in which Marsalis performed the Finale from the Hummel Concerto and then one of his own compositions, "Knozz-Moe-King (No Smoking)." While he was playing the Hummel Concerto on the E-flat trumpet, someone took his B-flat trumpet, which he intended to use for the jazz segment a few minutes later, and switched the valves around so he could not get a sound out of his horn when he went to play the introduction to the jazz piece. He had to stand there on live national television and fix his valves while his brother, Branford, had to begin the tune. The latest honor for Marsalis at this writing is the Pulitzer Prize for music, the first time a jazz musician has ever received this award. The great Duke Ellington was denied this prize in 1966! Wynton

Marsalis will undoubtedly go down in history as one of the greatest ever to play the instrument.

After finishing high school, Marsalis accepted a scholarship to study at the Julliard School of Music. Once in New York, he started to play in Broadway pit orchestras and sit in with bands led by Mel Lewis and Art Blakey. His joining Art Blakey's Jazz Messengers, however, began his incredible career and rise to the position of the most popular and perhaps the most important jazz musician in the world. He followed in the tradition of the great trumpeters Clifford Brown, Lee Morgan, and Freddie Hubbard, bringing to the group a fresh fire and seriousness of purpose rare among his peers. He was eventually appointed musical director and his recordings with the group, especially the 1981 release *Straight Ahead* (Concord), display his awesome command of the trumpet. His solos, especially on the standard "How Deep Is the Ocean," sound like no one else. That someone his age could play so much improvisational trumpet was astounding.

During Marsalis's tenure with Blakey, the world began to notice—other musicians, such as Herbie Hancock, began to notice. Marsalis soon joined the former sidemen of Miles Davis—pianist Hancock, bassist Ron Carter, and drummer Tony Williams—on a worldwide tour. That the former rhythm section for Miles Davis's great band allowed a twenty-year-old trumpet player to front the group spoke volumes. Only Davis, Freddie Hubbard, and Eddie Henderson had done that before. The group made a recording under Hancock's name, simply titled the *Quartet*, on the CBS/Sony label. Had Wynton's career stopped at that point, it would have been enough to establish his position in the lineage that began

with E. W. Gravitt, Buddy Bolden, and others. But Wynton Marsalis had only begun.

Some of the elements of Marsalis's playing, but not all, have been written about since he made his remarkable debut with Art Blakey in 1980. Speaking as a trumpeter myself, the degree to which he has been able to master the fundamentals is one of the first things that places him above even seasoned professionals. When Freddie Hubbard said to me that even Clifford Brown didn't have as much technique as Wynton Marsalis, I really understood what all the fuss was about. Not to belittle Clifford in any way, it is merely to make a point for comparison. As for saxophonist Charlie Parker, trombonist J. J. Johnson, and pianist Art Tatum, such mastery of technique has opened the door to pure musical exploration.

Marsalis has recorded prolifically since his career began and several of his recordings as a leader are very important in the annals of jazz history: *Wynton Marsalis*, *Black Codes from the Underground*, *The Majesty of the Blues*, *Marsalis Standard Time* (all volumes), *The Midnight Blues*, *Live at Blues Alley*, *Live at the Village Vanguard*, *City Movement*, *The Marciac Suite*, *Reel Time*, *Hot House Flowers*, *Blood on the Fields*, *All Rise*, and John Coltrane's groundbreaking *A Love Supreme*. They are important because they deal with all the major aspects or movements found within the entire history of jazz music. *All Rise*, recorded with the Los Angeles Philharmonic and the Lincoln Center Jazz Orchestra, and combined choirs from Morgan State University and Cal State Northridge, is Marsalis's most ambitious and perhaps his most important work to date. With the enthralling and majestic voices of the two choirs, the intricate but appropriate interchanges between the Philharmonic and the Jazz Orchestra, it is a true milestone in music. Yet again, a jazz trumpeter attains a new level of artistry.

Without all forty or more of Marsalis's recordings, it may be impossible to get a clear and precise view of the true scope of his talent. I cannot emphasize this enough and this goes for all other musicians regardless of instrument. It is always a good idea to have at least the early, middle, and later or present phases of a musician's recorded output.

Furthermore, one of Marsalis's most important contributions has been his consistent output of recordings that cover just about all of the phases associated with being considered a jazz master. His discography, unlike any other trumpeter of the 1980s and '90s, includes several volumes of standards, New Orleans music, strings, ballads and blues, live sessions, different phases of original music, extended pieces, small suites, the spoken word, music of the church, music for film, music for dance, and music for children.

As a musician, Wynton Marsalis has a beautifully even and controlled tone, a perfect embouchure that allows for his ease of execution, and technique at the highest level. Being classically trained, but having the desire and motivation to practice and improve, and having mastered all of the trumpet fundamentals to a greater degree than even the most accomplished professional, he enjoys the freedom to explore the unknown and the infinite in his music. The one thing I noticed immediately upon hearing him was his natural feeling for swinging through his horn. It is this quality of his playing that I appreciate, and it is infectious. From his earliest recordings to his most recent, he displays a understanding of the complete history of jazz trumpet.

In June 1990, while on tour with pianist Marcus Roberts, trumpeter Nicholas Payton and

I went to Marsalis's home in New York for a lesson. He demonstrated how, for trumpeters to really learn how to play jazz music, they should be able to take any tune, whether a blues or standard, and play it in the style of Louis Armstrong, Sweets Edison, Miles Davis, Dizzy Gillespie, Woody Shaw, and others—all the while completely outlining the harmony. This was the first time that I understood what I needed be able to do as a jazz trumpeter. This changed my playing, starting that very night onstage at New York's Bottom Line. It is the most crucial information I can pass along to any student. I had finally received information that would allow me to practice and make continuous progress and allow me to eventually reach the level of freedom to make music.

At this writing, Marsalis continues a whirlwind schedule of recordings and tours and has been very active and visible in his role as one of the founders and the artistic director for Jazz at Lincoln Center. This institution is the first in the world devoted exclusively to the perpetuation and education of jazz music. Marsalis was the pivotal force behind the development and construction of this $130-million project in the center of New York City. I honestly believe that no other person could have made this happen. From the brothels and smoky clubs in Storyville in New Orleans at the start of the twentieth century, to all of the major concert halls in the world, to its own venue complete with every tool needed for its operation, jazz has come a long way.

Jazz at Lincoln Center's educational seminars for kids have continued a trend in the United States and around the world. Jazz is in vogue to teach, understand, and play. Marsalis has mentored and sponsored hundreds and thousands of young musicians and students in their efforts to learn jazz. I have been the recipient of his generosity in the form of one of his custom-made Monette trumpets in 1989. As another example, in 1988, Wynton allowed trombonist Wycliffe Gordon, tenor saxophonist Herb Harris, and me, all college students at the time, to sit in with his band during a concert in Tampa, Florida. We had driven the six hours to hang out and hoped to get a lesson, but were actually given the chance to walk onto his bandstand and play with him and the group. As if this weren't enough to further stimulate our commitment to truly learn the music, Marsalis instructed his road manager to pay us!

That is but one way he has been of generous assistance, which those who have criticized him prefer to ignore. Musicians really know what the deal is, and Marsalis's contributions to jazz music and to building respect for it is already secure. His work as a classical trumpeter and his concentrated forays into the world of composing are just as important.

A solo for technical study of Wynton Marsalis is from a live recording from his Village Vanguard sessions in 1995. It is the standard "Rubber Bottom" (disc 3, track 9) by Duke Ellington. It is based on the chord changes to "I Got Rhythm" and contains all the elements commensurate with being a jazz master: maturity, swing, reckless abandon, playfulness, seriousness, and complete control of the instrument. I consider this solo to be one of the best two or three he has ever recorded and a milestone in rhythmic mastery. Marsalis has recorded so many other pieces that display the same elements of mastery that it was difficult to choose one to discuss in this book.

The Jazz Trumpeter and Vocalists: A Unique Collaboration

One of the pleasures of good jazz, for those playing and those listening, is when a trumpeter or any other horn player accompanies a vocalist. I have had the honor of playing solo fills (improvisation woven into the lyrics) with Frank Sinatra, Joe Williams, Tony Bennett, Rosemary Clooney, Dianne Reeves, Jon Hendricks, Natalie Cole, Melissa Walker, Pam Laws, Neena Freelon, Patti Austin, Nancy Wilson, and others. This type of playing is unique in that it requires tremendous concentration and unselfishness.

Louis Armstrong, during the early 1920s accompanied more than twenty of the greatest blues singers of the time, including the legendary Bessie Smith. I'm sure that the collaborations with singers (he was also a singer) influenced his genius and allowed him to go on to record some of the most incredibly melodic and perfect solos. One of the reasons is that he was forced to edit his solos perfectly when performing with vocalists. There was no room for error and unnecessary ideas. This type of discipline seems to be a lost art today, as often soloists and vocalists (with some wonderful exceptions) want to play over instead of with other performers.

One of the more famous trumpet-vocalist collaborations was that of trumpeter Harry "Sweets" Edison and singer Frank Sinatra. Edison had a way of playing just the perfect one or two-note fills in the spaces between Sinatra's phrasing adding a special and irresistible delicacy to the moment. Listen to him with Sinatra on "Live at the Sands" and "It Might as Well Be Swing." Edison told me that he arrived at his famous quarter note phrasing behind Sinatra because "That was all the space I had to play in!" Sinatra loved the way that Edison played behind him so much that he requested him constantly for recordings and tours. When I had the pleasure to work with Frank Sinatra in 1994, I was amazed to open my music folder and find my parts all had

Jazz vocal legend Tony Bennett.

"Sweets" written on them! I had studied Edison's playing with Sinatra and Billie Holiday (Verve Silver Collection) and knew what I could and could not do as a soloist while Mr. Sinatra sang. That week at New York City's Radio City Music Hall will remain as one of the highlights of my career, and it cemented my love for working with great vocalists.

It is always a challenge to try to make the trumpet do things that the human voice can seemingly do with ease. While living in Tallahassee, Florida, in the early 1990s, I worked regularly with a wonderful vocalist, Pam Laws, who is also an instructor in English and jazz history at Tallahassee Community College and has been a source of invaluable historical insight in the preparation of this book. At the now defunct Tallahassee jazz clubs Andrew's Upstairs and

Spiritz, it was routine for us to trade phrases on a blues or a standard with her leading the way with some incredible scatting, the style of singing that Louis Armstrong created and made famous on his recording of "Heebie Jeebies" in 1926—although, as James Lincoln Collier points out in his book *The Making of Jazz*, humans have probably been mouthing nonsense phrases to music since the beginning of language. With Pam Laws, I had the perfect opportunity to learn how to accompany a vocalist and make music. I found that on particular songs, there were different amounts of room for me to maneuver around her phrasing. But the key was to never get in her way. Doing what the music tells you is of paramount importance. In other words, listen.

After Louis Armstrong, vocalists Jon Hendricks, Leon Thomas, Richard Boone, and others would take scat singing to a new level. To stand and play Cole Porter's composition "Night and Day" with Hendricks's scatting as the only accompaniment was an honor, a wonder, and a lesson I will never forget. His generosity as an artist willing to make music with me spontaneously again serves as an illustrious example of and respect with which our jazz elders treat those who want to continue to learn this vastly rich and beautiful music.

Of further importance, working with vocalists regularly over a period of time, helps a trumpeter build the added dexterity necessary for interacting with a saxophonist, pianist, drummer, or player of any other instrument.

Photo by author

Frank Sinatra at Radio City Music Hall, New York, 1994

Photo by vocalist Chris Murrell

With Jon Hendricks on Cole Porter's "Night and Day." He is improvising a bass line to the chords while I solo over them.

And the influence and lessons can go both ways. The great vocalist Tony Bennett told me during a conversation we had in Italy that the legendary trumpeter Bobby Hackett was his inspiration for singing. He wanted to sing the way that Hackett played the trumpet. Hackett also influenced Miles Davis. Bennett's is but one example that continues to connect trumpeters and vocalists.

There have been many instrumentalist-vocalist collaborations throughout the history of jazz, such as Lester Young and Billie Holiday, Oscar Peterson with and Fitzgerald, and Roy Eldridge and Anita O'Day. One of the most incredible recordings is by vocalist Bobby McFerrin and trumpet great Wynton Marsalis, performing their original tune, "B 'n W," with only the acoustic bass of Avery Sharpe as their accompaniment. It was recorded live in New York in front of a very appreciative audience in 1982, and is on the album *The Young Lions* and is on the CBS/Sony label. Two of the most technically proficient and swinging musicians in jazz history trade phrases back and forth with stunning originality and sophistication. This piece proves that working with a highly skilled vocalist can help a musician make discoveries that will take the art to new heights. The more instrumentalists work with vocalists, the closer we can get to that original instrument—the voice.

Photo from author's collection

With Rosemary Clooney after a concert in Concord, California. Left to right: Author, Rosemary Clooney, Dr. Eddie Anderson, Lois Anderson (partially obscured), Jennifer and Tony Coleman.

Photo by Beth Klein

The author playing fills behind vocalist extraordinaire Neena Freelon.

Photo from author's collection

The author with Joe Williams.

Finally, I simply state again what Miles Davis said: "Music is not about competition, but rather about cooperation." The great vocalist-instrumentalist collaborations I mentioned above are testament to this and provide an example of what jazz music is all about—giving.

Photo from author's collection

Trading fours with Pam Laws.

Photo by Marshall McDonald

The author with Tony Bennett at Umbria Jazz Festival. Perugia, Italy, July 2005.

Photo from author's collection

Trading fours with Basie vocalist Chris Murrell.

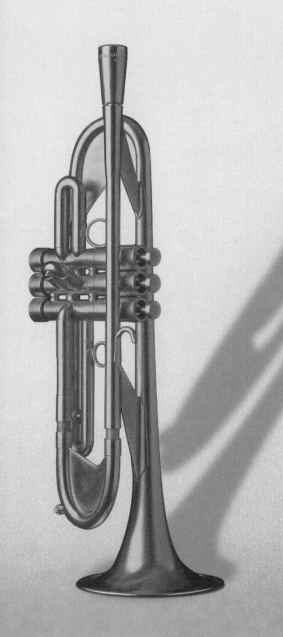

PART II
TRUMPET
TO
TRUMPET
The Interviews

Trumpet to Trumpet: The Interviews

It became apparent to me very early on, especially after meeting Wynton Marsalis and the great Basie trumpeter Sonny Cohn a few weeks apart in 1982, that simply performing with my band would not be enough to guarantee that I was making significant strides—or even holding down the fundamentals of jazz trumpet.

The two worlds which Sonny and Wynton represented were the worlds that would combine and become my own. Cohn represented the incredible history and legacy that Count Basie refined with his orchestra for fifty years, one that is still continuing, and if studied closely will reveal elements of standard musical practice that can be found in jazz bands everywhere—attention to dynamics, providing a good foundation for the soloist, playing the blues at many different tempos, and ensemble flexibility, to name a few. Wynton represented the promise of a new generation of serious and practicing musicians, and the wisdom that if they paid close attention to what musicians like Cohn and his contemporaries had to tell them, they too would find themselves invited into the incredibly sophisticated world of jazz royalty, and accepted, based on *music*.

It was never enough for me to learn a Freddie Hubbard trumpet solo, or a Sweets Edison solo, or even one of Wynton's. I wanted to know how and why they chose the notes they played. What were they thinking? One of the paradoxes of jazz is that a solo can be at once difficult but easy to listen to, beautiful but harsh. In some of the interviews you are about to read, some of my questions are not answered directly. Perhaps therein lies the truth—the *conversation* can be the answer. If you read these interviews carefully you should be able to *hear* the unspoken thoughts of these musicians. That is key to getting up on the bandstand and knowing exactly what to do. Given this knowledge, one can move forward, using history as both an unshakable base and a springboard, and hopefully join these pioneers at the vanguard of jazz trumpet.

I enjoyed doing all of the interviews—some of which were unfortunately unable to appear in this book—and cannot express enough how much gratitude I have for all of those that gave of their time and efforts to talk with me. From Sweets Edison to Terry Clark to Wynton Marsalis, Freddie Hubbard, Clora Bryant, Maynard Ferguson, Ted Curson, Chuck Mangione, and Arvell Shaw, I believe I have been able to put for the first time in one volume extremely varied and valuable information. The next time you see these musicians in performance, or listen to one of their records, I think you will have a better appreciation for their contribution to the world of music and the world of jazz trumpet.

Arvell Shaw on Louis Armstrong
"You cannot fool an audience."

To speak with anyone that was a part of Louis Armstrong's music is indeed a blessing. Without Pops, this book could not exist.

Arvell Shaw was Louis Armstrong's bassist for twenty-five years. I had seen him on television talking about Armstrong, and hoped that someday I would be able to meet him. That day arrived in early November of 2002, in the Grand Cayman Islands.

I had settled into my room on the *SS Maasdam* on the first day of a week-long "jazz cruise" through the Bahamas I was on with the Basie orchestra, and I decided to go up on the main deck to look around. I noticed an older gentleman being helped around—his sight was not good and he used a walking cane, but he otherwise seemed fine. As he got closer to where I was sitting, I realized that it was Arvell Shaw, Louis Armstrong's legendary bassist! Once again I was that kid in the candy store,

and I promptly introduced myself to him. I couldn't believe my good fortune. I knew I had to interview him for this book: He was as close to Louis Armstrong I would ever get.

Meeting Shaw on that cruise was incredibly fortuitous. The sun was shining very brightly and I could feel the spirit of Louis Armstrong in this great man. He was truly a living legend and an absolute goldmine to any jazz musician who is serious about their craft.

Arvell Shaw with All-Stars. From left to right: Earl Hines, Jack Teagarden, Louis Armstrong, Sid Catlett, Barney Bigard, and Arvell Shaw on bass.

Photo Courtesy of Jack Bradley

Exactly one month later on December 6, 2002, I was watching CNN and the bulletin came across the television screen announcing that Arvell Shaw had died. This turned out to be his very last interview. We are all very fortunate to have the following.

What was it Miles said about Louis Armstrong?

Miles Davis said that "whatever you play, Louis has already played it." Louis is the fountainhead. He's the teacher, the creator.

Wynton Marsalis said he used to put Louis down. But after he tried to play some of his solos, after two or three hours his chops were hanging down to here. He said it took him years to learn them—and he still can't really play it.

See, what Louis did, the main thing that he did, even without his singing or his personality—he made jazz into an *art form*, an *improviser's* art form. Before Louis they would play a tune, they would state the melody of a tune like "Dinah" [*sings the melody to "Dinah"*]. Then on the second chorus, they would get more heavily syncopated [*sings the same melody but with more syncopation and variation*]. That's what they called the "hot jazz." Louis was the first one to start improvising on the *chord structure* of a tune. And that was the beginning of jazz as we know it. That was what made jazz into an art form that spread around the world. It became the most played music in the world. No matter what country you went to, no matter where you were, when you turned on the radio, you heard some form of jazz. See, there are so many things that are the offspring of jazz. Broadway musicals, for instance. Movie musicals. Rock 'n' roll. Rhythm and blues. All that is the offspring of jazz. Jazz came from African chants, and the chants of the slaves. The field chants, the African drumming, the African syncopation mixed with European

harmonies, that was the beginnings of jazz . But the roots are African American. One of the things that has irked me all of these years is that this country did not recognize jazz. They called it "junk music" or "whorehouse music," so much so that the Europeans were the first ones to recognize jazz as an art form.

Jazz is more appreciated in every place of the world except right here. We don't know the value of what this country has given to the world. It is the only art form America has produced. Classical music is European. Opera is European. Jazz is American; an American creation that is the most played music in the world.

Who was the first jazz musician that you heard? Was Armstrong the first person you heard?

He was the first musician that impressed me. My father was a Baptist preacher, and jazz was a no-no in my household. My folks called that the devil's music. We were not allowed to have jazz records. A whole lot of black people were like that in those days. They had a very low opinion of jazz because they thought it was only played in bars. But my father took me to see Louis. He used to come through St. Louis, which was a completely segregated town then, and all of the black bands would come to play the Plantation Club there. Of course after I joined Louis, my folks changed their opinion about jazz.

So what year exactly did you join Armstrong?

After I was discharged from the Navy in 1946. That was Louis' big band. And that was the last of the big bands—most of them disbanded for financial reasons, and the public decided that they wanted Louis to play the music he grew up with in New Orleans. So they tried a Town Hall concert to see if it would work with a small New Orleans type of band, and it was so successful that they decided to disband the big band and let Louis form this all-star group. That was the beginning of the Louis Armstrong All-Stars. The original All-Stars were Jack Teagarden on trombone, Barney Bigard from Duke Ellington's band on clarinet, Big Sid Catlett on drums, and Earl "Fatha" Hines at the piano. And out of the big band, Louis kept me and the singer, Velma Middleton. That was the beginning of the All-Stars.

Do you recall your first meeting with Armstrong?

Yeah, it was with the first job with the big band in Kansas City. The first job was a dance at the auditorium in Kansas City. So I got onstage and was getting ready, you know, opening the book to get the music ready. The last bass player, Al Moore, had been there so long with the big band, he knew all of the tunes and he didn't even have to open the book. When I opened it, it was all completely, you know, number one was at the end... [*Laughs*]

I was scuffling to get the arrangements together. Then Louis walked on the stage and sat down. He didn't even look back at me. He just sat down and was getting ready to stomp off the band. I started playing and I noticed that everybody in the band started looking at me strangely. I said, "Uh-oh, this is going to be a short gig."

So I'm playing, and the set went down, then Joe Gordon, the straw boss (paymaster) and musical conductor, came up to me and said, "What the hell are you playing?" I said, "I'm playing the arrangements." The bass player before had been playing his own parts, but the arrangements were written by Benny Carter, Don Redman, those types of arrangers. That was the first time that the band had heard what the arrangers wrote for the bass part! After the first set Louis looked back at me and smiled.

Can you describe what his trumpet sound was like from where you were on the stage?

It's hard to describe. You stand on stage and play next to a man for twenty-five years, six, seven nights a week, but every night was completely different. Louis could do more with *one note*; he could bend a note that would make chills come over you. And sometimes, he would play a tune like "That's My Home," or "Nobody Knows the Trouble I've Seen," and you would have to fight to hold back the tears. And this is *every night*. And talk about power. After Jack Teagarden left, Trummy Young came in, and between Louis and the front line with Trummy and Edmund Hall on clarinet, who came in after Barney Bigard, they could play as loud as any big band you ever heard. Not just loud, but power. *Big*. And Louis had such phenomenal range that he was playing higher than it actually sounded, because his sound was so big and fat.

There are a lot of band leaders, if they gave you a solo and you got too much applause from the audience, they wouldn't give you any more solos. But Louis was not like that. In the All-Stars, everyone had their own feature spot. And when he put you on, he wanted you to go out there, and if you got a standing ovation, he loved it. Because he knew all he had to do was walk on stage, unfold that handkerchief, smile, and wash you away like you had never even been there. No matter *who* you were.

Whoa! How did he act with other trumpeters?

Oh well, if they asked him questions, he tried to teach them, you know. Dizzy Gillespie, and all of the other trumpeters, every time they were in town they came to see Louis. Because they all knew that whatever they did, Louis was the one who taught them how to do it.

Is there a memorable concert with Louis that stands out in your mind?

So many, so many. We played in Africa. We landed in Leopoldville [now called Kinshasa, capital of the Democratic Republic of the Congo] three days after the assassination of Patrice Lamumba [January 13, 1960], and we were the guests of his successor. The first night we played a concert for the VIPs, and the next night we played a concert in the soccer stadium to the largest crowd we had ever played for—about 175,000 people. There was a war going on, which was world news, and while we were there, both armies laid down their arms and sat side by side in the stadium. They were dancing and having a ball. Two days after we left, they started fighting again. The American Ambassador said that he had never seen anything like that in his life! That is when they started calling Louis "Ambassador Satch." The U.S. State Department found out, and that is how we started touring for them.

Then we played for the Independence Celebration of Ghana, and we were going to be the first ones behind the Iron Curtain, but because of what happened in Little Rock, Louis told Eisenhower "How can I go over there as a representative of the United States government with the way they are treating my people?" [In 1957, Arkansas Governor Orval Faubus called out the state's National Guard to surround Little Rock Central High School and prevent any black students from entering.]

Benny Goodman was the first to go to the Soviet Union, because Louis wouldn't go, and he had five trumpet players. One of them, Billy Butterfield, said that, "It takes five trumpet players to play what Louis played." [*Laughs*]

What would you say to the younger generation of trumpeters who are aspiring to be jazz musicians? What would Louis Armstrong say to a young guy?

Play what is in your heart. Do the best you can, and be yourself. He was the first man who said there are only two kinds of music—*good* and *bad*. He said, "If it sounds good to you, whether I like it or not, it is good music. If it sounds good to you, it's good."

Did Louis have any favorite trumpeters?

King Oliver. That was his mentor, his teacher, his father figure. He always talked about King Oliver. He mentioned Buddy Bolden, but Bolden was more of a legend, because I don't think there are any recordings of him. They said you could hear Bolden for miles. But King Oliver was his man.

What were his views on people like John Coltrane? What kind of music did he listen to?

Louis listened to everybody, but he never would discuss whether he liked or disliked a musician. He never would say, *I like him* or *I don't like him*, or *he's better*. He never would get into that. But he would listen. He listened to classical music, too. Louis liked all types of music. He was very open to music. He listened to records to see what he could improve on. If he had been doing a tune for thirty years, he would listen to it and say, "How can I improve on it?" That's the way he was.

What is the most important thing you learned from him?

"You cannot fool an audience." They will know when you are sincere. Show them that you are honest and sincere and that what you are doing is coming from your heart. We would travel to different countries and different cultures, from the most underdeveloped ones, to, Japan, and

India. Wherever he played, no matter the race, color, or culture of the people, they would react the same way—when this man walked on stage and smiled, they knew that this was an honest and sincere man, and what he did came from his heart. He was truly a world citizen. Everybody seemed to adopt him as their own.

I understand that he was a very generous man.

Oh, yes. He gave away millions of dollars. Money didn't mean that much to him. When he died, he was a multimillionaire. He could have had an estate somewhere in Beverly Hills or the East End of Long Island, or wherever, but he stayed right in the house he lived in, a very modest house in Queens. He stayed there for the last forty years of his life.

He used to hang out with the kids on the street, go to the barbershop. People didn't realize who they had in the neighborhood. They didn't realize it was *Louis Armstrong.* I mean, here is a man who they named an airport for. He has stadiums, schools, parks, everything named after him, and if someone had told him this would be happening to him, he would have said, "You're crazy." He knew that he was a special talent, but his mind didn't run on about how great he was. He didn't think that way.

I've got to tell you, a lot of guys in my generation, guys under the age of forty, try to bypass history and Louis Armstrong.

That is why classical music is great. The people that like Stravinsky or Schoenberg, they don't put Mozart down, you know? Stress that in your book, man. Without the history of your art, we have nothing. You can't build a building without a foundation. How can you become good if you don't understand where it came from?

John Coltrane came out of rhythm and blues bands. Dizzy Gillespie came out of the big swing bands. Charlie Parker came out of Kansas City, in Jay McShann's band playing the blues. You talk to them about their music and they will tell you where it came from. And they would stress the roots. And a lot of people have ignored Earl Hines. He did more to help people in his day— Look at the people who came out of the Earl Hines band! Miles, Budd Johnson, Dexter Gordon, Dizzy, Billy Eckstine, and Sarah Vaughan. Hines got those people started. Jazz did not begin with Miles Davis. You have to go back. We are all standing on the shoulders of giants.

Louis Armstrong's home in Queens, New York.

Photo by author

Harry "Sweets" Edison
"The notes were going by so fast…nobody knew the difference."

Along with Count Basie, Harry "Sweets" Edison epitomized the notion of a musician being able to be recognized by playing *just one note*. His was a trumpet sound that was deeply rooted in the blues, as well as the intense but subtle fire of saxophonist Lester Young. It was Young who gave Edison the nickname of "Sweets" while they were both in the band of Count Basie in the late 1930s.

Sweets Edison (1915–2000) was a rare breed of jazz master that stripped away the fat from his playing. He could say more with one note than most musicians could with fifty. His tone was lush and beautiful, and with a Harmon or bucket mute, especially, he was completely original. He had a way of bending notes that was uniquely his. His solos just oozed of the blues, but he could also play harmonically advanced trumpet. Sweets never let the innovations of the modernists pass him by either, but his use of the quarter note, such as playing one fat quarter note on each beat for five or six bars, shows just how much he was influenced by Louis Armstrong. And he could make a phrase sound easy just by his clever displacement of rhythm.

Born in Columbus, Ohio, in 1915, Sweets began to play the trumpet around the age of twelve. Interestingly enough, he would move to the great trumpet town of St. Louis and remain there for a couple of years before moving to New York in 1937. In New York, Edison joined the orchestra of Lucky Millinder. Several months later he would make a move that would change his career forever.

That was the year Count Basie made it to New York from Kansas City, under the care of John Hammond. Basie's orchestra was about to take the world by storm with its unique mix of blues and American popular songs driven by the irresistible Kansas City pulse. Sweets joined Basie, and soon would become one of the orchestra's most important soloists. His use of fanning "the derby," or metal hat, created a stir among all who heard him. As the great Basie saxophonist Earl Warren said, "He upset the people."

I first met Sweets in 1993. I had just joined the Count Basie Orchestra and was humbled to be a part of such an institution. During our performance in France at the Nice Jazz Festival, he walked straight to up to me and said, "You are sitting in the same chair I sat in 1938! I was making six dollars a week!"

After leaving Basie for the first of a few sabbaticals in the early 1950s, Sweets was in demand as a sideman, and toured with Jazz at the

Photo by Candy Augustine

Sweets Edison, center, with Wynton Marsalis, left, and Scotty on right. Tampa, Florida, 1996.

Philharmonic. He eventually moved to Los Angeles in the mid-1950s, and this would be his home until a year or so before he passed away. Once in Los Angeles, Sweets became one of the most in-demand jazz trumpeters for studio recording dates. Around this same time, he also began to make recordings with Frank Sinatra, which would bring him even more worldwide acclaim. The Sinatra and Sweets clique was legendary—Edison's light but definite fills were the perfect compliment for Sinatra's behind-the-beat phrasing.

Edison led his own group but would rejoin Basie in the mid-1960s for a short while. He always joked and told Basie that he would never be without a job, as long as Basie had a band. He said that if Basie didn't pay him, he would simply sleep in Basie's bed until he did.

In the 1970s, Sweets continued to tour the world and make significant recordings with jazz masters including Count Basie, Oscar Peterson, Eddie "Lockjaw" Davis, and Benny Carter. (He also became the musical director for the late comedian Redd Foxx's X-rated Las Vegas act!)

I recommend every recording featuring Sweets, but a few of my personal favorites are *Ben and Sweets*, which contains one of the most perfect improvised solos ever captured on tape on "Did You Call Her Today?" Every trumpet player in the world should know this solo. I also love *Oscar Peterson and Sweets Edison*, *Edison's Lights*, *Sinatra and Basie at the Sands*, *It Might As Well be Swing*, *The Complete Decca Recordings of Count Basie*, (the last three are under Count Basie's name), and various live recordings.

I was fortunate to know Sweets Edison for several years. He lived only ten minutes from me in Los Angeles, and we spent a few afternoons at his apartment talking, laughing a lot, and playing our trumpets. Sweets Edison was one of the most gracious and funniest human beings ever to walk this earth. And Sweets didn't care how much horn you thought you played, he would be sure to remind you at every instance that he was one of the all-time trumpet masters.

Listening to Lester Young every night had to be incredible.

Lester was the one who made the Basie orchestra popular. Also Hershel Evans and Joe Jones. They were the three stalwarts of the band. I was back there having so much fun *I* should have paid Basie!

As far as trumpet players go, you were one of the first cats to become a star with Basie—as far as the excitement, and with that style of swing, using the derby hat and all. How was it to be in a section with Buck Clayton and Ed Lewis?

It was something man, and I think the two greatest first trumpet players I ever played with were Ed Lewis and Snooky Young. I just tried to develop a sound I was comfortable with.

I'm dealing with that derby and plunger all the time. Right now, I am trying to figure out how to use my plunger so that I am not always doing the open and close sound of doo-wha, doo-wha. There is this one lick that you play where it sounds like two trumpeters playing at once… [I start to play a little of the phrase]

That's it! Now another thing I can show is this. Start on your low E with the third valve, and go on up using the first and the third valves. And you don't have to change valves. A G comes out. An A comes out with the third valve. Stay on the first and third. That's what you call *skatin'*. It sounds so effective because the notes are going by so fast, that's the way Dizzy used to do. The notes were going by so fast 'til, *shit*, nobody knew the difference.

[Laughs] Dizzy could play so fast. Standing next to Bird had to affect him.

I met Dizzy in 1939. At the time he was playing just like Roy Eldridge. He started playing like bebop when he was with Cab Calloway. Cab used to say, "What kind of shit is that?" Tad Dameron brought down a [modern] arrangement for Basie. It was kind of difficult. Basie had to go down on a lot of those chords and he wasn't used to that so he threw it away. I'll tell you one thing, Basie was successful with tempos. That son of a gun could swing anything. In those days, if you didn't hit the right tempo to make them dance, you didn't get work. And he would mess with the tempo until he got it right. Then the guys could come in. Sometimes guys would get mad and say, "What are you doing?" Basie would just say, "I'm trying to get it *right*."

It doesn't have to be a big band. It can be a small group and the tempo can make or break the tune.

The wrong tempo takes away the spirit of the music. In the old days, there were two bands for swing; Basie and Jimmie Lunceford. And Benny Goodman used to swing. Basie used to tear his ass up. We used to tear his ass up all the time. There was one time at Madison Square Garden in New York. Benny played the first set, and after we got through playing the second set, shoot, we had sent his band home.

How was Bennie Moten, compared to Basie?

Basie had a more modern band. It was the same notes but more modern. Basie had Lester, Herschel, Hot Lips Page—that was a little swingin' son of a gun on trumpet. He could take a plunger and *kill* you. Kill you, kill you, kill you. He ran Dizzy off the stand many times.

Damn!

Yeah, playing the blues. Hot Lips was a mean trumpet player. He would take that plunger and hang you out to dry.

Did Dizzy ever use the plunger?

Nahh. Dizzy was no real blues player. Not like Hot Lips Page and guys like that. Not like Jabbo Smith. Jabbo was a mean motor scooter. He could play. He could play. Basie also had a trumpet player named Louis Metcalf. Aw man, when I first got here, he had a crown on his head. He was the king. He had a hell of a name in New York. Roy Eldridge pulled that crown off of him.

I heard the story that Dizzy outplayed Roy Eldridge so bad one night that Roy started crying.

He did. I was there. It was at a place called the Spotlight. It was the end of an era. At that time Little Jazz [Roy] was playing at the Strand with Artie Shaw. He had those weird chops. Just play his solo and get off. At the Spotlight, they had these jam sessions every Sunday afternoon where you could get your ass cut. Charlie Shavers and I played together, and after that, here comes Dizzy and Roy. Man, Dizzy had those tires burning. You could see the steam coming from the bell of his horn.

And Roy evidently didn't expect that. Because Roy could play fast, too.

Shit, yeah, he could play fast. And Roy sat down on the stage there and cried. It was the end of an era.

I heard that Dizzy said he went and told Roy not to feel bad because he would have not been able to do that had it not been for Roy…

Dizzy didn't say anything before or after he cut his ass. He didn't say, "I'm sorry." After that, Roy always wanted to stand next to Dizzy. Whenever there were two or three trumpeters playing together, Roy would always want to stand next to Dizzy. He would tell you to move over if you were next to Dizzy.

And Roy couldn't *stand* Erskine Hawkins. Roy used to carry his horn around everywhere he went, looking for Erskine to cut him. They had a placed called Anchors Away on Seventh Avenue that all of the trumpet players used to go and play. It was between 126th and 127th Streets. Roy used to go there looking for his ass. Whenever there was a new trumpet player in town playing there, somebody would get Dizzy or Roy and they would run that son-of-a-gun out of New York.

That is one thing I never saw Pops do—be at a jam session. But you know, everybody would go down and bow to him.

Do you think that one of the reasons Armstrong ended up having such a big sound accounts for the fact that when started learning how to play, he was largely teaching himself? …I mean, he didn't have like a private teacher that would sit him down and say…because when you are first starting to learn how to play a brass instrument, you are automatically going to play louder than the next player who has a teacher.

A trumpet is the loudest instrument that you can play. And the hardest. When they used to bring kings and royalty in, they had those big long trumpets, you know. That got attention, man. That got attention.

Clark Terry
"One man is not a prayer book!"

Clark Terry is one of the most incredibly versatile musicians to ever live. He is a jazz trumpet master that played with the greatest names in the history of the music, from Duke Ellington, with whom Clark spent nearly ten years with, to Count Basie, the U.S. Navy Band, and dates with Thelonious Monk, Ben Webster, NBC's *Tonight Show* Band, Quincy Jones, Ella Fitzgerald, Oscar Peterson, Dizzy Gillespie, Dinah Washington, Ben Webster,

Jazz trumpet master Clark Terry performing on flugelhorn.

Thelonious Monk, Billie Holiday, Sarah Vaughan, Coleman Hawkins, Zoot Sims, Milt Jackson...the list is endless. Clark Terry has performed for seven U.S. presidents, and was a jazz ambassador for State Department tours in the Middle East and Africa. He is a Grammy Award winner, and has received thirteen honorary doctorates, was knighted in Germany, and is the recipient of the French Order of Arts and Letters.

Clark is also an important educator and his books include *Let's Talk Trumpet: From Legit to Jazz, Interpretation of the Jazz Language,* and *Clark Terry's System of Circular Breathing for Woodwind and Brass Instruments*.

I first heard Clark on an album that I bought while in high school, called *Oscar Peterson and the Trumpet Kings: Jousts*. On the first track, "Danish Pastry," Clark demonstrates a very unusual combination of technical finesse—with his use of rare, improvisational triple-tonguing—coupled with his unique sound and approach to the blues. It is just another example of the pioneering technique for which he is famous.

I first met Clark Terry in 1990 at the first Thelonious Monk Trumpet Competition, where he was one of the judges. He immediately put me at ease with his friendly manner, and answered every question I asked about jazz trumpet. I didn't win that day, but Clark sent me a check for $100 from his personal account as a consolation prize, along with a note to keep my spirits up! He told me that my day would surely arrive and not to be discouraged about the contest. I wasn't the least bit concerned—others who didn't win included Nicholas Payton and Tom Williams—but the generosity of Clark stunned me. I didn't even know that he knew me.

I always made it a point to get any recordings featuring Clark—he had to be someone special to have both Duke and Basie hire him. The way that he plays the blues, as well as extremely fast tempos, is amazing. And he makes it look effortless, the sign of a true master. I wanted to learn as many of his solos as possible. Some of my favorites are Clark with pianist Oscar Peterson on the record *Oscar Peterson Trio + One*; *In Orbit with Thelonious Monk*; and various dates where he is the leader, such as *Serenade to a Bus Seat*, *The Happy Horns of Clark Terry*, and *Spanish Rice*. But his Pablo dates with Norman Granz as producer truly display his command of the instrument, playing alongside other trumpet greats like Dizzy Gillespie, Roy Eldridge, and Freddie Hubbard. The recording *The Alternate Blues* that features Terry, Hubbard, and Gillespie, is one of *the* most important jazz albums.

In 1995, I was with the Basie orchestra in Holland to play the North Sea Jazz Festival. They were also honoring Clark Terry and Benny Carter that evening with Lifetime Achievement awards. It was nice to see Clark, it had been a few years, and I just wanted to hang with him and talk with him after the concert. I was helping him with his cases and he said, "Get your horn and come and play this gig with me." I was speechless. The great Clark Terry was asking me to do a gig with him!

My knees were shaking. He then asked me what tunes *I* wanted to play.

Backstage, Clark pulled out his flugelhorn and plays something that sounds like a human voice speaking. They were not "notes" as we know them. I had never heard anyone do that before or since.

We took the stage with a trio behind us, and just me and Clark out front. He gave me his blue plunger to use. He let me call the first number and I chose "Mack the Knife." I don't remember too much after that, except I used the plunger behind him as he sang one tune. We played five or six numbers. I was in absolute heaven—and glad that I had studied his playing. It was one of the highlights of my life, and I was humbled that I was allowed to share the stage with such a man and musician and bring a smile to his face.

On July 7, 2002, I finally was able to make it to Clark's Haworth, New Jersey home to talk with him about his career for this book. When I walked into his living room, I was astounded by the awards and photos that blanketed the walls and floor. In the in the middle of the floor was a bass drum for a coffee table. The tom-toms doubled as coasters and a place to put the telephone. Clark came into the room with the aid of his wife Gwen. He was a bit frail, but he looked great and still does for a man some eighty years of age. I was honored to be his guest.

Do you know how rare that is for someone with your technique, the refined technique you have, to not have had a teacher? How did you learn how to play?

Never had a teacher in my life. I'm from a big family and my dad couldn't afford a teacher. It was 10,000 questions for 10,000 people. I got 5,000 answers, and most of them were wrong. [*Laughs*] I'll never forget when I asked one old dude about trying to improve my tone in the lower register. And this old fucker said, "Son, do you have a mirror at home?" And I'm naïve and I said, "Well, yeah." He said, "Get in front of the mirror in a chair. Sit back in the chair. And make sure your arms are up enough to allow ample room for the air column." I said that all sounds good, yeah. OK. Then what? [*Speaking in the voice of the old trumpeter*] He said, "Now sit in that chair and wiggle your left ear and grit your teeth." Now you know damn well that ain't got shit to do with playing the trumpet. Then he probably went home and said, "Well, I got rid of another one of them little motherfuckers." Because they thought that everything they taught would be a threat to their livelihood.

[Laughs] That's insane! But did you go through some of the method books, like the J .B. Arban method and others?

Yeah, the Arban. And I used to also practice with a clarinet book.

You know, Freddie Hubbard used to do that. That is some hard stuff. You've got some technique if you can do that. Guys have said to me that you must have studied with some top cat, because everything about your embouchure is just perfect. Cats have been trying to copy that for years—the horn placement, the attack, the triple tonguing, all of that stuff.

One man is not a prayer book, you know. I tell students that all the time. The secret of the whole thing is to look at, observe, and listen to as many different methods as you possibly can. Then draw from there that which works for you. Whatever is good enough to make it possible for you to give vent to your feelings, in the proper fashion, so that you don't hamper your feelings with a fucked-up embouchure. Those cats in New Orleans, when they got a hold of instruments that

were left in the pawn shops by the symphony players, they put the horn over here, up there, up their noses, up their asses, anyway they could find [*laughing*]... One thing that came out of that was very important, one of the main ingredients for the colorization of jazz and the perpetuation of the craft–the *buzz*. Somebody figured out that in order to make your sound bigger, you could *hum* while you played. It became known as "buzzing" and it is still very widely used–Ben Webster did it, Vic Dickenson, Miles, everybody that you can think of.

Miles was a little funny cat when he was coming up. His teacher, Elwood Buchanan, used to be a student of Joe Gustav of the Saint Louis Symphony, and he used to tell me to come over to the school to hear "Dewey Davis." So I went over to Miles's school to meet him, and he was thin enough to ride a rooster. If he stood sideways, they would have marked his ass absent. He was very, very shy. He couldn't look you in the eye, either.

How old was Miles when you first heard him?

He was a teenager. He was still in high school—maybe twelve or thirteen. I heard him play and he had one thing he would always do, and that was to play with a wide vibrato. He loved Harry James.

Buchanan told him to stop shaking that note, because he was going to shake when he got old anyway! Anytime he shook that note, Buchanan had a ruler and he would go "Bam!" and hit him on the hand. So he's responsible for Miles having that straight sound. That, plus the fact that Joe Gustav used to insist that all of his players play Heim mouthpieces. I could never play it because my chops were too big for them. Miles had the thinner chops.

I figured out at some point how to fix my valves so that the springs would make them come up faster, so I wouldn't have to pound them down so hard. Miles used to see me and ask me to fix his horn for him. He had a flugelhorn and he used to call it "Fat Girl." He'd say, "Hey man, take my Fat Girl home with you tonight and fix the valves." Miles, Shorty Rogers, and Emmit Berry all had flugelhorns with trumpet mouthpieces in them. It let them play higher. But that's like putting hot sauce on ice cream.

When did you start playing flugelhorn?

The first one I got was in November 1957. We were on a date, at the Blue Note with Ellington, and Billy Taylor came to town and recorded a big band date using the whole Ellington band except Ellington. The whole sphere. The title of the album is *Taylor Made Jazz*. I was staying with my buddy Sike Smith from St. Louis, a trumpet player, who used to let me play at the Plantation. [The same club where bassist Arvell Shaw heard Louis Armstrong when he was a kid.] He'd let me take his solos sometimes. We were on this recording session down at Universal when the horn arrived—we had worked on it in the basement of Keith Ecker, who was the technical advisor of brass for Selmer. Have you seen the Selmer flugelhorns called the K-Modified?

Yeah.

Well the "K" stands for *Keith*. Keith was a good buddy of mine. His dad was a great wine maker, and we used to go to their basement and drink up some wine while trying different things with the flugelhorn. I always told him that I wanted to see if I could get the flugelhorns back on the scene again. So we kept putting different portholes together, and different lengths of tubing.

I didn't know you were involved like that.

Yeah. We finally put something together, and he said, "This sounds like it is going to be it." We sent it back to Selmer in Paris and they corrected whatever needed to be done. They finessed it and sent it back to Chicago, and Sikes brought it down to the session. It was gold plated, too, man. It had such a gorgeous sound. Billy Taylor said, "You should play that on the date." I said, "I intend to."

They sent it back with the flugelhorn mouthpiece?

Yeah. Of course, later, I had Giardinelli make a flugel mouthpiece, a 7F. By this time, all of the trumpet players had decided to convert to the French horn principle—no bowl cup in the mouthpiece. Flat rim and straight. You never saw a French horn mouthpiece with a bowl for the cup.

I took the horn to the gig that night with Duke and he said, "Man, you ought to keep that in." I said, "I intend to." So he wrote the only piece for me from the left hand corner and it was called "Juniflip."

Did I tell you that Sweets showed me how to squeeze the plunger, which I had never done before? Normally, I just kind of go in and out.

Yes, you have to caress it. So many cats try to play the blues and can't play the plunger. They don't know how to handle it.

Well, I always tell everybody if you want to learn how to play the plunger, listen to Clark Terry, listen to Cootie Williams, and listen to Snooky Young.

And Ray Nance. There are several different theories about intonation and the plunger. I find that when you cut out the hole and leave the hole open, it is much more in tune. You can even touch the bell.

Completely closed?

Closed. You can even temper it long enough until you find the correct pressure. That's important too—to find the correct pressure. If you bang on it and jam it up in there, it will be out of tune.

That's one of the things I found, too, that if I play an open middle C, then put the plunger on completely closed and play the same C, then if it is tune, the plunger is cool.

Yeah.

That's what I found. But I've never played one with a hole in it, though. I have the one that has the little finger hook on it so it doesn't slip out of my hand while playing it.

You have one of those plastic ones?

No, it's rubber, but I find if I put it flush on my bell, it is still in tune.

Then you have found the proper pressure. If you jam it up there it won't work. I need to get another one. I bought up all the blue plungers I could find...

Blue?

Yeah. In Sweden. I used to give everybody a blue plunger. Some cat over here has them, but they are too big. They go over the bell of my horn.

Have you been traveling lately?

Yeah, but my pinched nerve in my back has been bothering me. I was supposed to be leaving Wednesday for the place where you and I played together that time. The North Sea Festival. And you were smokin' that night, too! How is the book coming?

Scotty with Clark Terry, right, after their performance at the North Sea Jazz Festival in 1995.

It's a lot of work, but you know, I was tired of reading books by critics who don't know what they are talking about. This one cat said that ballads were an area that plagued Clifford Brown!

What? Couldn't play a ballad? What the fuck does he know?

I learned the entire Clifford Brown with Strings record. That is one of the ways I learned how to play a ballad! And here is this guy talking about somebody like that, and he couldn't blow a note if his life depended on it.

I'm hip.

I have a list of over 800 trumpet players— I've tried to find everyone that I could, whether they were famous or not.

You know much about this cat in Milwaukee? He was parking cars there for years. They finally brought him back in a Broadway show called *One Mo' Time*. Old-timer. Yeah, what is his name? Shit. A brother, too. Old Spanish trumpet player...

It wouldn't be Jabbo Smith, would it?

Jabbo! Yeah!

95

See, it's guys like Jabbo that a lot of the younger guys don't know about. Man, I have some recordings of him, and this cat had great technique and range.

That cat could play his ass off. Duke Ellington offered him a job, and he laughed at Duke!

What?!

[*Imitating Jabbo talking to Duke*] "You must be fucking kidding me!" He was one of those cats that, while the New Orleans cats would be playing simple quarter-note and eighth-note rhythms in their solos, Jabbo would be playing sixteenth and thirty-second note rhythms in his solos. [*Clark sings a very fast solo*] He was running changes and things back in those days.

I did read where he was Armstrong's only rival.

Satchel [Armstrong] had a whole bunch of tapes on him that nobody else ever had. I don't know where he got them. He was a funny cat, man. We used to hang out. And he loved chicks. I'll tell you his favorite saying, but you'll have to edit it out of your book...

Humphrey Lyttleton
"Let it build."

Humphrey Lyttleton is a part of the British lineage of jazz trumpet that began with Nat Gonella, "Britain's answer to Louis Armstrong."

Lyttleton has been hosting *The Best of Jazz* show on BBC Radio for about fifty years, and has interviewed trumpet legends from Louis Armstrong to Wynton Marsalis. Because he is a jazz trumpeter himself, he has a unique insight into the art.

His trumpet playing reminds me of a youthful Louis Armstrong in its bounce and swagger, but also hints at the subtleties of Buck Clayton, whom Lyttleton knew very well. He provided me with valuable insight into the attitudes of British jazz musicians, and also painted a picture of a career that has been full of exciting musical adventure. I found Lyttleton, who is almost ninety, in his native England, preparing for a gig.

Tell me about when you got started.

There was a guy named called Nat Gonella. Nat was like a star footballer is today. He moved from one club to another. From one big band to another. He was the first guy in this country of any note who used to play in the Louis Armstrong style. Musicians in the '20s used to play in a kind of Bix Beiderbeck, Red Nichols-style, and Nat was the first one who was a great devotee of Louis

Armstrong. And that was what attracted me. He used to play what we called *hot choruses*. And he sang a little bit with an accent that was peculiar a bit to the east end of London, but with a bit of a Louis Armstrong's gravelly voice to it.

In the late 1930s when I was listening to a lot of jazz on record, it was the time of the Dixieland Revival. Muggsy Spanier, who had a very simple

Humphrey Lyttleton.

Photo courtesy of Humphrey Lyttleton

style, was a good one to start with. And a big idol of mine for many years was Max Kaminsky, who again had a very direct and simplified style. Little bits of them brushed off onto me. And Henry "Red" Allen, and Yank Lawson. They were the early influences of mine.

How did you and your friends view the American jazz musicians? Did you view them as kind of a separate entity from what you guys were doing?

American jazz was the source of it all. It took quite a while in this country for each individual musician to have a style of their own. The tenor players were all into Coleman Hawkins and Lester Young, the trumpeters were into Armstrong.

There was a stupid kind of a trade ban that went on between Britain and the U.S. I don't know who started it, and it doesn't matter, but it was like, *I won't play in your country if you won't play in mine*. Very childish. This lasted well into the middle '50s.

The first American musician I played with was Sidney Bechet. It was like smuggling contraband. They got him in ostensibly on a holiday. He did a concert with my band. It had to be rigged up where the guy would say we have a special guest here, as if it were a spontaneous thing from the audience. We'd been rehearsing all afternoon.

What was the difference in approach between the British players and the Americans?

One of the big differences, a fairly obvious one between British players, and American players, is that we British have always tended to hold back our emotions. We had a lot of men in the '30s who played like Coleman Hawkins, but they never allowed the emotion to come through like Hawkins did. It's different now, but in the early days, you couldn't get a British band to do the same

riff for more than two choruses. It has taken them some years to get to the point to where they can play the same riff for twenty minutes. Let it build.

We still do that in the Basie orchestra, and it's great.

When they did the exchange thing, we went to the United States in 1959. Since that time, I have employed a lot of musicians who came up in the modern field. And that kind of brushed off on me. I am a self-taught musician, and I used to say to my pianist, "I'm a musical illiterate and if a flatted fifth came up and hit me on the nose, I wouldn't recognize it." He told me that I played a flatted fifth at least fifty times a night. I've played with a lot of trumpet players who switched from traditional style to bebop who had to change their embouchures to get the speed and the lighter sound. I've always played with a layered tone, or several layers of sound, so I've never really sounded much like a modern jazz trumpet player.

Do you remember when you first saw Louis Armstrong?

At the beginning of 1948, at the Nice Jazz Festival, with the All-Stars. It was the first international jazz festival on the continent of Europe. The big writer and critic Huges Panassie staged the concert. There were the All-Stars, a band led by Mezz Mezzrow, Rex Stewart had a band, and Django Reinhardt was there.

First, this French band went on that played very much in the revived King Oliver style, with two cornets. It was quite a loud noise. We all played too loud then. I was talking to some people when the French band went off, and Louis' band was on next. Somebody said, "Hang on...they have started." The All-Stars had started, and there was this music that was far quieter and far richer in tone than any of the European bands.

That was a big lesson to me. One of my great musical experiences was hearing Louis Armstrong. It was like the sun in orbit.

Did you get to know him very well?

Insofar as anybody did. If you had written something nice about him or gone to meet him at the airport or if he felt you were in his corner so to speak, he would never forget. And I have memories of when he used to prepare for concerts. He would often have on very little, other than a very complicated jock strap and a stocking thing to keep his hair in place. Then he'd cover his lips with this lip salve, so all in all you couldn't really hold a conversation.

How you feel about more modern, or more contemporary players? Miles Davis? Wynton Marsalis?

I like Wynton's playing and I like Wynton. I've seen quite a bit of him over the years. I've heard his various bands and he gets a lot of criticism for doing the repertory stuff, but again, if somebody gets such beautiful music out of a trumpet, I think you are doing yourself a disservice if you allow yourself to start criticizing. It is best to remain sort of an ignoramus and just enjoy it.

I've been listening to the latter day Miles, a lot of the "rock fusion" Miles. I like the intensity. It is like if you would light a campfire with a magnifying glass. He had that spare style, with focus, with a little bit of smoke coming from it. That's him.

Describe the importance of trumpet technique as you see it.

Well, I'll give you a quote that I overheard Duke Ellington say. I heard him being interviewed by some students and one of the students said, "How come in your trumpet section you have a guy who plays all over the instrument like Clark Terry and then you have a guy who obviously doesn't have that kind of technique, like Ray Nance?" And Duke Ellington said, "Let's be like a business man and talk percentages. Nobody plays one hundred percent of the instrument. Some play ninety-nine percent of the instrument and it sounds great. Some play ten percent, but what they do with that ten percent, no one else in the world does."

Clora Bryant

"If you want to learn, you have got to be there."

Clora Bryant is by far the greatest woman I ever heard play improvisational jazz trumpet. And her work proves that she is worthy of the stature afforded Louis Armstrong, Dizzy Gillespie, Miles Davis, and Clifford Brown.

Clora Bryant possesses all the elements of the most advanced and seasoned jazz trumpeter—a complete understanding of tradition, an inner desire to tell a story and make musical sense, a natural talent cultivated and expanded by many years on the bandstand, and a love for passing knowledge down to the next generation of musicians.

On her album *Gal with a Horn*, Clora sings with grace and style, and her trumpet sound is all at once brilliant, bright, commanding, warm, bold, and beautiful. She sounds like a perfect mixture of Roy Eldridge and Sweets Edison, with a little bit of her good friend and mentor Dizzy Gillespie thrown in, especially on "Gypsy in My Soul," in which she directly quotes a favorite Gillespie phrase (that he actually got from Eldridge).

I first met Clora after a concert at the University of Southern California and ended up giving her a ride home. Once back at her place, she showed me footage of her on *The Ed Sullivan Show*, as well as footage of her playing at various jazz festivals. She could go on anyone's bandstand and hold her own, and even lay down a law or two. Dizzy Gillespie said, "I called her up to play a tune since it was her birthday, and when she started playing so good, I hurried up and grabbed my horn back!" She is the only woman to ever play with Charlie Parker...and Clifford Brown. And did I mention that she also played with Louis Armstrong?

Clora was born in Denison, Texas in 1927, a time when it was not easy for a woman to be a part of a man's world, especially when one was also a perpetually oppressed minority. Undeterred, she practiced and developed her talent for playing the trumpet to such a high degree that doors could not help but open for her. She reached as high as the men in power would allow her, never losing her grace as a woman and as a human being. That she managed to raise her children as a single parent while touring and traveling is a testament to her strength.

Just as we owe a debt of gratitude to Louis Armstrong for showing us "The Way," to Dizzy Gillespie for elaborating and extending the art of jazz trumpet improvisation, and to Clark Terry, Sweets Edison, Freddie Hubbard, Miles Davis, and others for giving a unique voice to the music, we also owe a unique debt to Clora Bryant.

Clora's influence is not only as a jazz trumpeter, but as an ambassador to jazz musicians everywhere, and especially to all women of jazz. In 1989, she was the first woman to travel to the Soviet Union to play jazz. More recently she was honored at the Kennedy Center in Washington, D.C., and a full-length documentary was completed on her life and premiered at the Schaumburg Museum in New York.

There are not enough superlatives to describe Clora Bryant.

How did you begin to play the trumpet?

My uncle had played with Buddy Tate [great tenor saxophonist who also played with Count Basie] when Tate was with the territory bands. My uncle was also a saxophone player, but he knew about the trumpet. He told me to pucker my lips and blow. The first thing I did was play a G. He was floored. I was fifteen. I graduated high school when I was fifteen—they let school out early in those days so that the kids could pick cotton.

You got out of school early because you had to pick cotton?

I didn't, but my two brothers did. They would be up at four or five o'clock in the morning to catch the truck. My dad would never let me go, and I was so glad. But that is when I started. I bought one of those little books so I could learn "My Country 'Tis of Thee."

My dad was my knight in shining armor. He was a frustrated trumpet player, and he loved Louis Armstrong. He loved "West End Blues," and whenever it would come on the radio, he would hold the trumpet like he was playing it. And when I started playing the trumpet, I became his everything. He would praise me, he was so proud. He would listen to me play and go into the bedroom and cry. He was very sentimental. When

I started to play the trumpet, he became a different man. He could relate to me better, and I could relate to him. The first thing I learned to play was a solo by Harry James called "I Had the Craziest Dream." I did that without any real effort. And then I went to UCLA. It was 1959 to 1961 when I took lessons there.

Do you remember the first trumpet player you ever heard?

It wasn't Louis Armstrong. In my home in Texas, we heard the white bands on the radio. I don't remember exactly, but the bands were Woody Herman, Tommy Dorsey, Artie Shaw, and Glenn Miller. Then after midnight, we would start to hear the black bands. My brother had this set of headphones and he would put on one ear and I would put on the other and we would sit there at the radio listening to Duke Ellington, Count Basie, Andy Kirk, Jimmy Lunceford, and Fletcher Henderson. But the trumpet players would have been the white trumpet players with the white bands simply because they came on earlier in the evening on the radio broadcast. When I heard the black bands, I heard Sweets Edison with Basie, Cootie Williams with Duke.

Do you remember the very first jazz record that you heard at your house?

Yes, it was Andy Kirk, and pianist Mary Lou Williams was with them. This was in the 1930s. Then my dad started taking us to the one dance hall to hear Jay McShann with Charlie Parker, Tee Bone Walker, and Bessie Smith, who had Teddy Edwards with her in some sort of minstrel show. I remember that because Teddy Edwards told me that was the first time he had ever seen pickled rattlesnake in a big jar. See, all of the carnivals had minstrelsy shows, you know, the guys with the big painted lips and big shoes.

How did you meet Dizzy Gillespie, how did your friendship begin with him?

I met Dizzy in 1956, but I knew about him. When he played "Things to Come," I couldn't believe it. I said, "How do you play that so fast?" I was hooked. I was a Dizzy nut from then on. Then I met Dizzy at a club out here on Sunset and Western. Melba Liston, Lee Morgan, and Quincy Jones were with him. Al Grey was also in the band. I was sitting at the bar between Charlie Barnett and Sweets Edison.

That is some heavy company.

Hey, I'll tell you. I hung with the biggies. If you want to learn, you have got to be there. The guys used to say that I was forward, and I used to say that the only way I am going to learn is by being here. You can't sit back and wait for somebody to come to you.

So, were you ever in jam sessions where you had to cut some people?

Shucks, I used to find myself having to hold back from doing that. [*Laughs*] I had balls, because I *knew* I could play. I was young, but I had sense enough to know that I could do it. See, my daddy had really stamped into my brain that I could be the best. And when he heard me play, he told me I was the best and to never let anybody tell me that I was not.

How did you meet Clifford Brown?

Max Roach had just brought Clifford out here to join his band, so we went to the California Club to hear them. I was sitting in a booth with my husband and his friends. Rolf Ericson, the trumpet player from Sweden was on the bandstand with Carl Perkins on piano and Frank Butler on drums, and I told my husband I was going up to sit in. Clifford came in while I was

playing. He sat with my husband with his back to the bandstand. Clifford must have heard something he liked. He looked around and saw that it was me and did a double take. He said to my husband, "Man, who is that woman up there playing? That chick can play." When I came down off of the bandstand, he was standing there with his arms out.

Did I tell you about what happened with me and Charlie Parker? I was the only female that played with Charlie Parker. Max and Clifford were playing at the Lighthouse Café. Charlie went out to see them there. I was playing next door at the High Seas, with a tenor player, who later married Mahalia Jackson. I would always go to the Lighthouse on my intermissions. Charlie knew who I was. So I went into the club and spoke to him, and then I had to go back to my club. The next thing I know, Charlie is coming into where I was playing, with all of these people following him. He came up on the bandstand and asked the tenor player if he could play his horn. This guy had just gotten a new Selmer. Bird took that tenor and looked at me and said, "Well, Clora, what do you want to play?" I said, "Let's play 'Now's the Time.'" That was his tune. We had a good medium tempo, and got down on that. Then he said, "Let's play some 'Tickle Toe.'" He counted it off so fast, and I said, "Oh, shit. I'm in trouble now." He said, "Clora, you know I love you, and I love the way you play, but don't try to double up if you can't get outta shit." [*Laughs*]

And you played with Louis Armstrong?

In 1960, we were playing Las Vegas. We were in the lounge and he was playing the big room. On their breaks, they would come and sit in the back of the room where we were playing. And one night I am up there doing my act playing "Basin Street Blues," and I looked up and there was Louis and all of his band marching up to our stage. They played my whole act with me. I don't know how he knew to do that, but he broke it up. He didn't tell anybody he was going to do that. And Dizzy, too, would just walk up there and start playing.

What do you think the solution is to getting jazz back into the mainstream?

The schools. The schools don't have the right teachers to educate the students. I did a master class, this was in the 1980s and I was still playing then. I told the rhythm section backing me up to play a riff behind me while I played. They didn't know what a *riff* was.

I am glad I came along when I did. The music was lyrical and it was mind-boggling. You'd be popping and foot stomping. That's what we are missing. Musicians don't seem to move anymore. Move with the music and the audience will too.

Maynard Ferguson

"Oops. We are written to a high C."

6

When I was in eighth grade, at Gordon High School in Decatur, Georgia, the hit song "Rocky" was all the rage amongst high school bands. I had not even seen the movie yet, but I knew the trumpet solo. I was already playing along with it when I would hear it on the radio, which seemed like every day.

Our marching band director, Gordon Boykin, decided to determine the seating arrangements in the trumpet section, from first all the way to last, by seeing who could play it. Since I was the youngest, the only one there in the eighth grade, I was already sitting at the end of the section.

Boykin started picking people at random. The band room was packed and a hush came over the room as the first player began to play. He screwed it up and everybody began to laugh. The next player sounded even worse. More laughter. The next player did the same. I was the last one, and I played it perfectly. The whole room started whooping and hollering and giving me high fives. I didn't understand what the all the fuss was about, but I went ahead and took my seat next to the leader of the section, who was the only other one to play the theme correctly.

A few years later, I was given a trumpet solo called "Conquistador." My band director had the album, and on the cover was a drawing of Maynard Ferguson—the same trumpeter who played the solo on the theme to *Rocky*. I decided to do a little research on Maynard Ferguson, and I discovered that he has influenced thousands of trumpeters during his fifty-five-year career.

From his early days in Montreal, Canada, to his beginning with Charlie Barnet in 1949, to his great years playing Birdland in New York opposite Miles Davis, to his performances with high school and college bands around the world performing *Rocky*, Maynard Ferguson is simply a master of jazz trumpet.

Maynard Ferguson.

What was your first major break? Was that with Charlie Barnett?

Boyd Raeburn was my first band. Even Dizzy Gillespie played for a short while on that band—the chart I played for "A Night in Tunisia" said *Dizzy* on it. They wanted to make sure he got the solo trumpet part, because the personnel was changing every week on those kinds of bands. That was not a very successful band.

But one night I walked into this jazz club right on Times Square, downstairs, I can't remember the name of it, but Count Basie's band was there. Like 1948 or '49. I had just come in to join Boyd Raeburn's band for one three-hour rehearsal, get on the bus, and drive to Galveston, Texas.

Anyway, the owner of this club was kind of funny, let me walk in I guess because I had a young face and a trumpet case. And guess what happened to Maynard Ferguson the first time he went to hear a band on Times Square? Basie said, "Hey, you're from Montreal. What are you doing here?" I said I was going to stay here and try and find work with the bands. And he said, "Boy, your timing is unbelievable. Get up on the stage right now." I was astounded. I had the horn with me and everything... Harry Edison hadn't shown up yet. So suddenly there I was in Count Basie's band! [*Laughs*]

That's incredible.

I must have played about sixteen bars and the band was playing, and I was trying to sight-read a part, and there came Harry, and *oh my God*. I bet Harry wasn't late for a while.

Then I went with Jimmy Dorsey. And that was great. I had my feature tunes. Predominantly, other than the dance music and the girl singer and boy singer that he featured, he himself was a fine Dixieland clarinet and saxophone player. That wasn't my bag, but he had a sense of humor and he said, "Why don't we do just one bebop tune?"

And he had no idea how to do it himself, so it was me and some young alto player playing third alto on the band, and I bet we were pretty lame. [*Laughs*] But we were both Dizzy Gillespie and Charlie Parker fans.

Charlie Barnet is when the heaviness started. [*Laughs*] That was a wonderful band. 1949. Doc Severinsen was in it, and Rolf Ericson, the great Swedish trumpet player. We got in trouble for "All the Things You Are." We went so far off of the arrangement that Mrs. Jerome Kern objected!

Really?

Yeah, and there was a big lawsuit, they were going to sue Capitol Records. My first solo recording became a collector's item because she was going to sue them for three million dollars!

For what?

She said, "For defamation of my dead husband's work." [*Laughs*]

When did you begin to play?

When I was nine years of age, they made a terrible mistake and took me to a church social. And a little boy stood up, about my age, and played the cornet solo, I said, "Hey Dad, get me one of those." I might have been a victim of people thinking if you played the violin and you were a boy, you were a sissy, you know?

Who was the very first jazz trumpeter that you ever heard?

I'll tell you what happened. I was nine years old. My mother took me to a record store in downtown Montreal—and she was very lucky that she chose the right one. And she said [*using "mom" voice*], "My son is attracted to the jazz trumpet. And even though I am hoping he will be a classical musician, give me everything you have on great American jazz trumpet players." And I ended up with a collection that would knock your socks off today. I had all of the Ellington guys. Bunny Berigan was just in full start, and Harry James was doing those semi-classical things, *Flight of the Bumblebee* and all that kind of stuff, and it was a knockout. I seemed to prefer jazz over the *Carnival of Venice*!

Do you remember the very first jazz band that you heard?

My folks loved anything that was a big band. They would take me to every big band thing that we could see. I was just amazed by Ellington. A great band that never got recognized was Erskine Hawkins's. I watched them at the Paradise theatre in Detroit. I played there once. We were called the "Montreal High School Victory Serenaders." In the beginning our piano player was Oscar Peterson.

You and Oscar Peterson went to the same high school?

Yes. It was a small band and we worked and got ourselves a summer gig. My dad was, in spite of being a *banjo* player, he was screaming for hours at all of the Protestant school board meetings that we should be starting music education in the schools, other than the choirs, which were there forever, of course. He said it was time for instrumental music to be taught in the Protestant schools. He was one of the first guys to yell for that.

How did you learn to improvise?

I had a very small band and didn't realize how fortunate I was. I was playing in a French-Canadian nightclub. My mother would be arrested for this now. [*Laughs*] We were there seven nights a week, we would play all the Ellington things. I remember "Sophisticated

Lady," damn it gave me problems. If you were a teenager, that was pretty difficult. And what was nice is that those older guys would take me to one side and say, "Try this or try that", you know, and it's amazing that a small French-Canadian nightclub band in the north of Montreal played predominantly Ellington music.

What basic elements of trumpet playing did you realize were crucial in learning to get the desired results that you wanted in your playing? Which elements did you know that you had to have to be able to do in order to play?

Well, I'll tell you what. First of all, the formal thing got taken care of. I won a scholarship to the French Conservatory of Music in Montreal. My teacher was Benny Baker. They would fly him up from New York, where he had a trumpet studio in New York City. He was principal trumpet with Toscanini. He would say, "Play me some of them high notes. How do you do that?" This is my teacher, you know. Somehow I was blessed with the chops. There were a lot of stories about me just playing in the upper register. But he knew how to keep me straight, because he'd pick up a horn and play and I'd say, "Damn, how do you do that?"

How did you begin to develop your upper register?

Well, I tell you—simply by imitation. I had Bunny Berigan's "I Can't Get Started." I had Rex Stewart with Ellington. Louis Armstrong, of course.

My favorite thing was sitting underneath the bandstand at the Auditorium Ballroom in Montreal when I was thirteen, and there was Louis walking around in his undershorts. There was no air-conditioning in those days. I actually sat on Louis Armstrong's lap as he said to some of the guys [*with a heavy Southern accent à la Louis*], "Listen at this li'l white boy. Listen at this.

Come on, play it up an octave like you did for me before. Play it. Play me somma 'dem high notes."

You mean to tell me you were sitting in Louis Armstrong's lap playing the trumpet?

Yes! That was when he had the big band with Trummy Young and Barney Bigard. And Big Sid Catlett was on drums. I couldn't believe why I was getting all of that attention.

When I was with Johnny Le Rondo, he would take me to one side and say, "That's good, *but...*" I didn't know what a minor ninth was, and yet, I knew all the other, the classical. But it is a whole different game when you are talking chord changes. Dizzy heard me when I was a teenager and said, "Why don't you come to my home when you are in California and let me show you some things about playing changes?" I thought to myself, *that* was a critique. [*Laughs*] *You can play the shit out of the trumpet, but you can't play the shit out of the changes.* But he was too nice of a guy to say it that way.

As your reputation and your career grew, what direction did you see your music headed in, like from the mid-1950s? Did you see yourself staying as a big band leader or leading a small group as a soloist, or doing more studio stuff?

Well, I had gone in different directions. There was one point where I disbanded, got signed, got married, and went with Paramount Pictures. Those were the lucrative days when you had a yearly contract. You were set for life...they said. But a great thing happened, which finally terminated a lot of that, and that was they started doing those big epics. Instead of doing like forty movies a year, they started doing seven. *The Ten Commandments* was years in the making. I was on the lot with Cecil B. DeMille. I always laugh and say that when I was younger, I was Moses. As far as what you heard—the bugle calls—some of them were me. I love telling people I'm so old I was there when they parted the Red Sea.

You were definitely one of my early idols on the trumpet, because when I was in high school, I had to play the solo on Conquistador. How do you think you have influenced trumpet players over the last fifty years?

Well, I guess the upper register predominantly, and also to be fearless about it, because it was a stigma there—"Oops, we are written to a high C." [A typical comment heard in the early years of trumpet playing.] But if you stayed with those books, you stayed with a limited range, you know? It was just something in me, you know imitating Bunny Berigan, who you wouldn't think as a scream player, and of course the early Dizzy things. I was trying to copy them. It wasn't very good, but what the hell. I was seventeen and having fun.

So what advice would you give to a young trumpeter who is just beginning to learn how to play jazz?

I think that as soon as you find yourself favorites, unlock yourself and go out and find the other guys that don't sound like them at all. Sometimes when you get influenced by a lot of people, that's when your own identity comes out.

Sonny Cohn
"You've got to tell stories."

I was seventeen years old and had just attended my second Count Basie Orchestra concert at Atlanta's Fox Theater. It was June 1982. I went alone, and afterwards I waited for my parents to pick me up across the street from the theater. I had been waiting for a minute or two when suddenly I saw the silhouette of the entire Count Basie Orchestra crossing Atlanta's famed Peachtree Street. There were trombone cases, trumpet cases, tall men, short men, and the unmistakable image of Freddie Green's guitar, illuminated by car lights in stopped traffic. Unbeknownst to me, I had been standing near the entrance to their hotel.

I had goose bumps watching these incredibly distinguished men walk towards me. I immediately spotted Sonny Cohn. He looked just like he had moments earlier, during the concert, when he was walking down to the front of the bandstand to take a solo. In my mind, I can still see his leather trumpet and flugelhorn cases and his brown band suit.

I said hello to Cohn as he walked to the entrance of the hotel, and after I told him I was a trumpet player, he invited me in to have a bite to eat with him while I waited on my ride. He was the very first professional jazz trumpeter I had ever spoken with at length. That a man of his experience would take the time to spend a few moments with me is something I will never forget, and it only reinforces my belief that all artists—regardless of fame—should be so kind to youngsters.

Sonny Cohn.

Photo courtesy of Sonny Cohn

He told me that I needed to make sure I practiced out of the important trumpet books for technique and control of the instrument. But the thing I remember most from talking with Sonny Cohn on that warm summer night, was that I felt an immediate connection to what his life was all about—performing in the world's greatest, most swinging jazz orchestra; constantly traveling the world and meeting new people; and developing a certain and solid level of musicianship that only the road can teach. That feeling is still with me, but it has taken on an even greater dimension since I have inherited some of the very same trumpet solos he played for thirty years in the Count Basie Orchestra, including "Li'l Darlin'," "April in Paris," and "Blues in Hoss' Flat."

When I met Sonny I had a feeling that I would someday be in the Basie Orchestra. I didn't know how or when, but I knew it would happen, and that he would be one of the main reasons.

Up until this interview, which took place in Chicago on New Year's Day, 2003, I had not seen him since that summer day in Atlanta twenty years ago. I had called him over the years, but he was always on tour. The wonderful singer Carmen Bradford shocked me one day when she told me that she was at his home in Chicago and saw a picture of me on his dresser! I must have sent that to him right after I met him. Life is funny.

I met Sonny for the second time at his South Chicago residence. When he walked down the steps to meet me, those memories of our first meeting came rushing back, and I felt like a kid in a candy store all over again. I could see the wisdom on his face, wisdom from years and years of traveling the world, from an untold number of hours playing the trumpet. Sonny retired in 1991, but his wide smile was enough to warm the bitter cold Chicago weather.

We went to dinner, and it was wonderful and a little weird—I was then in my eleventh year with the Basie Orchestra, but I had always wanted to play alongside Sonny.

Do you remember when you got your very first trumpet?

My father worked at the post office, and he was friends with a guy that played alto saxophone with Earl Hines. I think he worked at the post office, too. He had something to do with my father getting his first trumpet. I was a kid in elementary school. I would hear my father practicing on the horn. He never did anything with it—he got tired of it. Anyways, he decided to save it for me. So when I got about nine or ten years old, I started taking lessons, and the guy that taught me was a guy that worked at the post office with my dad, Charles Anderson. But we called him "Baby." He was very good, too. Very good.

Was this classical training? Jazz, or what?

Nah, this was just basic fundamentals out of the Arban method.

So you played all through high school?

Oh, yes. You know the longer you play the better you get. [Laughs] Then I started playing in little bands around town, and at the different high schools, they would compete. Remember King Flemming? He's still around. And John Young had an orchestra. There were all these different bands, and we would compete against each other. This is when we were going to high school, but it continued when we got grown.

Do you remember when you first heard jazz?

Well, I've been hearing jazz all my life. [Laughs]

Do you remember the first person that made an impact on you?

When I first started playing, it was Roy Eldridge, Louis Armstrong, and different cats like that. Dizzy came later. But Diz and myself, we got to be very good friends, especially after I joined Basie. That worked out just fine.

What does Louis Armstrong mean to you?

I'll put it to you this way: *He was full of it.* He had it. He had it.

Did you ever meet him?

Yep, I met him. It was just like how we are sitting here talking now. Pops inspired everybody. He was one of the first ones to *do it*—to pick it up and do it. And he's been copied, but it's nothing like the real thing. Pops could play, and it seemed as though he never lost his chops. He played those high notes just like everybody else plays the low notes. And he told *stories*. That is something the average young musician does not do, they don't tell *stories*. You have to tell a story when you are taking a solo. You just can't play a lot of notes. For instance, if you are getting ready to say something romantic, that's where you play like you are *talking* to somebody. It's not all shouting, it has to have ups and downs.

Do you remember the day you got the call to join the Basie Orchestra?

It was just before the holidays, 1960. The guy that took Wendell Culley's place got sick. Wendell took the first solo on "Li'l Darlin'." The band was playing at the Blue Note in Chicago at the time and they called me to go down and fill in. So I went down and filled in, and a couple of weeks later they asked me if I'd be interested in joining the band. I said, "Oh, yeah." That's when I joined the band permanently. It just went on and on. I left town with them and I never came back. [*Laughs*]

You were on the road with Basie for all of those years—what was one of the main things you learned from working with him?

Basie was one of the nicest guys in the world. He was never a snob no matter what. Basie could be sitting here eating and enjoying his meal, and somebody would come up and say something to him, or ask him for an autograph, he was never too busy. Never too busy to give an autograph.

When you first started playing with the band, Snooky Young was on lead, Thad Jones was second, you were third, and Joe Newman was fourth, but on some recordings it sounds like you playing lead on the ballads. Were you guys passing different parts around, like certain guys would play lead on certain things?

Yes, I did mostly the ballads. And then the other one—Freddie Green's tune "Corner Pocket"—I played lead on that. I played lead on quite a few things.

Was that to just give the lead player a rest or just to spice it up a little bit?

It was to spice it up a little bit...

Would you recommend to younger guys in college and high school bands to do the same thing now?

If they are able to do that. Then also, you have to *think* like a leader. You have to take charge when you play it. It's more than just notes. You have to play with a *feeling*. That's what we all did then, played with a feeling. We would all set different riffs. You'd *think* that something was written, but it wasn't. It's not *what* you played, but *how* you played it. You know what I mean? And the band had certain ways of *phrasing* different things. It was like I say, *togetherness*—and that's where it was.

You mention "togetherness." How did you personally approach doing your shake? Did everyone approach it the same way when you first joined the band?

Well, more or less. You can do it by trilling your lips—*ah-ee-ah-ee*—or shake the horn.

One thing that the Basie band is known for is to make sure those shakes have a certain width to them.

Oh yeah, yeah! And if you notice back then, when the band played, everybody hit the note together, they phrased it the same way, and then they cut it off at the same time.

That just evolved over a period of years?

That came from guys just laying back.

A lot of guys don't understand that when they do join a band like the Basie band, things are already established.

Yeah. You have to learn how to play things like they are when you join. You can't be the new kid on the block. You have to keep your eyes open, your ears open, and...

...your mouth shut.

That's it. And *listen*, you know what I mean? Listen to what they're doing, and then join in. I don't care how it's written—how is it being *played*? Simple. *And anything that is right on the beat does not swing.* It's too mechanical. It's not what you do, it's the way that you do it.

You have to *feel* your way. I don't care how good a musician you are, or how good you can read—a lot of things are *not* played the way they are written. You understand me? This is a laid-back orchestra. Understand? It's a *laid...back...orchestra.* And anything that is laid back is *relaxed.* The people don't want to be out there dancing [*mimics stiff dancing*]. You know what I'm talking about?

Do you have a favorite trumpet player of all time?

Clifford Brown. Miles told some stories too. And Fats Navarro. Boy, he could do no wrong. I mean, he could *play*.

He was Clifford Brown's idol.

Well, Clifford Brown was like a young kid—he was excellent too. He could play his tail off. And there were other trumpet players who didn't play so much with the big bands, but rather with small groups. But the Master, the all-around master that could play any way—that was Dizzy.

Now I'm going to turn the clock back. I haven't seen you or talked to you in twenty years, and I am sure I asked then, when I was a kid, what are some of the main things that I need to do as a trumpeter, to make sure I'm a good trumpet player?

Well, you have got to play with confidence. You have to be very confident in what you do. And you have got to practice.

What kinds of things should I practice?

Things for your endurance, for one thing. I know you have that. Endurance is one of the most important things a trumpet player needs. Don't try to overplay, that's another thing. And a lot of people play too many notes. You've gotta tell *stories*. Try to talk on your horn, just like if you were romancing her. You wouldn't shout in her ears—it would be over and done with! [*Laughs*]

And sometimes when you are playing, especially when you're playing a solo on a ballad, you find somebody in the audience, a young lady. Not like you are trying to get, you know, just play to them. Just like you are whispering into their ears. It works! [*Laughs*] It works!

How did you approach your plunger playing?

I used to listen to different guys, like Rex Stewart and Cootie Williams, and try to do it the way they did it. And then you have to *growl* with it.

On a regular day, on a gig, or when you had a concert at night, did you play much during the daytime?

Well, one thing, I used to make sure that my chops were OK. I'd play some long tones, soft, or I would do a few lip slurs. Another secret is to swing soft. Not everybody can play soft. They think that because it's a trumpet you've got to blow all loud.

Any more little secrets or pieces of advice to learning how to improvise? How to tell a story?

You just can't listen to one person, and you just can't listen to trumpet players. You have got to listen to everybody, and listen to how they interpret things. Interpretation is one of the main things. You can listen to saxophone players, you can listen to violin players, you can listen to bassists, listen to what they do and how they do it. All of that stuff gathers up here [*pointing to his head*] and here [*pointing to his heart*]. And then you let it come out.

When you are improvising, you try to play around what is going on under you. And certain little things that you do, you bring them with you. Understand? That's it!

Did Basie ever give guys in the band advice on how to play?

Nope. Never. Nope.

That's a big deal.

See, Basie had his own style. But if you ever listen to some of the old Fats Waller records, you can see where he and Basie played similar. [Basie,

during an interview with Ralph Gleason, mentioned studying organ with Fats Waller.]

Who are some of the guys you enjoyed playing with in the section, and who was your favorite lead player to play with?

Snooky Young! Well, we had quite a few lead trumpet players, but I'll tell you another good lead trumpeter you don't hear too much about, Lenny Johnson. He was there sometime after Snooky left. He could play. He had the range and all that. Good trumpet player.

What was Snooky's range for lead? What would be the highest he would play?

Well, it all depends. You know he could hit a G [G above high C] like it was nothing. But a G was as high as he needed to go. See, it is not all high notes. It is what you put *in between* those notes.

What was your favorite solo to play in the band?

I used to like to play "April in Paris." There are lots of things you can do on "April in Paris."

Man, that's a hard tune. It's a trip because sometimes you have to play the "Pop Goes the Weasel" thing that Thad Jones made famous.

But you don't have to play "Pop Goes the Weasel" every time you play it. You can play another melody to the melody. My thing is, I wanted to be *melodic*. That's the way you tell stories, with melody. You don't have to put a whole lot of unnecessary notes in there. You pick out the right notes. You play around what you hear. You can't do it unless you are *relaxed*. You understand what I'm talking about? You have got to be relaxed. Then you can let it *flow*.

Ted Curson
"When you are a really good player, there are no mistakes."

Ted Curson came to prominence playing with Charles Mingus. Mingus, a virtuoso bass player who had played with Louis Armstrong, Duke Ellington, and Charlie Parker, was as much a visionary as he was a pragmatist, and wrote music that reflected the turbulent political times of the late 1950s and early 1960s. Curson's solo on "Fables of Faubus," a Mingus composition pointed at segregationist governor Orval Faubus, is at once haunting and forward-thinking. For Curson, it set in motion a career that has spanned the better part of fifty years.

Curson is a very honest musician, someone who loves what he does tremendously. His improvisations mirror his personality in daring, but he has figured out the true key to music and he can evoke pretty much any emotion he desires.

When did you first begin to play the trumpet?

I was born in Philadelphia in 1935, and I didn't get a trumpet until I was ten. It was an old one. Fortunately for me, I lived around the corner from the Heath family. I went to school with Tootie Heath (a top hard-bop drummer, the younger brother of bassist Percy and sax player Jimmy), and there was about ten of us that got started all around the same time. People like Tootie, Bobby Timmons, Jimmy Garrison, McCoy Tyner...

How did you begin to improvise on the trumpet?

I studied with Jimmy Heath a little. We listened to records. In those days we would take a hat and put it on the record to slow it down. My main man was Miles Davis, and also Dizzy Gillespie. I also liked Monk and was always trying to play the piano. When I was seventeen, I decided that I wanted to play somewhere in between Fat Girl (Fats Navarro) and Dizzy. I was working on something between those two cats. They both were great, and were so different

On the night of my prom, I was seventeen, and I was taking my girlfriend down to hear the Orioles. We were walking by this club and I heard this trumpet player, and I wanted to stop, but my lady said no. But I went in to listen, and to this day I don't know what happened to my prom date. She left. I was mesmerized by this trumpet player, man. That trumpet player was Clifford Brown. That would have been 1952 or '53. He was playing with the Blue Flames. And that's the way I wanted to play. I was already working on something, but that fucked me up.

How did you start playing with Charles Mingus?

It was a funny thing. In 1959 I had been working with Cecil Taylor, we had done an album called *Love for Sale*. That was some wild shit, man. [*Laughs*] I got a call from a trumpet player friend of mine here in New York, and he told me that he had gotten a call to go play with Mingus, but he was too scared to go, because, Mingus had been beating up on guys—knocking their teeth out and shit like that. He had just knocked Jackie McLean's teeth out. That was in the Philadelphia papers. And he had also knocked out Jimmy Knepper's teeth. But you have to remember, I'm a prize fighter. I was Golden Gloves. So I told this cat that if Mingus hit me, I would break his fucking jaw. I wasn't a big cat, but I had a guerilla attitude. And that is what you needed for New York, because every trumpet player who was anything was in New York.

I went over there to the audition for Mingus. There were like thirty guys there. This was because Mingus was the only guy who could keep a regular job in New York. If you were on a gig with Mingus, you could be there for two, three, four years. He made it his business to draw people. About two months later, I get a call at midnight. It was Mingus calling me. He said, "Is this Ted Curson?" I said, "Yeah." He said, "You are hired. Come to the club right now!"

I said, "Now?" He said, "As soon as you can get over here." On my way to the club I ran into Eric Dolphy. He said, "Where are you going?" I said that Mingus had just called me and he said, "Me too!" I asked Eric if he knew any of Mingus's tunes and he said, "No." Neither did I. We walked in the door and he had a band on the stage! The place was packed, too. When Mingus saw us walk in, he got on the microphone and said, "Ladies and gentlemen, these guys that are playing with me right here are fired! Here comes my new band with Ted Curson and Eric Dolphy!" He fired those cats right there on the spot. [*Laughs*] He told them, "Pack your shit and get off the stage and get out."

[*Both laughing*] I don't even know what we played that night. I was with him for two years, and made five albums with him. Five of the best ones.

One of my favorite Mingus records is Mingus Ah-Um, where you play the solo on "Fables of Faubus." Is that what made your name?

Yeah, the one with the singing on it. And also *All the Things You Could Be Right Now If Sigmund Freud's Wife Was Your Mother*. [The version of "Fables of Faubus" with lyrics was censored by Columbia Records on *Mingus Ah-Um*, and released without the vocal track. The "Original Faubus Fables," intact, was later released on Nat Hentoff's Candid label.]

Discuss the importance of trumpet technique as you see it.

The main thing about being a jazz artist or a creative artist is your *ideas*. That is the name of the game. You practice your scales and your chords everyday, in every key, so that when you are playing, things just come naturally to you. If you miss, you try to make a pattern out of it, because when you are a really good player, there are no mistakes. If I pick up a record today and listen to it, it will be clean and in tune, most of the time, and it's nice. And when they go for the high notes, they usually hit it. But I would rather hear a cat miss that high note. Because if he misses it, then I'll know he was *trying* for that motherfucker.

Freddie Hubbard

"You have got to say it and mean it."

I wanted to make this the most intimate and important interview that Freddie Hubbard has ever given: he was the first jazz trumpeter I had ever heard, and is my all-time favorite.

That Freddie Hubbard is acknowledged as one of the greatest jazz trumpet players in history is a given to anyone who knows anything at all about jazz. His sound is so big and pretty that on some of his recordings it is hard to tell if he is playing trumpet, or the mellower-sounding flugelhorn. His technique, during his most active periods, was nothing short of flawless, way above even the most accomplished professional trumpeters, regardless of idiom. Freddie was given a gift that very few other musicians have ever had: He is able to combine the elements of every major jazz trumpeter before him, from Louis Armstrong, Roy Eldridge, Dizzy Gillespie, Sweets Edison, Clark Terry, Charlie Shavers, Kenny Dorham, Fats Navarro, Miles Davis, Clifford Brown, and even Chet Baker, to create a style that was at once all his own and the envy of his contemporaries.

In 1958, after being set up and jailed by racist police for dating the daughter of a prominent white business man, Hubbard left Indianapolis and arrived in New York, setting the jazz world ablaze with his world-class technique, imagination, and daring. Once in New York, the word got around that a new young trumpeter was on the scene and setting fire to every bandstand he walked onto. Freddie so impressed Miles Davis at Birdland one night, that–according to Freddie–Miles told Blue Note Records president Alfred Lion to "sign him up." Freddie's career was aided by his work with

Freddie Hubbard playing the author's trumpet.

Photo by author

trombonists and fellow Indianapolis homeboys Slide Hampton and J. J. Johnson, and he would go on to replace Lee Morgan with Art Blakey and the jazz Messengers. A new and powerful voice on the jazz trumpet had arrived.

Hubbard has recorded on over three hundred albums, perhaps more so than any other trumpeter. He practiced with John Coltrane and Sonny Rollins, and was first call for many record dates led by the likes of Wayne Shorter, Herbie Hancock, and Dexter Gordon. In the 1970s, Hubbard began recording with record label CTI, material that was more a reflection of the times. In fact, Hubbard won his first Grammy Award for the album *First Light*. Although he recorded more commercial music in the '70s, it must be noted that he never lost sight of making music that was both cerebral and danceable, with such records as *Red Clay*, *Super Blue*, *Keep Your Soul Together*, and my personal favorite, my introduction to Freddie, *Bundle of Joy*. On top of all that, Hubbard was still playing great trumpet and extending its vocabulary, a point lost on many critics. Super Blue, for example, his band with Ron Carter, Joe Henderson, and Jack DeJohnette, further solidified his status as someone to reckon with musically—Hubbard clearly shows that he was the most skilled trumpeter of the 1970s. And he never stopped swinging, another point that critics of his work during the '70s refuse to acknowledge.

He knew that this was an important interview for him, coming at a time when he is struggling as a trumpeter due to some problems with his lip that have never fully healed.

Freddie Hubbard provided me with information here that will astound as well as delight and surprise. From his days practicing with John Coltrane, to his dealings with Miles Davis and Dizzy Gillespie, to

Wynton Marsalis, he was gracious in everything he said. An entire book needs to be written on the career of Freddie Hubbard.

Did you come from a musical family?

My sister Mildred played trumpet. She had a beautiful sound. Non-pressure. But she wouldn't play outside the church. She and my mother were real religious. They wore me out with that! My brother played jazz piano. We would play together. He was crazy about Bud Powell. He used to play all of those things from Bud, and couldn't read a note. He refused to read. I learned a lot from him.

When I was in junior high school I used to play my trumpet in church—"Nearer My God to Thee." But I never could play like my sister did and it used to make me mad. That's when I started becoming serious about the trumpet. My first trumpet was a Blessing. The same kind Clifford Brown had. It had a dial on it where you could change keys. I practiced on that for a long time, and then I met this guy named Max Woodberry. He played first trumpet with the Indianapolis Symphony. We became tight.

Did he play jazz at all?

Nahhh. He had me in the Herbert L. Clarke book. The Amsdon.

Was the trumpet always easy for you to play?

No, because I never had the right approach. I always had my own way of doing things. Maybe that is what caught up with me later—I started to stretch my embouchure. Slide Hampton said I needed to keep my corners down. But my corners were down then, like they are on the cover of *Body and the Soul*. I started having too much movement. I started rearing back like Kenny Dorham. Don't do that!

How did you learn to improvise on chord changes so well?

I always played the piano. The Callichio book was good for me for jazz. Stuff like that. I would take some of those things and try to fit them into my solos. [*Sings a phrase*] The notes are coming down chromatically, but you mix it up. Like "Take It to the Ozone"—see, I practice that on the piano and would play it on the trumpet.

Did you transcribe solos from Clifford Brown or any cats like that?

Man, I have a tape where I am sounding so much like Clifford, you would laugh.

How did you meet John Coltrane?

I met Trane after I got to New York in 1958. He wouldn't let me sit in for four months. I'd be up there standing next to the bandstand at Count Basie's club and he would forget about me. So one night I just jumped up out of the audience and started playing. I played for about a half an hour. It was crazy. When I got off the stand, Larry Ridley introduced me to Coltrane.

Trane wore me out. Trane would practice so much that his lips would be bleeding. With those cats, man, it would be *all music*. That was the Golden Age. A great period. I would go to Sonny Rollins's house, he would be something else to be around. He was a huge cat and he had that Mohawk haircut. Sonny was *the man* during that period. But he would ask me, "What is Trane doing?" And Trane would ask me, "What is Sonny doing?" They were into each other.

Who else were you hanging out with?

I remember Richard Williams, he would play that high stuff and I'd ask him how he did that. Lee Morgan used to come around like *this*. [*Mimics Lee Morgan with his nose in the air*] Bill

Hardman was making it. I became friends with him and used to go over to his house. When I met Kenny Dorham, now that was an experience. He wasn't bitter, but kind of upset at not being accepted like Dizzy and Miles were. He played some stuff back then that was inside, but he never had the *big tone*. He could play some stuff inside, like a saxophonist. I never could play like K. D. I remember he taught me a different way of getting to the D7 bridge (rhythm changes). He had some slick stuff he would play, man, like the subdominant A-minor-seventh to the D7, instead of D7 for the entire time... He would come down through there (the D7) and it would be so pretty.

Brooklyn was the place. We all lived near each other. You had all the cats—Max Roach, even Miles for a little while. Everybody came to Brooklyn. Wynton Kelly was around the corner. Kenny Dorham around the corner, Grant Green around the corner, Doug Watkins. Paul Chambers. Paul told he me thought like a tuba player. It was something about that tuba for him that got him that sound. And when he and Philly Joe Jones would get together, man, it would be something else, on and off the bandstand.

How was it recording with Dexter Gordon? Doin' Alright *is some of the baddest stuff I've ever heard.*

Dexter played so far behind the beat, but it was a joy because he was such a giant. I used to go out to Sarah Vaughan's house in Hidden Hills, California and hang with Dexter, Billy Eckstine, and Sarah. When I was in New York I met Cannonball Adderley when he was doing his thing. Nat, everybody. It was when everyone was *trying*. They had some trumpet players you never heard of that could play their asses off. You'd go to jam sessions and cats would be playing so much trumpet that you'd say, "Who is that?" It was about the music. You couldn't play a wrong chord change. Cats would talk about that.

Damn! How would you describe your style?

A mixture. Clifford, Sonny, Trane. Trane was something else. Beautiful. I used to be at his house. He would drive me home—and he couldn't drive. I'd be scared as hell in the car. He'd be driving all over the place not even paying attention to what he was doing. He would drive us over to see Eric Dolphy. He was so nice. They told me about the old days when he was a junkie, but by then he was cleaned up and the straightest guy you would meet.

How did playing with Ornette Coleman and Don Cherry affect you?

I met them out here in L.A. I had been out here with Sonny Rollins. They came by my hotel room one night, Ornette and Cherry. They put some music out on my bed and they started playing this *stuff* man. [*Laughs*] I said, "Y'all ain't reading it like it says on the paper." Ornette said, "We give the notes any value we want." Their music had no bar lines either. They had their own way of playing. It wasn't like it was written. I started hanging out with them, and also with Archie Schepp. Man, I had a headache.

That was back during the revolution days. But Ornette, I could understand what he was doing on the records. Some of his stuff was almost kind of conventional if you paid attention, except when it came to the solos. When it came to the solos, you played what you would feel, and play around some part of the melody.

What are some of your favorite records that you've played on?

I like *Ready for Freddie*, and that record I made with Herbie Hancock, *Empyrean Isles*.

Yeah, that's some baaaaaaaad shit... And also the one with Wayne Shorter, Speak No Evil.

I made a lot of records with Wayne. Wayne and I became tight during that period. We made about six records together. What do *you* think about swing and playing outside chords and stuff? Are you into that at all?

Well, the way that things shaped me were that I heard you, and I heard Basie at the same time...

So you love some *swang*?

It's a challenge just to play a D-flat blues with the plunger for one chorus!

You have got to say it and mean it. Quick. No time for messing around. When I speak at schools, they rush out and get my records and want me to dissect them. They use terminology that is so academic, the flatted-fifth of this chord, and the altered this-of-that, and I have to tell them that I don't ever think about it like that. I think it takes away from it, the real swing and the essence. They get too technical with it. The kids today, they practice so much that they are not *creating*. You have got to leave some room for creativity.

I'd much rather hear a cat play a wrong note than trying to be too perfect in his solos...

Miles would do that on purpose. Miles would play a bad note on a chord, then another weird note, but he knew how to come out of it. I used to think that Miles wasn't a good trumpet player until I went over to his house. He played some chords on the piano, *wheeeewwww*! Man, I said, "Where did you get this from, Gil Evans?" He said, "No, I showed Gil Evans this." He knew a lot of music.

He came to one of my gigs in D.C. and afterwards we got in a taxi and went to the Howard

Theater to his gig, and he played "Two Bass Hit" in D-flat. Man, he played faster than Fats Navarro did. He played some high notes, and was making difficult runs and shit, too. Coltrane asked me, "What did you do? What's wrong with Miles?" He was showing me that he could play like that.

I heard Dizzy take Miles out one night. They were playing together and Diz said, "Watch this." He was playing a duet with Miles on "Round Midnight." It was during the time that the Village Gate in New York was getting ready to close in the early '80s. Dizzy was playing some shit from Turkey, Iraq, and Iran. Aww man, it was so *deep*. Dizzy could sound like he was messing around. But that night he got the biggest ovation. I was a witness.

Backstage they had a room where you could watch whoever was playing on a TV. I would sit back there with each cat and listen to what they had to say about one another. Miles said to me, "Dizzy is playing sharp. He plays sharp all the time." Miles could say anything and Dizzy would say to me, "See, they wouldn't let me get away with that shit." [*Laughs*]

Miles didn't want to play long passages, he liked to play the scale. I can't do that. I mean, I can do it, but it doesn't make any sense to me. I like to run like Clifford.

That's what Wynton was talking to me about, your speed. You and Booker Little. The way you cats can think that fast. That's one of the things I love about Wynton's playing. This cat can think so fast.

We had a gig at Carnegie Hall, and Wynton came backstage and brought all these musicians with him. I knew they were building him up to come and play for me. He played some of my stuff and I said, "What?!" So, I did something I *knew* he couldn't do, and that was to play my slur thing. That's the only thing that saved me! But

he's bad. He was down there at the Blue Note when I split my lip. Did he tell you?

No, he didn't tell me that.

I had a knot on my lip bigger than Louis's. Wynton looked at my lip and said, "Your lip is fucked up." It was, but I kept playing. Then I went to Helsinki and straight to a rehearsal, did a TV show, and got through it. I was hoping I didn't mess with the tissue. But it started working on me psychologically. I started scaring myself. Never do that, you know, lose faith in yourself. I was one of the baddest cats out here in L.A.

You were the baddest cat out here, man. Anywhere.

I popped my lip and couldn't play. It was murder, man. I got ready to move to Hawaii or somewhere. I still feel weird. What happened—it goes back to keeping the corners of the embouchure down, taking away all of that pressure, and using the air.

How much do you play these days?

Not everyday. I'll pick it up and do a couple of notes.

Do you still have the same feeling in your lips?

No, it's not the same feeling. I had a "grip" when I was young. I could just put that trumpet up there and play. When I came back, a lot of fundamental shit that I used to do was missing. I haven't really done anything major in the last ten years.

If you could put together a rhythm section with any of the players in the history of jazz, who would you have?

It's hard. Between Herbie Hancock and McCoy Tyner, and Elvin Jones and Art Blakey. Art Blakey gave me so much confidence at Birdland.

He made you play. Sometimes too much. When we had that band it was crazy. I used to soak my chops in a bucket of ice. He wore out Lee Morgan, Bill Hardman, Kenny Dorham...

What was the biggest lesson you learned from Art?

How to stay out of his way! [*Laughs*] When he made those rolls, man. When he first did that on me, it scared me to death. I was trying to play through it and I got to the point where I would wait until he came out of that before I would keep playing. He would bring so much excitement. Can you imagine how loud it was in the studio? He would be so loud the place would be *vibrating*.

What's the one thing young cats need to understand about jazz? What's lacking?

I hate to say it, but it is feeling. Now, I don't expect them to be like me or Miles, but for cats to be more serious about what we were *playing*, and not just thinking about the notes. We played linear, with leaps and bounds. With the technical facility of kids now, they can get through things easier, where as it took us a lot of trial and error, but they are not playing with the passion, you know? I heard Trane and them play and I tried to play it on the trumpet. I got to the point where I could play some real difficult things. Sonny called it "playing on the air." You are not right on the beat. I didn't know if it was different or right or what. Half the stuff then, I was just trying for the first time.

Bobby Bradford

"Anyone out there who had any ears was listening."

Bobby Bradford is best known for his work with the master musician and innovator, Ornette Coleman. Coleman, of course, beginning in the mid- to late 1950s, was one of the pioneers of the avant-garde movement known as "free jazz." Coleman and his cohorts, which included both Bradford and that other wonderful cornetist from Los Angeles, Don Cherry, practiced together and experimented with different ways of achieving a goal that had been the same since Louis Armstrong truly defined it—to make a musical statement based on sincere personal expression through the new music called jazz, which at its core lay the blues and swing.

Bobby is one of the few people left who was a direct part of the group of musicians that surrounded Ornette Coleman. The music that Coleman and Bradford gave to the world of jazz has influenced all that came after it, and can be traced directly through the music of Miles Davis, Archie Shepp, Wayne Shorter, and Woody Shaw, up through to the present generation, including Wynton and Branford Marsalis, David Murray, and a few others.

I caught Bobby with his octet in a club in Los Angeles back in 2002 and was able to witness first-hand his music and his improvisations.

Although the term "free" is readily thrust upon him and his group, their music had structure and form. But with Bradford, such things as being in different keys on the same tune are second nature. This requires a cultivated talent that not everyone has, but allows musicians like Bobby to further explore the infinite wonders of individual

Photo courtesy of Bobby Bradford

Bobby Bradford, who still performs today in Los Angeles, is a true representative of the style pioneered Ornette Coleman, but he has his own personal style of improvisation.

and collective improvisation on a very high level. I learned quite a bit, and my head is still spinning from some of the things shared with me.

When did you first hear Ornette Coleman and Don Cherry?

I first heard Ornette in Texas. He is from Fort Worth, near Dallas. I went to a little black Methodist school along with [drummer] Charles Moffett, who was a senior. When Charles got married, Ornette came to the wedding as his best man. There was already a rumor about Ornette's playing, and after the wedding we had a jam session. That was the first time I heard him play. There was Ornette, alto saxophonist Leo Wright [from the Dizzy Gillespie Quintet], and tenor saxophonist John Gilmore [from the Sun Ra Arkestra]. They were smokin', and after four or five tunes, they started playing Ornette's music. Most of the guys got up and walked out. But I said to myself, "Hey wait a minute, I don't know what you all are talking about, but this cat is playing some real hip music." He played a couple of his blues lines and some of his rhythm things and he was already moving outside. This was 1953.

That early?

Yes, and you could still hear where he was coming out of the bebop tradition. But he was definitely hearing some other stuff, too. He told me he was organizing a band and asked me would I like to come and play. So I would go to his house and we would rehearse his tunes. I didn't meet Don until maybe the start of 1954. Don didn't start playing with the band proper until I left. See, a couple of years earlier, Don was still in high school along with [Ornette's would-be drummer] Billy Higgins.

So you were the first trumpeter with Ornette Coleman?

Yes, during the period when he was putting the band together. We played little clubs around town, and then I went into the military in late 1954. This is when Don became the main trumpeter in the band. I think Ornette got his first break in 1958. And of course, by 1959, he had gone on to New York. But when I saw him at that wedding, he was playing some things that were conventional, but would mix it up with sounds like the whinnying of a horse. The people would look at him and say, "What the hell is he doing?" Then he would play some Charlie Parker licks, but over and over, and a half-step above where they should have been. And he didn't give a damn about what you thought about it either. But he knew that anybody out there who had any ears was listening.

What kinds of discussions did you guys have musically?

This is what people always want to know. Like, did Ornette have a sort of pencil and paper philosophy about what he was doing—he didn't. He definitely had a system, but he didn't know how to articulate it, to tell you what he was doing. He knew about eight bar phrases and all of that but he didn't think that was the gospel, and didn't want to get caught playing in that fashion. He was harmonically more adventurous, and he also had in his system something that was kind of folksy that still had blues in it. Most people stuck on Charlie Parker would ask when was Ornette going to get to the swing part, but Ornette wasn't stuck on strict and straight-ahead patterns. He had his Tex-Mex thing, too. He was real sure of what he was trying to say, and was trying to get past the obstacles. He was the kind of guy who couldn't be stopped. The first time I heard him, I said this guy has got something. When we played together, there were no chords. All he gave us was the melody with no key signature, only accidentals, and sometimes no bar lines, and would tell us that this music is about *feeling*. So when I played the melody it made me feel a certain way. That was all we had to go on.

He had trouble writing down in a conventional sense what he was trying to get us to play. He had a tune that he wanted me to play, and it had a pick up to it, but he notated it on the beat. Then I knew he really had his own system for what he wanted. He'd say that if the first two notes are a fourth apart, then it must be a pickup.

Wow. That's a trip. Damn!

It's getting real deep now isn't it? He said the interval of a fourth dictates some kind of rhythmic response, and that's true. A lot of guys told him to go and learn how to read. I wasn't interested in arguing with him. When he got ready to copyright some of his music, I had to notate it for him. He might have a beam with an eight note on it, but he would also have a half note on that same beam.

What the fuck? [Laughs] So, how would he count a tune off?

He wouldn't do that. We would rehearse so much that we could simply look at each other and know what to do. All we did was get up in the morning around ten and play all day.

When you got back from the military and heard Don Cherry for the first time, what were your impressions of him then?

Don was a talented guy, man. Very talented guy. But he couldn't play for twenty minutes without having serious problems. His embouchure was way down here in the rim, in the soft

part. He got comfortable with his embouchure, but after a while it caught up with him. You know, it's like if you play golf with the wrong type of grip on the club and have early success, you think you can do it forever that way. You hold it like a baseball bat and you'll get more power, but you have no control.

That's a great analogy.

You might hit the ball farther than the guy that is trying to teach you, but you don't know where it's going. Finesse is the key. But Don, to me, was still a bebopper. When you listen to his lines, even after a solo by Ornette, he would eventually play something along those lines. But one of things I learned to do with my band, was have every instrument play a different time, but along with the soloist. We don't always have to play ballads and standards in the conventional 4/4 structure, but rather free things up. For example, the drummer doesn't have to keep time, but rather just play *rhythms*.

As if he is breathing.

That way, you can play whatever tempo is in your head. You just get a texture and then there is no way for you to play a conventional bebop line. See, now you have got to be creative. The first thing you notice is what you *can't* play.

Damn!

So when a guy asks me if I play *free*, I say I play music that I *like*. We can play standard tunes like "All the Things You Are" or "A Night in Tunisia," then we might play something that has the drummer doing a complex rhythm with the bassist doing octave D's—but not in an even rhythm. So then he is not accompanying *you* anymore, and you are forced to enter where it makes musical sense. When you are playing rhythm changes or a conventional standard, the rhythm section is accompanying you, right? But with this sort of piece they're not. Maybe *you* are accompanying *them*.

I'm so glad you explained that.

The reason I explained that is that sometimes it is hard to listen to. A lot of people say, well, then anything you play is OK. I say no, it is not. Because when it is not happening, you will know it, too. Ornette once told me that once he knew he could play something that was wrong, he knew he was on to something.

Wow. So, how do you define playing "in" versus playing "out"? Or is there such a thing in your mind?

When people say "out," what I think they mean is somebody who plays like Joe Henderson, who would take a standard and take it outside. He is playing really very remote notes, but he is still being guided by a set of chords. I never heard Joe Henderson play free like Ornette, where you don't have a harmonic base of some kind. What Joe played was great, but it was always in relationship to a chord, and you can see how the solo falls into harmonic groups. The solos also had a *harmonic rhythm*. Ornette Coleman's solos don't follow that kind of logic. What I consider "out" playing is a guy like Eric Dolphy. I still consider Dolphy a chord player, but who chooses to play a lot of remote things in relationship to the chord. Just like the band Charles Mingus had with Ted Curson and Dolphy. Mingus said that he was showing Ornette how free it was supposed to be. That wasn't a free band. They were playing tunes that had chords, except that they chose to play *outside notes* against a *chord reference*. That is what I consider "out."

The free thing, in my mind, is that it might not even be about the notes you are playing so much as it is just the *rhythm*. The great thing about playing with Ornette was that you had the tune itself as the point of reference. But when you have a bass player doing one thing, and the drummer doing something against that, and you have to play something, the first thing that I am thinking is what rhythm can I play. Then I find some notes.

That's a beautiful way to think.

Sometimes we play tunes that are just rhythm. Some people will say *that's the drum part*, and I tell them that's a mistake—*I don't get to play any rhythm?* Sometimes I'll tell the trombonist to play a rhythm against what I am doing. He can play whatever note he wants. Then I tell him to morph it later on. Sometimes it doesn't work—but when it does it is breathtaking.

You took me to church today, man. That is a whole different way of thinking.

That is what I learned from Ornette Coleman. He made it clear that you can reduce everything down to its least common denominator. We'd ask ourselves, well, what are we doing? I'm sitting here blowing hot air through a long piece of metal pipe. And the drummer—you are a grown man sitting over there beating on a piece of animal skin. We are out here trying to make music and not compete. We're not trying to out-blow anybody. I might do something to make you sound good. That's the love in the music.

11

Chuck Mangione

"You couldn't play the flugelhorn in the trumpet section…"

People are always shocked when they hear recordings of Chuck Mangione made before his 1977 hit "Feels So Good" turned him into a pop star. Even Chuck himself gets a kick out of it when others find out about his beginnings as a purely jazz trumpeter.

"Feels So Good" is still one of the most played and requested instrumental classics of all time. But think about this: "Feels So Good" is part of the lineage of jazz trumpet that began over one-hundred years ago, and elements of all of the great attributes of the masters of jazz trumpet can be found in the way Mangione delivers the melody. I don't mean this in the strictest sense, as in a swing or bebop interpretation, but rather the *ever present sound of the optimist based on the collective prowess of the group*. It should be no surprise that Chuck has a very rich and unusual historical connection—he played with Art Blakey and the Jazz Messengers, a gig he got through a recommendation from none other than Dizzy Gillespie. Blakey needed a replacement for Freddie Hubbard, and…

One of the things that impressed me about you when I heard you live is that in the middle of your set, you put the flugelhorn down, picked up your trumpet, and played a bebop tune. I think it was one of Dizzy's tunes. I didn't expect that at all…

Well, a lot of people think that "Feels So Good" was my first record. There were a whole lot of other things that happened along the way.

Chuck Mangione.

Photo courtesy of Chuck Mangione

How did "Feels So Good" happen? How did you write it? I heard that that Herb Alpert signed you to A&M records.

Actually, Jerry Moss signed me. He came to see me at a club in New York. He knew that my time with Mercury Records was passing. I had always chosen the music I would record and went into the studio and made the record. With Mercury, after I had done the *Land of Make Believe* album, they said that was enough of me doing my own stuff, they wanted to find a pocket. They wanted me to record a movie theme. That was enough with that company.

Jerry Moss said, "I'll give you a budget, you go into the studio, hand me the tapes, and that will be the record." I had recorded *Chase the Clouds Away* and *Main Squeeze*, and I was beginning to put together a new band. The guitarist was Grant Geisman. We went into the studio with this new band, with six songs. They didn't even have titles, they had numbers, and we recorded very quickly. We went on tour somewhere up in Portland, then came back to the studio and finished up a few things and gave the songs names then gave the tapes to the record company. They said [*Chuck mimics the nonchalant attitude of a record executive*], "You did a nice album, but we don't hear any singles in here." Then someone at A&M performed major surgery on "Feels So Good," which was a nine-minute version on the album, and got it down to three minutes and twenty-seven seconds. The Bee Gees had completely saturated radio with the *Saturday Night Fever* thing at the time. Six out of ten songs on the radio were Bee Gees songs. I guess program directors were looking for something they could put on in-between, and they started playing "Feels So Good." I ended up selling over two million albums.

I remember the first time I heard that tune. I went and asked my parents for a flugelhorn immediately. I ended up getting the same kind of flugelhorn I saw you with on the cover of your album Fun and Games. Of course, high school bands started having arrangements of "Feels So Good," and every trumpeter wanted to be you.

At least you knew it was a flugelhorn. [*Laughs*]

How did you get started?

I was born November 19, 1940, in Rochester, New York. I happened to see a movie called *Young Man with a Horn*, with Kirk Douglas and Lauren Bacall. It was the life story of Bix Beiderbeck, so I said "Give me one of those." That's how I started playing the trumpet. From the age of ten there was nothing in my life but music and baseball. I would play three ball games a day and change my clothes in the car while my mother drove me to play an Italian wedding or a bar mitzvah, an amateur hour contest, or whatever. I think if we had been into medicine, they would have taken us to hospitals, but we were into music. Whenever somebody came to town and was playing my dad would take us to hear them.

We would hear Art Blakey and the Jazz Messengers, maybe the next week Horace Silver came through town, maybe Roy Eldridge might come through, Sonny Rollins might have been there, Carmen McCrae, Sarah Vaughan, Kai Winding...I'm almost sure I heard Billie Holliday. I heard Kenny Dorham, Bill Hardman...

You had an ideal childhood as far as musical experiences, man.

Sometimes groups were there for a week. We would stop by early in the week and my Dad would invite the musicians over to our house for spaghetti and Italian wine. I think people knew

PART II – Chapter 11: Chuck Mangione

about our place before they got to Rochester, the word got out. They knew about a house that had some real good home cooking and a good record collection. And when you are that young, and it happens on such a regular basis, you think every kid must be doing this. One week there would be Art Blakey and the Jazz Messengers, Dizzy, Cannonball Adderley, Ron Carter—it's still kind of mind-boggling.

It was kind of a weird way of networking at a very early age. Dizzy became like a member of the family. He sent me one of his turned-up trumpets. I remember Art Blakey, I think I was about sixteen, said, "Why don't you come and move to New York?" But I had seen enough cats come through town who were just *dying* to come off the road. They had been out there so long, and there was nothing else they could do, and I decided I was going to get an insurance policy. I was going to go to the Eastman School of Music and get a degree in public school music as a teacher so I would have something to fall back on. I certainly wasn't mature enough to be running out with Art Blakey at sixteen.

I studied trumpet, theory, and piano. *Jazz* was a four letter word—they didn't have anyone there who had knowledge of jazz on the faculty, so it was intimidating to them. Those of us students who were into jazz, we'd get together on Saturday afternoons and put together a big band. And people who were arrangers would transcribe stuff from records, and we would play their music. At the time, Miles and Gil Evans were collaborating on those wonderful records, *Miles Ahead*, *Sketches of Spain*, *Porgy and Bess*, and all those things. Miles was playing flugelhorn, and I wanted to play those parts. I fell in love with the sound and the feel of the flugelhorn. Back then, flugelhorn was the odd man out, you know. You

couldn't play the flugelhorn in the trumpet section, and a freelance person had to play trumpet. Eventually, trumpet players started carrying flugelhorns just like tenor players started carrying sopranos [after John Coltrane made it popular].

Miles Davis is as important a musician as I can think of. Not just from a trumpet point of view. I adored his playing. Believe it or not, I still stick a mute in my flugelhorn from time to time.

When did you move to New York City?

The way it happened was that I was in New York City over the Christmas holidays, I had come down to hear some music or whatever. I was in a place called Jim and Andy's. It was pretty close to where the *Tonight Show with Johnny Carson* was taped, and musicians like Snooky Young would come by there. Kai Winding comes over and says, "Aren't you that kid from Rochester?" I said, "Yes." He said, "Are you in New York now?" I said, "I am right now." He said, "Good. I have a gig for you."

The gig with Kai Winding turned out to be somewhere in Ohio. But after I had been in New York trying to make it for a year, I get a call from Art Blakey. He said, *"I want you to be a Messenger."* Freddie Hubbard left and Art Blakey called Dizzy for a recommendation. Dizzy said, "Do you remember the kid from Rochester?"

How long did you play with him?

About two-and-a-half years. Playing with him was just an indescribable feeling. He had so much swing. People might think of him as real powerful, but it was *simmering*. All of a sudden he would do one of those press rolls that would lift you off your seat and then come right back down.

What are some of the things that you are thinking as you are improvising? Do you think in colors or anything like that?

I don't think in colors, because I grew up at a time when there were great voices and great melodies that have lasted—and still stick in my brain. I saw an interview with Quincy Jones once and he said, "Music is a talent and a gift, but melody is a gift from God." I've always tried to create songs that are melodic, and in improvising, try to create another melody. Hopefully nobody says, "Boy, the drummer was great." You can walk away remembering a melody.

Well, your music is definitely melodic. You can hum it and remember it.

Well they tell me that "Feels So Good" is one of the most recognized songs of all time. It's funny, because it is not easy to play on the horn—that high D.

Did you ever have a flugelhorn custom-made for you?

The first flugelhorn I played was a Cuesnon. The mouthpiece I use is a copy of the mouthpiece that came in the case with that horn. Then I played a Yamaha, right off the shelf. And lately I've been playing the Callichio.

Hasn't anyone ever offered to make you a flugelhorn?

Just give me the basic B-flat kind of horn.

What advice would you give to young jazz trumpeters?

To any young musician, really on any instrument, you should be listening a lot. Not so much to things that are happening today, you go back and listen to the older things and check them out and learn how everybody got to be who they are today. And listen to the Zen masters of the music. And, obviously, to put the time in you need on the instrument. Always try to play with people who are better than you. In other words, if you are a tennis player and you are beating the other guy all the time, then you aren't really learning anything. Surround yourself with something that's challenging and educational. And generally, as a musician, be like a human sponge and soak everything in, try everything.

And then, [Laughs] all you young guys out there, don't put yourself in a position where you will have to choose the financial side rather than the artistic side. You know, you're just getting excited about music, but now you want that car, that apartment, you want to get married and do a lot of things, and before you know it, when you could have been playing a gig with some very creative people, you are out there playing some watered-down gig at the country club because you gotta pay the rent.

That's great advice, man.

I wish I had taken it. I wish somebody had given it to me.

[Both laugh]

Valery Ponomarev
"I knew this was my music."

12

To actually have to *escape* one's country to have the freedom to play jazz music is as serious as you can get. This is the story of native Russian trumpeter Valery Ponomarev. Being a jazz musician saved his life.

Valery followed his dream and became trumpeter for the Jazz Messengers in the mid-1970s, and as fate would have it, provided the opportunity for Wynton Marsalis to enter the spotlight.

Valery is one of the world's best jazz trumpet soloists, and also happens to be a very warm human being with a keen sense of humor. His experiences are an inspiration to anyone who needs to be reminded that there is light even at the end of the darkest tunnel—if you do not give up.

You have an incredible story...

I was born in Moscow, Russia. And I escaped the Soviet Union in 1973 with the expressed idea to play with Art Blakey and The Jazz Messengers. To most people it sounded crazy that I loved that music so much. I used to go to my friend's house to listen to jazz music. One day I said to them, "I will be playing with Art Blakey and the Jazz Messengers." I was only sixteen at the time.

How did you become exposed to music when you were a kid?

My first exposure to trumpet came when I was in summer camp when I was six years old. I heard a bugle for the first time and I was shocked. I was at the far end of the camp playing with a ball. I remember it as if it were yesterday. I heard the bugle playing this fanfare, and I dropped the ball and ran to where the sound was coming from. That was in 1949. He gave me the horn and I grabbed it like it always belonged to me. I put it to my chops and played exactly the same sounds. They were all shocked. That was the first time I tasted applause. The very next year I was the official signal giver on the herald trumpet.

What was the first jazz band you ever heard?

The first real trumpet player I ever heard intimately was Clifford Brown. I was seventeen, I had already begun to play professional gigs in dance bands, and at one of the gigs a friend of mine told me that he recorded something off of the radio and I would love it. It was the song called "The Blues Walk." Imagine the shock I had! It was incredible. It was total truth—total beauty. From that point on, that was it for me. I knew then that this music was there for me, and not some classical music. I knew this was my music.

Photo courtesy of Valery Ponomarev

Valery Ponomarev, age seven, playing his first trumpet at summer camp. Moscow, Russia, 1950.

I can't possibly imagine what growing up in the Soviet Union was like. Tell me, was jazz forbidden there to listen to and to play? Was it an underground kind of music? How was it perceived there?

I'll give you one clue—when I wanted to go to music college when I was seventeen, they didn't accept me in the college in Moscow because I was interested in *jazz* music. So I entered a college *near* Moscow where they didn't know my reputation. [*Laughs*] I entered school in the late 1950s, but by the early 1960s, they already had a jazz club open to impress foreign tourists. It was called the Youth Café.

To impress the tourists?

Yes, to show them that we have freedoms here like in the West. But in reality, anyone who was involved deeply in Western culture was under suspicion. The interest for jazz music was always there, and people were drawn to it. Incidentally, now, as I predicted years ago, Russia imports more jazz now more than any other culture including Japan.

How did you get your jazz records?

I had an enormous collection of nine records! [*Laughs*] Clifford Brown's *Study in Brown*, *The Magnificent Thad Jones*, *Charlie Parker with Strings*, and I had three or four others by Clifford Brown, but that was all I could get on the black market. But on tape, I had a zillion recordings. I used to tape them off of the Voice of America radio program. I went all over Moscow looking for more tapes, and guess which was the first one I found? [*Valery sings the melody to "Moanin',"* *which was major hit for Art Blakey and the Jazz Messengers.*] When I heard it I identified with it somehow. I knew it was my music. Nobody could tell me anything differently.

You told me that you escaped from Moscow. Tell me about that.

In 1973. At that time it was a deep closed society. You couldn't change apartments easily, let alone travel to a foreign country, and especially a Western country. You couldn't just go somewhere. It was a long process to even go to a socialist country, but to try and go to America, you could likely end up in jail. So you literally had to escape. But during the early '70s, there was a huge exodus of Jews out of Russia. It was some kind of deal between Israel and the Russian government. I got a false visa, because I am not Jewish. I didn't have any family in Israel, so I had to lie and say that I had some relatives there. I went to New York to meet Art Blakey. When I actually joined the Messengers, there were shockwaves all over the world. They used to come to the airports to get a look at this phenomenon from Russia!

You took Bill Hardman's place?

Yes. I sat in once, and then I got the call. It was very early in 1974. Someone told Art that I was from Russia and that I could play like Clifford Brown. When I showed up at the club to sit in he said, "Play anything you want." I began to play "What's New." When I played the cadenza, I played Clifford's cadenza. I guess I sounded good to him because, I ended up playing three songs in a row! Blakey never let anyone play more than one song...When it was over, the crowd was going crazy, a standing ovation. The next day, the papers all over New York were talking about the Russian trumpeter who sat in with Art Blakey.

Did you go to Russia with Blakey?

No, I could not go back until the collapse of the Soviet Union. For seventeen years, I could not go back. When I left, my mother was a good looking lady, standing upright and strong. When I returned, she was stooped over and weak with totally gray hair. She had heard a rumor that I was killed in a car accident. It was circulated on purpose by the KGB.

Oh my goodness...

And when she first talked to me on the phone, she broke down in tears so badly that I couldn't stop her. She heard my voice and said, "Val, is that you?" I told her it was me. She kind of knew that the rumor was not true. She couldn't really rest until she heard me live. I would send her postcards from Brazil and all over the place. I also sent her postcards from Paris, and left my phone number on it. When I got home to New York one day from a tour, the phone rang. It was my mother. She said, "What are all of these postcards? Are you in some kind of trouble?" I told her that I was with Art Blakey, and we were on tour. She said, "What Art Blakey? Who is that?" I asked her if she remembered the pictures on my wall. She said, "Yes...now I understand. That handsome guy with the trumpet?" I said, "Nahh, that's Miles Davis."

You introduced Wynton Marsalis to Art Blakey.

When I first heard Wynton play, he was eighteen years old. Sensational command of the instrument. Great tone production, chops setting, range, you name it. I was shocked. I thought he was the new Louis Armstrong or something. I actually thought I had witnessed the next trumpet messiah. I asked him to sit in, and he told me that people didn't do that in New York anymore. I told him that this is *exactly* where you are supposed to sit in. I introduced him to Blakey, and then he came up and played on a tune called "Along Came Betty." He didn't know the tune and he played it by ear. It's not one of those tunes you can play by ear, but his tone was there, right away. The next tune was "Blues March." Man, now that was sensational. He started playing so much trumpet, double high C's, incredible tone, technique, and it was totally sensational. He became my sub.

What advice would you give to young trumpeters who want to learn how to play?

I would tell them that the most important thing is the learning *process*—you learn what you *hear*. What language do you speak? If by some crazy circumstance you had been kidnapped at birth and taken to China, you would be speaking

When did you begin to play the trumpet?

I wanted to be like Louis Armstrong. I saw him on *The Ed Sullivan Show*, probably around 1958.

Do you remember the very first jazz record that you heard?

Louis Armstrong singing "St. Louis Blues." My parents wouldn't let us play jazz in the house, so I would go down to the neighbors and wear my welcome out. And then in high school, I got in the jazz band and my band director would put on Maynard Ferguson. I was fortunate enough to have a good band director. And he showed me how to build chords, theoretically. So, back to my neighbor's house because they had a piano, and I would go down there and practice doing that until I could play in all of the keys, and all of the ninth chords. And I would just wear out his records, a Hank Crawford record called *More Soul*. It had Phil Gilbeau, Bud Brisbois, and Marcus Belgrave on trumpets, but the soloist I would listen to was Hank! I would pass the trumpet players up. I *heard* them, but Hank, with that bluesy sound attracted me.

Do you remember the very first time you heard the Duke Ellington Orchestra?

I wouldn't remember that. But the very first time I saw them was 1972, they were playing down at the Shamrock Hilton Hotel here in Houston. I went with Arnett Cobb [great jazz saxophonist] to the concert and he asked me if I wanted to meet Duke. On the break, Duke comes up to Arnett, and Arnett tells Duke I am the trumpeter with the Texas State University Jazz Ensemble, and Duke says, "Oh, yeah? Well how come you aren't playing in my band?" And he takes my name down.

The next night—I was a newlywed then, and we were staying with my wife's mother—and

about three o'clock in the morning my mother-in-law comes into the bedroom and wakes us up and says, "Barrie, there is some 'Duke' on the phone."

Oh, my goodness...

[*Laughs*] Duke asked me to come to Columbus, Ohio, that same morning. But I didn't go. I wanted to go, but I was still in school. I would keep track of them all over the country and they would call me and tell me that I was still on their minds, and that I was indeed going to be in the band. I had told everybody. The whole town lit up too. It was amazing.

How do you think Duke helped evolve jazz trumpet?

I'd say it is the plunger. And there are very few who are keeping that going. I know people play it, but I am talking about people for whom it is a *part of them*. You know? Where it is not just an implement, but it is a part of *who they are*. I think I am one of the last ones. Me, and Clark, and Snooky.

Describe your experiences in the trumpet section with Cootie Williams.

He would be quiet on the bandstand, very serious about the music. Off the bandstand he was a clown. He was a sweet cat. He didn't play any parts, he'd just wait for his solos. I have his last horn, you know, a Conn Connstellation. It's actually a double horn. It is a trumpet-cornet. It uses a cornet mouthpiece. And I have his plunger. And his pixie mute.

He used a cornet mouthpiece?

No, but this horn uses a cornet mouthpiece. He got a great big walloping sound out of that thing. I would be on stage with him, man, and he never played in front of the microphone.

That's something… What things in particular, as far as the plunger goes, did he ever show you anything?

Those guys didn't show you stuff, man. They had a code of ethics. *You call yourself a pro? I ain't got time to teach you nothing.* They never would. But Paul Gonsalves, I would sit next to him on the bus and he would rattle off something about what he was doing. Paul said, "I'm just doing thirteenths." What the hell did that mean? *Now* I understand it. But no, they would not show you, and you wouldn't dare ask. So you hit the sheds, man. I remember one time with Duke, we were in Atlantic City playing the Steel Pier for a week. Six shows a night. Thirty-minute shows, but six a day. It was grueling. And Duke says, "Ahh, now, we have a long tall Texan," he calls me up, "and we are going to do a tune called… 'Spacemen!'" And he lets out a scream and counts it off going a thousand miles-an-hour. My one and only solo. And all I can remember about that day were my knees shaking.

After I had thoroughly embarrassed myself, I went to Duke's dressing room. I said, "Duke, on 'Spacemen,' you think you could play it a little slower? It's a little too fast for me." And he said, "Awww, baby, you don't like my song?" I had no more words after that. You know, you think something is fast, but actually you just have to shed it. We were on the road like 280 days a year, so I just took my tail to the room and started shedding like crazy until I could I could play that thing, and then I didn't care what tempo they called it.

Wow. What other trumpet players did you learn from?

Clark Terry. He's just the consummate trumpeter, just born with the horn in his mouth or something. And after Mercer died, he called me up, because you know, he was encouraging me,

and he said, "Now you have got to be assertive, because you are the one that needs to run the band." It brings me to tears in how he encouraged me. He just called me up out of the blue. I didn't really think he knew me like that, but those old cats, they be knowing folks, man. They know you, they know your work.

I was also having struggles with my chops and I knew he would have the answers. I said, "Clark, what's happening when your chops feel like there is a film on them, like something is on them, and they aren't flexible, and I can't get it off and I can't lick it off…" I'm just going on and on, and he says, "Well, what's happening is"—I wasn't prepared for this—"you aren't playing enough. What you can do to get past that is to do lip buzzes like I do." And he starts lip buzzing the Clarke studies! [*Sings one of the most basic of the Herbert L. Clarke study exercises*] But wait—it sounds like he is pressing valves down.

Damn. That is a very difficult thing to do…

It was ridiculous. Impossible. I pride myself on being able to do whatever on the trumpet and I can't do that. He was doodling it. And *fast*.

Did you know Cat Anderson?

I only met him once, and it was at a place in Los Angeles at a club called Dantes. That was right after Duke died and so everybody came there to hear us. I remember Cat, Art Farmer, *everybody* came to that gig. Just stars in there. So when we got through playing, Cat came over to me and gave me some props, and he just sort of befriended me and decided to show me something about playing high notes and all that. He took my horn and did his Cat Anderson thing on it, in the extreme upper register. And he said, "It ain't the mouthpiece." I was playing on a Giardinelli mouthpiece. [A big mouthpiece, and the bigger the mouthpiece, the harder it is to play high on the trumpet, and it also requires your embouchure muscles to be stronger.] It was *insane*. Then he said, "Look, go home and practice playing your horn while your teeth are clinched, and develop that." That was Cat's secret.

Playing with his teeth clinched?

No, he didn't *do* that, he just practiced that way. What it does is teach you that you can't play with pressure on your chops.

What advice would you give to young trumpeters just starting out who want to play lead, solo, and work within a good trumpet section?

You know, playing lead and being a soloist, that is a big bite. But I'll tell you, the youngsters just don't want to do the work. You are trying to learn a foreign language. You have got to practice speaking it. I wanted to learn how to play fast, clear, and articulate. I would sit beside Clifford Brown records and they would intimidate me. First I thought it was impossible—*I can't do that!* But one morning I woke up, I said, Well, shoot, he is a just a man, just like me.

Photo courtesy of Jack Bradley

Cat Anderson, left, the great high note specialist with the Duke Ellington Orchestra, flanked by Ellington alto saxophone master Johnny Hodges.

Wendell Brunious

14

"A lot of people can't play a New Orleans style, because they want to play too many notes."

Wendell Brunious is from one of the first families of jazz. His father, John Brunious Sr. was an extraordinary musician and was one of the very first African-Americans admitted to the Julliard School of Music in New York in the 1930s. Brunious Sr. also played lead trumpet for Jay McShann, Billy Eckstine, and Cab Calloway.

Wendell, born on October 27, 1954, exactly ten years to the day before me, is an important figure in present day New Orleans music, representing *The Truth* as sent forth from men such as Buddy Bolden, Louis Armstrong, Punch Miller, and Alvin Alcorn.

Wendell demonstrated to me how the true New Orleans trumpet sounds today, with elements from all styles of jazz, including bebop, but you can still hear the style that has been perfected in the cozy clubs and hot streets of New Orleans over a period of one hundred years.

(Author's note: During the last week of finishing up this book, the worst natural disaster to ever hit the United States in the form of Hurricane Katrina completely destroyed the city of New Orleans. The homes of Wendell Brunious and many others were totally destroyed, and are still under ten feet of water or more as I write this. The priceless artifacts of perhaps the most important jazz archives in the world, at Tulane University's Hogan Jazz Archives, which was invaluable to me during my research, were blessedly saved. But the status of the original cornet of Louis Armstrong that is housed at the U.S. Mint in the city is unknown, along with thousands of other priceless materials, documents, and

Photo by author.

Musically descended straight from Buddy Bolden, Wendell Brunious is a shining example of the present day New Orleans jazz trumpet master.

oral history recordings that told the story of how jazz began in the Crescent City. This interview with Wendell took place in a restaurant and in his car, driving along the bridge on Interstate 10 East to his sister's house in Slidell. Slidell was also devastated, and the fate of Wendell's sister and her home are unclear at this writing. The bridge was completely destroyed by the hurricane. Listening to the tape of this interview, with the sounds of the car riding along the bridge mixed with discussions on the history of New Orleans jazz, has become a particularly profound experience.)

Discuss the role your father, John Brunious Sr. played in your development.

Well, my dad was a killer trumpet player. He graduated from high school when he was fifteen years old. He was a really smart guy. He skipped two grades—they skipped him from the third to the fifth grade and from the seventh to the ninth grade. His first semester in college, he went to Pinewood Mississippi, and that summer, his cousin Harold Dejon had a gig on the *S.S. Dixie*, going to New York. He told my dad, "Look, if you really get your reading together, I'll take you on the boat." My dad practiced that whole summer, getting his chops together. He went up to New York with Harold and auditioned at Julliard—he won a scholarship to Julliard in 1935! That was a wonderful, wonderful thing, man. And, you know, for my dad being the mixture of blood that he was, basically French and Mexican. He had a kind of status, it wasn't really a black status type of deal going on, so he could go to Julliard.

He worked with the Jay McShann band when Bird was there. Then he went on to the Eckstine band. When Cab Calloway fired Dizzy Gillespie, my daddy took that spot. I used to talk to Dizzy and he used to tell me, "Man, I went on to be somebody. I'm glad your dad took that job." [*Laughs*]

Who was playing second to your dad in Billy Eckstine's band?

Fats Navarro was playing second in 1942. My father was the sixth-ranked trumpet player in the *Downbeat* poll that year, and that year he developed arthritis in his legs and he couldn't walk for two years. He was only in his twenties, and boy, when you have three children at home, and you can't work for two years, man...but my dad was such a great writer. He could write in *bed* for a thirty-one piece orchestra with no piano as a guide—and in ink!

But man, that guy could really play. He was such a big influence on my older brother, John Brunious Jr. He is fourteen years my senior. When he was fifteen years old, he played for his sophomore recital "Flight of the Bumblebee!" My dad bought him a brand new trumpet—an Olds Ambassador. Student model horns were very good in those days. I mean there was pride in the work, and ingenuity. I'm not sure if we have that anymore. One time Dizzy was at John's high school giving a master class. Diz said, "Anybody wanna come up here and play?" My dad was there. He and Diz were friends, so my dad told John to get his horn out and go on up there and play. Man, John had learned every solo Dizzy had recorded. So he went up there, at fourteen or fifteen years old, and nailed this tune called "Shawnuff." After the performance, my dad went up and said, "Diz, my son tore your ass up." [*Laughs*]

Describe the role of the trumpet in New Orleans music.

New Orleans music accentuates the melody. The solo is basically a *counter*melody. All the way from the time of Buddy Bolden and Bunk Johnson, there has always been a strong demand to play melody in the New Orleans vein. And by the time Louis Armstrong came into his heyday, he had the technique to take it somewhere else. Armstrong's introduction to "West End Blues" is the greatest thing ever recorded for its time.

How did you learn to improvise?

My dad used to give us "assignments." And we didn't really know we were learning to improvise. He had this record that he recorded with Paul Barbarin, and it had many musicians on it, including bassist Milt Hinton and the clarinetist Willie Humphrey. He would say, "When I come home, I want to you to sing me one of Bob Thomas's solos from this record." And we'd be so excited to do it. We'd be at the record player all day. I can still hum that solo, it was from "Bourbon Street Parade." That was our ear training. We didn't realize it at the time, and it is probably a good thing...

You would have probably looked at it as work! Describe soloing on top of New Orleans music versus soloing on top of bebop.

With New Orleans music, you stick to more of a "two feel." It is so closely related to gospel music, you keep that low key feeling in there. This is why a lot of people can't play a New Orleans style, because they want to play too many notes. It is like chocolate ice cream. It is good, but it doesn't go with everything.

Do you think that was one of the reasons that Louis Armstrong put down bebop when he first heard it?

Louis came out against it at first, because to him, it was just a lot of notes—he wasn't really hearing cats get to the essence of a song. When you play a slower style, you had better hit more right notes.

Who do you consider to be the most important New Orleans musician?

By far, Louis Armstrong. He put American music on the map. And this was a black man. He was not a Creole. He never got any break for any reason, and they tried to push him under the table. And he rose above everything, to not only become the most recognizable face, but his imprint is on everything after him and especially music. He redefined the world, man. Single-handedly.

And Buddy Bolden was the originator of jazz. The guy who combined gospel music, cocktail music, society music, and other things, then added a dimension of pimp to it and became one cocky trumpet player.

If Louis Armstrong came back to life today and came back down to New Orleans and heard the cats playing today, what do you think he would think about it?

He would be very disappointed. What he would think would be, *Where is the melody?* Even on these supposedly modern gigs, he would walk up there and say, "Where is the melody, man? Where is it?" He would be impressed with the technical ability of the trumpet players today, but he would be concerned with the heart and the love. When you listen to Pops sing a tune like "Give Me a Kiss to Build a Dream On," he was singing to somebody. We don't hear that anymore. People don't even know those kinds of songs. Most people don't give a flying shit. And that is dangerous.

Wynton Marsalis

"The best, when corrupted, becomes the worst."

My musical life was changed in April 1982 when Wynton Marsalis made his national television debut with his quintet on NBC's *The Tonight Show Starring Johnny Carson* (Bill Cosby was the host that evening). His explosive trumpet playing and seriousness of purpose bore the hallmarks of nearly a century's worth of cornet and trumpet innovation, from E. W. Gravitt to Buddy Bolden to Louis Armstrong, Dizzy Gillespie, Miles Davis, Freddie Hubbard, and Woody Shaw. I knew then that my life would take a turn into an area that would provide me with the richest foundation upon which to grow as a human being and as a musician.

Wynton Marsalis is in constant pursuit of the truth. His wide media coverage allowed all of us to learn his thoughts on the most profound and even trivial, and his celebrated relationship with Miles Davis would prove that Wynton would call it as he saw it, regardless of who it was concerning. This would enamor him to many, and cause ridicule and scorn from others.

This interview took place on March 30, 2005. Wynton was at home in New York, I was in Tallahassee finishing up a semester of teaching at Florida State University and preparing to go back on tour with the Basie orchestra. He answered the phone in his usual relaxed Southern manner—"Yeah, man." Our conversation was illuminating, and also very funny, and I learned a great deal. I am only one of thousands of trumpet players who have benefited from Wynton Marsalis.

Wynton Marsalis in Rose Hall in Lincoln Center.

Photo by author.

Wynton and Scotty at Florida State University, 1985.

Do you remember how you felt when you got your first trumpet?

I liked it because it was gold—well it was lacquered, but I thought it was gold. It had engraving on it. And it had a gold jet-tone mouthpiece with it. It was an Al Hirt mouthpiece. I actually got my first trumpet from Al Hirt. This was 1967.

Did the trumpet always come easily to you?

No. Man, I couldn't really play at all when I was younger. I was afraid to get the ring around my lips. Cats always had that titty on their lips. [*Laughs*] I was afraid to get that. So it wasn't easy. I was *sad*, man, playing the trumpet. I didn't get serious about playing until I was twelve.

Was there something that triggered you?

Like everybody else, I was listening to pop music. For some reason I started listening to John Coltrane that summer. I started listening to the *Giant Steps* record and that was the first time I could *hear* what a jazz musician was playing. This would be like 1973. The style of music we *thought*

was jazz, was *fusion*—which was mainly electronic instruments. I could hear that something about that wasn't like the *real* jazz. I liked it, because it was what we had growing up, but I could see that it wasn't like Trane and them. And then I started listening to Clifford Brown, Miles, Blue Mitchell. I could hear what they were playing. Between twelve and fourteen, my playing improved 150 percent. I got better very fast once I started to practice.

But even before I started listening to Trane, I used to get into jazz. When I was eleven I'd go see my Daddy play at Lou and Charlie's on Rampart Street. It was just a swingin' and soulful-assed club. They used to have good hamburgers and I would go there to throw darts and listen to all the older musicians talk shit. They would tell me stuff about pleasing women. I loved it. They would be corrupting me with all kinds of old bullshit.

What jazz trumpet masters gave you advice early on, advice that you understood when they gave it to you?

Clark Terry was the nicest. He called me "Demon." Clark looked out for me. He told me to just "sing it and play." He was the first cat I saw play that really was *playing*. I saw other musicians, but they were playing funk tunes and bull-shittin'. So I love Clark. But the first cat that I ever sat in with was Sonny Stitt. That was a bad motherfucker. I sat in with Stitt when I was fourteen. He told me, "Man, I had a dream that you are going to be one of the badddest motherfuckers that ever played."

Sonny Stitt told you that?

I swear. I said, "Man, this cat is patronizing me." I sat in with Roy Eldridge when I was like fifteen. I was playing the flugelhorn, and he said, "Man, you ain't playin' shit, you young motherfucker. I brought that fucking instrument over here from Europe."

He said that?

I didn't take it the wrong way. You know, I grew up with that. It didn't affect me. It was like I was one of them. And I *wasn't* playing shit. As I got older I realized that I didn't really know who the man was.

Damn!

I thought that jazz was for old people. We were playing funk and we always had girls around. They had all old people and no women at their gigs. Our funk gigs would be packed—we always had three or four hundred people. It was dancing, so sometimes it would be a thousand, maybe fifteen hundred. These big dances at the top of Gaylord's in New Orleans, there would be four and five bands.

How would you say that jazz trumpeters have extended the range and vocabulary of the instrument over the last one hundred years?

Well, the first achievement was the elevation of a personal style. What that meant was that any person who had a unique way of playing had invented *another whole trumpet*, because you were playing, and then you were *composing*. Buddy Bolden did that. It was not just embellishing melodies, Buddy Bolden elevated the whole personality. King Oliver didn't want to play like Buddy Bolden—he understood that in order for him to be as great as Bolden, he had to invent *his* own way of playing. Then Bunk Johnson had to invent *his* own way of playing. Then Freddie Keppard had to invent *his* own way of playing. Manuel Perez had to invent *his* own way of playing. That wasn't a prerequisite for trumpet players before that, you just had to develop some

technique that would stand you apart. You would double-tongue or triple-tongue faster than somebody, have a sweeter sound, some characteristic. But now you had to have an overall way of playing and inventing music that could identify you.

Right.

Now, when we start talking about specific techniques, you talk about the fact that each individual human on Earth has some originality, something they like to do, and they can vent that through music. Bunk Johnson would have a real smoky tone and a thick attack. King Oliver could be like a master of mutes and making sounds and laughs and a certain logic of syncopation. Buddy Bolden could be the master of a kind of sanctified church sound, like a combination of one of them big heavy sisters in the back of the church shoutin', and a field hand's cry. He could play notes that would make your heart break whenever you heard him. Freddie Keppard could play with so much power he could blow a mute out of a horn and make it sound like people laughing. Louis Armstrong could do all of that.

Umph!

With Louis Armstrong, you had the first person who combined all of that with the virtuosity of a traditional cornet player. People don't talk about that too often. But you know, you never hear Pops double-tonguing and shit like that. Cadenzas and the flourishes and embellishments of playing high and playing low, that's American cornet tradition, that has nothing to do with jazz. He was a virtuoso at that style of playing. It's just that he never played in that style, but he had that concept of virtuosity in his playing. That is what set him apart from everybody. I mean he wasn't any more soulful than King Oliver, but he played way more trumpet. He also sang through his horn like an opera singer. So he started to combine all different styles of music in his horn, but he had the personality to project that and to absorb it. He's a bad motherfucker.

How has your classical training influenced you, as it pertains to improvising in a jazz context?

Jazz influenced me more than playing classical music. That's because my daddy played jazz and I was always around musicians. In the funk bands, the gigs we did, nobody ever read music. I mean, who ever came to a funk gig with a music stand? Maybe there was one gig I played where they had a *Real Book*. But that was always in concert key, so you know... [*Laughs*]

But playing classical music effected my concept of the *solo*. When I studied the music of Bach, the music of Beethoven, the music of Stravinsky, Richard Wagner, when I started to listen to all of these people, I started to learn that there are many ways to develop themes. I started to perceive how you can organize your music in a solo, then I started to perceive it in jazz music; how Coltrane would organize his solo, or how Miles Davis would organize his solo. Like that.

That's a very clear understanding. OK, this is the name recognition part... I'll give you the name of a trumpet player and you just tell me the first thing that comes to your mind. The first person is Dizzy Gillespie...

[*A beat*] Intellectual.

Rafael Mendez.

[*A long beat*] Original sound.

Chet Baker.

[*A very long silence*] I'm not going to say what I think. We had a fucked-up exchange. I don't

want to comment on him. I might be biased, you know?

It's cool. I'll go on to somebody else. Miles Davis.

[*Another long silence*] The best, when corrupted, becomes the worst.

Clifford Brown.

Beautiful.

Bix Beiderbeck.

He could play, man. He had a golden attack, and he had a plaintive sound. And he played with tremendous originality. He was a good musician, he could hear. He had great ears, and not only that, he wrote very interesting original piano music, too. He was an indispensable part of the Jazz Age, an indispensable part of the spirit of jazz.

Jon Faddis.

Complete musicianship. He is somebody who loves the trumpet and he has unbelievable skills that no other trumpet player has ever had.

I know exactly what you're talking about. He can play in the extreme upper register of the trumpet as if he were playing in the normal middle register, and he does this with ease, unlike anyone. How about Freddie Hubbard?

Ah, big sound. Great velocity. He and Booker Little probably played with the best velocity of any trumpet players.

Wendell Brunious.

Wendell, he plays with a real light, a real nice attack. He puts a lot of tone on the note, and he uses a combination of New Orleans music and modern jazz, and he plays all the styles at once.

If you had to put a trumpet section together for a big band, and you started with yourself, who would the other three trumpeters be? Of all of the trumpet players in jazz history.

Snooky Young. Ray Nance. And Booker Little.

Whoo! That's a hell of a section there. How do you think the work of Duke Ellington effected the vocabulary of jazz trumpet?

Well, I think that he orchestrated the music of King Oliver. I also think that he had an ear for great trumpet stylists. He basically heard Louis Armstrong and King Oliver. Those were his two models on the trumpet. You take all of the cats that he hired, they all had something of Oliver and Armstrong. Then later on, Dizzy. He liked Dizzy too. And Dizzy loved Duke.

That's right.

And you can see that Bubber Miley was trying to play like King Oliver. Cootie Williams came in trying to play like Bubber Miley and Pops. Rex Stewart played like Pops, but with his own style, with the tricks and half valve, and all of the bent notes. We can go through Freddie Jenkins, Artie Whetsol, Shorty Baker. Ray Nance could play anything, man—just one of the unsung heroes. He played with more personality—he could bend a note better than anybody. Just the different colors and sounds and effects he used to get on the trumpet, it was unbelievable. Now that was a heck of a trumpet section. Cat Anderson, Clark Terry, Ray Nance.

How do you balance your traveling schedule with keeping your chops up? Do you find that difficult? Do you have any routines that you go through? You work all the time, man...

I'm playing almost every night, you know? It's just keeping it up by playing. Sometimes I have problems with my chops, like I'm overplaying, because I have tendonitis or something from playing too much. I have to return to long tones and stuff, warming up real good.

What do you consider to be your best recordings?

I think the best recordings I played trumpet on were *Live at Blues Alley, The Midnight Blues, Live at the Vanguard...* To be honest with you, I never really listen to my records. But I'm going to tell you, to me, some shit I played that nobody else did. First would be the solo that I played on "Delfeayo's Dilemma" on the recording of *Black Codes*. The logic of the solo. Even on the *Live at Blues Alley* recording, I'm getting to a certain thematic thing. Thematic in terms of the organization of the ideas. I thought that on *Live at Blues Alley*, on "Knozz-Moe-King," where I was playing real fast, and playing an internal melody inside of that? I never heard nobody play trumpet like that. And then, on *Marsalis Standard Time, Volume 1*, the way I played in time on "April in Paris." I played in four, but a third above the time, I don't think any other trumpet player did that. And "Majesty of the Blues," with the plunger mute, I'm not playing it like anybody in Ellington's trumpet section. I feel like on the record *The Midnight Blues*, I do a lot of shit nobody has ever done on the trumpet. Different ways of scooping notes and playing with them and bending them and doing shit to 'em.

Absolutely right about that. That's why you're the last interview in this book! So how does it feel to have become the "spokesman for jazz"... Do you think that an unfair burden that has been placed upon you?

Nahh, I don't really care about none of that, man. Martin Luther King Jr. gave us the ability to speak—he taught us that we don't have to be quiet. If somebody asks what I think, I'm going to say it. I'm not trying to be a spokesman for anything. You ask me a question, I'll answer it, and I'll try to be truthful when I answer it. And if I learn something different, or more, or better, I'm going to try and change. But it's just an opinion, and every opinion is not the same, because some opinions are more informed than others. It's not like I'm lobbying to be anything. I just play, give concerts, I teach and do and give what I can. Whatever abilities I have, I try to share. But I'm not afraid to say what I think and I don't care what the repercussions are. These last twenty years, I've loved it. I wouldn't take a second of it back. That would mean I'd have to be less than who I was, to get along with the establishment. I didn't want to do that, and I don't do it. And even now, I'm forty-three, I feel like I'm twenty, with all this selling out and bullshittin' these younger musicians are doing. They're keeping me young, man.

PART III
THE JAZZ TRUMPETER
Theory and Application

The Trumpet Section in a Jazz Band

The trumpet section in a jazz band is unique. There are usually four players, occasionally five. In some high schools I have even seen six and seven, and I applauded the director for not leaving anyone out. The trumpets have several roles to fill, and one of the most important is to bring absolute fire to whatever is being played. There is such joy in hearing a strong section swing its way through a good arrangement that covers a good range from the fourth chair to the lead chair.

Generally, the lead, second, third, and fourth chairs all have different functions with the soloists normally playing the second, third, and fourth parts. In the better bands, the lead player also is a strong soloist. In the Count Basie Orchestra, I believe we have one of the strongest sections anywhere in the world. One reason is the length of time we have been playing together. To my knowledge, there are no other bands that come close to our uninterrupted sectional tenure: at this writing, three years for the fourth chair, eighteen years for the lead chair who once played fourth, thirteen for the second chair (yours truly) who once played fourth, and nine years for the third chair. Add to this a schedule of plus or minus thirty weeks a year of touring the world, and you get an idea of how easily we can anticipate every move of each person in the section.

Members of our section regularly play parts from other chairs. This allows for the lead player and others to rest on a lower part when needed and it makes for a balanced section that does not

Count Basie Orchestra trumpet section rehearsing in San Juan, Puerto Rico, in 2005. From left to right: Scotty Barnhart, Mike Williams, Shawn Edmonds, and Endre Rice.

Photo by Bill Flowers

151

fatigue easily. Also, some of us may have a natural affinity and prettier sound for playing lead on ballads or certain other types of tunes. Just because someone has a greater range doesn't necessarily mean they automatically should be placed on lead every time. As an example, the late great Cat Anderson, Duke Ellington's high note specialist, sometimes played the fourth chair and not lead. Sonny Cohn, who to my knowledge sat in a trumpet section (in the Count Basie Orchestra) with uninterrupted tenure longer than anyone in jazz history—thirty-one years, became the primary lead trumpeter on ballads, although he was usually in the third chair.

Trumpet section of the Lincoln Center Jazz Orchestra. From left to right: Wynton Marsalis, Sean Jones, Marcus Printup, and Ryan Kisor.

Intonation is one of the main problems facing any section at any level as well. On any given day it can be great or terrible. So the best thing to do is to just listen and constantly adjust as necessary. The main factors that effect intonation are the state of readiness or warm-up of each player, fatigue, and the temperature of the room or place where the group is playing. Normally it is good to tune to the piano, because it will remain at the same intonation whether it has been tuned or not. If the piano tuning is terrible, then use the other lead players or guitarist, who may use an electric tuner sometimes. I have also seen several musicians place electronic tuners directly on their music stands so that they can monitor and adjust their tuning.

To play together all of the musicians in a trumpet section must be willing to listen to one another and appreciate one another's talents for what they are. If your lead player is consistently nailing triple C's among other accomplishments, then tell them what a good job they're doing. If a soloist in the section is swinging and playing some hip improvisations, then say so. If anyone plays with a closed mind or attitude, the music will suffer and the necessary camaraderie will not develop to a level that is commensurate with being professional. This is crucial to a successful section and especially one that will be together for a while.

One crucial fact that needs to be understood by directors and lead players in a jazz orchestra is that if the lead player is not a seasoned soloist, then he or she should defer to players in the section who are when it comes to interpretation. This is because the language of the jazz *soloist* has been and continues to be the model for which the music is written and arranged in the first place. Every jazz phrase written down on paper for a section to play has come from an accomplished jazz soloist, regardless of instrument. These phrases should be played just as a soloist standing

Photos by author

Trumpet section of Osaka, Japan Jazz Orchestra.
From left: Hiroshi Igami, Katsuji Shirai, Hiromitsu Ogaki, and Shozo Okuda.

Trumpet section of the Oresound Big Band of Sweden, 2004.
Left to right: Per Augustsson, Patrik Ekdahl, Marten Lundgren, and Jan Stahl.

in the middle of a hard swinging rhythm section would play them. Furthermore, the types of phrases Louis Armstrong played in the mid-1920s changed the way everybody else played and also the way composers and arrangers wrote for their orchestras. Thus, he almost single-handedly developed the style for the swing era. Every soloist of note from the swing era can be traced back directly to Louis Armstrong.

If the lead player is not familiar with the vocabulary of the jazz soloist, then his or her playing will never have a natural feeling of swing. The good news is that if the others in the section are soloists, the lead player can learn from them the best way to interpret the material. So in this instance the lead player may in turn follow the soloists and others in the section for correct interpretation and not continue the outdated "follow the leader" mentality so prevalent in college and amateur bands, but not necessarily the protocol of an established orchestra. This also holds true for the trombones and saxophones. Both the lead player and the director have to have integrity about this. How is a lead player not experienced as a soloist going to truly swing an entire orchestra?

In jazz, playing the lead trumpet chair is not about playing ear-piercing high notes; rather, it is all about style and good taste. An example is a recording of Snooky Young on the composition "Who Me" from the Basie recordings *The Complete Roulette Studio Sessions* (Mosaic) (live and studio versions), and especially *Count Basie Live in Europe* in 1962. Snooky's solo on this tune shows how his ability to improvise, especially on the blues, greatly enhanced his effectiveness as a lead trumpeter of the highest caliber.

The Shake

The shake, or lip trill, is one of the most effective ways a trumpeter can add to the feel of any note. To the layman, it sounds similar to a horse or someone laughing. To my knowledge, this method of "shaking" the note was introduced into the big band by trumpeter Sydney DeParis of McKinney's Cotton Pickers around 1930, as well as by Ed Lewis, lead trumpeter with Count Basie in the late 1930s. Snooky Young and Sweets Edison sat next to him in the section. It is a stretch, however, to say that the shake was never used before then, although it doesn't appear on recordings made before 1930 that I am aware of. Just as the accidental sticking of a valve may have created the smear effect, there must have been

153

Sydney DeParis, perhaps the first trumpeter to use the shake in a jazz orchestra with McKinney's Cotton Pickers of the late 1920s and 1930s.

Ed Lewis, powerful lead trumpeter who introduced the shake to the Count Basie Orchestra, circa 1935

times when the horn slipped in such a way as to make the sound that the shake produces. The player could have begun to laugh while playing or done any number of other things. (King Oliver and Freddie Keppard are known to have introduced all manner of effects on the instrument.) Whatever its origin, the shake has become an integral part of the vocabulary of jazz trumpet.

There are basically two ways of producing the shake. One way is to literally shake the trumpet (mainly with the right hand) while playing the note. The other is to utilize the lip trill exercises found in nearly all of the basic trumpet method books such as those by J. B. Arban, Max Schlossberg, and Herbert L. Clarke. The exercises use the syllables *ahh-eeh-ahh-eeh-ahh-eeh*, while varying the speed. From experience, I have found that the shake should be done according to the tempo of the piece being played. For example, to do a shake at a fast tempo of mm=284 the same way as if the tempo were a slower mm=96 doesn't make musical sense.

The Count Basie Orchestra and the Duke Ellington Orchestra both seem to have had a near patent on the use of the shake. As there is almost a seventy-year *continuous* history of the Count Basie Orchestra, however, it is easier to follow the shake's evolution there. The shakes do not sound the same on the 1979 album *On the Road* as they did on the 1953 album *April in Paris*. Over time, they became varied in width and the players seem to have become much more relaxed while playing them. Some of the recordings that showcase the shakes by the Basie Orchestra are *On the Road* (Pablo 1979), "Blues for Stephanie" (cued at 1:36–1:50) and "In a Mellow Tone" (cued at 1:30 and especially at 3:20); *Basic Basie* (MPS 1969), "Blues in My Heart" (0:00–0:08) and "Ma, He's Making Eyes at Me" (0:07); *April in Paris* (Verve 1953), track *Shiny*

Stockings (2:55 and 3:44 through the end).

In 1990, I had the pleasure of sitting and talking with three giants of jazz trumpet, Snooky Young, Clark Terry, and Nat Adderley. To be in the midst of so many stories was incredible. Among the tidbits was how the widow of Rex Stewart gave Snooky or Clark, Rex's social security card and mouthpiece. Another interesting story was how Clark Terry was in line to succeed Skitch Henderson as band leader on NBC's *Tonight Show Starring Johnny Carson.* Because of the color of Clark's skin, the prestigious spot went to Doc Severinsen, who, along with Snooky and Clark, was in the trumpet section under the direction of Henderson. (At this time period in U.S. history, discrimination on the basis on ethnicity was the order of the day.) However, when the subject of the shake arose (I may even have brought it up), the information was most interesting in that they all seemed to have a slightly different opinion of how the "best" shake was done. Someone said that it will not swing unless it is done with the hand to which someone else replied it should swing *regardless* of how it is done.

I did a clinic at the University of Kansas with Jon Faddis, who over the last thirty years or so has become one of the world's best lead trumpeters, and Mike Williams, the current lead trumpeter with the Basie Orchestra. A student asked how we all do our shakes and which was the better method. We all gave basically the same answer in that it varies, but I proceeded to demonstrate

Photo by author

Jon Faddis, the best lead trumpeter in the world. He is the only instrumentalist who can approximate the harmonic and rhythmic particulars of Dizzy Gillespie.

how one should let the *tempo* determine how wide the shake should be which would ultimately determine the method used to produce it. And, as far as whether the lip or hand method swings, I believe that if the musician is swinging in the first place, it won't matter which way the shake is done. And, of course, the opposite is true.

To prove this point further, listen to a trombone section doing a shake and it is nearly impossible for them to shake their instrument. They must use the lip trill method and as a result the shakes they produce are almost always the smoothest and they don't have that rushed, rigid, or uneven sound. Bill Hughes, the great bass trombonist, who joined the Count Basie Orchestra in 1953, and is currently our director, informed me that the shake was originally done *without* the shaking of the instrument but rather with the lip thrill method. His experience is invaluable in that he has been such a key force in one of the all-time great brass sections in jazz history.

The vibrato is something that I have found to be a dilemma for many directors on all levels.

Since this is jazz music, it seems to me that one should play each part as if it were a solo, but of course, within the confines of the group's balance. "Vibrato-less" sound is not in keeping with the freedom and the spirit of optimism that the pioneers of this music worked so hard to develop. Simply listen to the hundreds of recordings from the 1920s and later, and you will hear the individual and collective vibrato constantly. The earlier generation of jazz musicians had a better appreciation for the vocal contributions to music, it seems, because most of the prominent soloists and bands in general could be identified by their vibratos alone.

All of the great masters such as Louis Armstrong, Sidney Bechet, Charlie Parker, Roy Eldridge, Coleman Hawkins, Ben Webster, and the orchestras of Fletcher Henderson, Jimmy Lunceford, Duke Ellington, Benny Goodman, Glenn Miller, and Count Basie had that personal sound of the eternal optimist, attained through the collective. I cannot imagine any of them without a vibrato. Unless the composer specifically calls for no vibrato in the piece, I would urge all trumpeters to use it as naturally as possible, as if singing through the instrument. Lastly, you should be able to produce a vibrato without holding the trumpet yourself.

The Role of Jazz Trumpet in a Small Group and the Big Band

The practical applications and requirements of being a jazz trumpet soloist vary greatly from the small group—such as a quartet (trumpet, piano, bass, drums), quintet (trumpet, saxophone, piano, bass, drums), or even a duo or trio—to those of the big band, in which there are normally four or five trumpets and each trumpeter has a specific role. These two musical canvases call for different levels of musical awareness and preparedness.

A soloist in a small-group setting must master all facets of musicianship—including control of the instrument, melodic invention, harmonic and rhythmic reflexes, and adaptability within the

In concert with the quartet in Opperman Hall, Florida State University. Kevin Bales, piano; Author, trumpet; Rodney Jordan, bass; Leon Anderson, drums.

group's direction—to a degree that allows him/her to give as a natural performance as possible. In my experience, playing in a small group will raise the level of his/her musical abilities in every area because it exposes any deficiencies. You don't have three or four other trumpets or trombones, saxophones, and the rhythm section as in a big band to cover up those flaws. If your goal is to become a jazz soloist, then you must work hard to perfect all facets of musicianship, including knowing infinite ways to deliver a melody, being acquainted with harmony so well that you are able improvise consistently and with increased depth, incorporating the harmonic and rhythmic contributions of the other musicians in the group into your ideas, and taking those ideas to make a broader statement based on the collective thoughts of the group. If you incorporate ideas from members of the group, then your instrumental technique would develop, because when a trumpet soloist responds to the harmony and rhythms of other instruments with good technique, he/she can offer another level of harmonic and rhythmic proficiency.

Let's examine this theory in a more practical way. Wynton Marsalis's recording of "Chambers of Tain" from his *Live at Blues Alley* (disc 1;

157

track 7; cued from 2:14 through 2:51) is an example of how the entire group of four musicians (trumpet, piano, bass, and drums) can incorporate the ideas of their leader and vice versa. Marsalis takes what Jeff Watts ("Chambers of Tain" composer) suggests on the drums in the introduction and then arrives at a point (beginning at 2:14) where a longer and uninterrupted phrase is required to respond to the group. Marsalis accomplishes this extended phrase via circular breathing. While Watts provides the rhythmic spark and inspiration to match his fire, Marsalis then adds the percussive and harmonic shifts and rhythmic accents of pianist Roberts to his already developing solo while bassist Bob Hurst holds down the foundation for it all. Between 2:30 and 2:43 and until the end at 2:51, they set a precedent for small-group performance that, to my recollection, is the first time on record that this occurred with a trumpeter. When I heard this and studied its implications, I was able to add this method to my own group and it improved my harmonic and rhythmic reflexes as well as my trumpet technique.

Playing a simple duet (trumpet and piano; trumpet and drums; trumpet and bass, etc.) can also be the way that these types of harmonic and rhythmic reflexes can be enhanced. I have made duets a regular part of my small-group performances, even if the group is actually a quintet. During my solos and even during my introductions with the melody, I routinely like to play only with the bassist, pianist, or drummer. When playing with only one at a time, it forces me to hear in my mind the accompaniment of the other two parts of the rhythm section. For example, when I began to first learn the composition "Giant Steps" by John Coltrane, after a week or two playing it with the group, I began to break it down and play choruses with the drummer alone.

This forced me to continue my melodic improvisations on top of the chords, but to also respond in kind to the many different rhythms that the drummer was now freer to provide.

Moreover, the smaller the group the more responsibility each performer has to carry more of the melody along with its harmony and rhythm. I recommend all inspiring jazz soloists, even those that have not spent much time in these types of settings, to participate in a small ensemble. This is where one truly learns how to play as opposed to only getting sporadic solo space in a big band. But the big band has its own unique requisites of the soloist that, if fulfilled, can add a level of musicianship not easily attained elsewhere.

Being a trumpet soloist in a big band such as the Count Basie Orchestra has given me the great opportunity to sharpen the skills needed to deliver my improvisational statements within the specific parameters of this particular orchestra. Since this orchestra began in 1935, it has provided its many soloists with a foundation of the blues and Kansas City swing that has inspired jazz master soloists like tenor saxophonist Lester Young, trumpeters Buck Clayton and Sweets Edison, trombonist Al Grey, and Count Basie himself at the piano. What these men have in common is a marked level of refinement—and blues sound—in their solos, which is an art in itself. They could play one or two choruses (twelve bars of a blues or thirty-two bars of a standard) and say everything they needed to, whereas the small-group soloist has the freedom to take five, six, seven, or more choruses to get to the essence of their idea. My solos on Basie standards like "Corner Pocket" and "Moten Swing," for example, are only one chorus each, so I have to know exactly what I want to play when I am at the microphone. Of course, I have a theme in mind,

Photo by Stefan Anderson

Author with Count Basie Orchestra in Stuttgart, Germany.

but it can be twisted and altered in many ways, which means I have no idea of what I am going to play until I play it, since I would be affected by the background parts played by the orchestra during my solos. I have to find areas of the arrangement that allow me to develop my ideas, but also leave room for the orchestra to play. In reviewing the tapes that I made of my performance during the many years I've been the Count Basie Orchestra, I can see how I was forced to mature quickly as a soloist and how I have become able to get straight to the point in my solos. My small-group work with Marcus Roberts and my own quintet has also given me the opportunity to develop my ears to a level where I could hear the chord progressions

and background parts with the orchestra and use them to my advantage. If you don't know the chord changes, you had better be able to hear what they are as quickly as humanly possible. Working with the small group prepared me for working with the big band and performing regularly with both will refine your musicianship regardless of style.

Instructional Philosophy

3

"One should teach what one has learned rather than what one has been taught."
—Bruce Lee

Instructors on all levels have one of the most important jobs in the world. There are some who give as well as teach, and I have been fortunate to have several great ones such as Gordon Boykin, Lindsey Sarjeant, and Kevin Eisensmith. They taught me what they had learned as musicians themselves. But there are some teachers whose approach can be detrimental to their student's development. Most of the time it is due to the fact that the student is talented enough to reach levels that the teacher never attained or the teacher doesn't provide the correct environment for the student to mature.

Each time I visit a school and work with a jazz band, I am introduced to the students who are the best soloists. Sometimes, the others seem to have been given a subservient role, much to their dismay. What I stress is that each person is important, especially in a jazz ensemble, and that no one person should ever take all of the solo space. In the bands of Ellington or Basie, for example, everyone has a solo at some point or another. There are great records that feature soloists on the same instrument on every tune, such as the Roy

Eldridge/Dizzy Gillespie/Clark Terry album *The Trumpet Kings at Montreux* (Pablo), the Bobby Shew/Tom Harrell *Playing with Fire* (Mama Foundation), or the Nicholas Payton/Wynton Marsalis/Roy Hargrove session from the Payton disc *From This Moment* (Verve). These combinations seem to produce an unusually high level of performance and to push all involved to reach new heights of creativity.

I once heard an all-star high school jazz ensemble giving a concert in Santa Monica, California, as a part of their tour. The program

The author giving a master class in Hong Kong.

Photo from author's collection

161

was long enough to have featured each soloist, but the director only let a few play. I told him afterward that I could tell the others were itching to play (I'd confirmed this by talking to them) and that he could have easily let them have at least a chorus or two. His reply was that there was not enough time even though on several tunes soloists stretched for five and six choruses and the program lasted for more than an hour. To me, there is no excuse for this at all with students, especially in an all-star type of band. They all deserve a chance to play, even if some of them may not be as advanced as others.

If directors teaching jazz have practical experience on the road with a major group or orchestra, then they will have a better understanding of the importance of team play instead of the "star" syndrome. There will always be students too shy to request a solo, and it is incumbent upon the director to sense this and solve the problem. This is what great teachers do. It may be a much better performance if a couple of trumpeters or saxes or trombonists are trading fours (this is when one soloist plays four bars then the other soloist

Photo by author

Cenobia "Snow" Marquez, right, and her trumpet section at Satellite High School, Satellite Beach, Florida. The future of jazz is with such dedicated students as these.

"answers" with four bars and this cycle repeats throughout the form of the tune) or choruses rather than one person playing five or six choruses alone. A soloist will rise to the occasion if prodded along and challenged by trading with someone, even if their abilities are worlds apart. In fact, trading is one of my favorite ways to play as the ideas tossed back and forth are not entirely my own and therefore make for a broader canvas to create from.

Directors who do not have practical experience on the road should consult those who do to ensure the success of the program. There are so many things that are only learned from being on the road night after night for years. I have seen directors present a program in which there is no music by the greats who set the standards for big bands, such as Duke Ellington, Count Basie, Fletcher Henderson, Woody Herman, Thad Jones, Jimmy Lunceford, and others. It is perfectly okay to do music by contemporary composers, but in jazz you must deal with the Ellingtons and the Basies. If not, you are denying the students their history.

Furthermore, I would ask jazz band directors on every level to give students who may not yet realize their potential a chance to improvise. One student told me that because she played clarinet, she could not participate in her school's jazz band! When I thought of Jimmy Noone, Barney Bigard, Russell Procope, Benny Goodman, Eddie Daniels, and countless other master clarinetists, I felt sorry for her and asked to see her director immediately. This type of teaching is both unprofessional and ignorant. No one should be left out of a jazz band because of what instrument they have chosen to play. This music is for every instrumentalist, and especially youngsters, who are its future.

Encouraging students to "go for it" can reveal surprising talents. When I was with Marcus Roberts during the first weeks of his first band back in 1989, I was always afraid and nervous about really opening up and playing the things I knew I could. Nightly meetings about how we were playing did not help either. This was understandable, though, as Marcus had gone from being an integral part of Wynton Marsalis's band to leading a quintet of neophytes who showed promise, but were not really ready to go on the road as mature artists.

When the criticism far outweighs the praise, this can have a powerful effect on the musician regardless of the level of talent. However, two things were crucial to my development and feeling comfortable and free to create without fear. The first was playing night after night for an extended period of time. This allowed me to hear my progress (I taped each gig) and to really learn the material we were playing inside and out. Still, there was a certain level of apprehension in my solos and I hadn't begun to "go for it." This was finally nipped in the bud by master drummer Herlin Riley, formerly with Wynton Marsalis and the Lincoln Center Jazz Orchestra.

We were doing a video shoot for the recording of "Deep in the Shed," which is now only available on Laserdisc or DVD. I was warming up just before we were to do a take on the title track, simply doing lip trills with varied use of the plunger. Riley came to me and said, "What you are doing is killin' and you should do some of that on your solo." I had never had anyone of his level encourage me like that before, and it immediately erased all nervousness and apprehension. I was being appreciated for what I could do, and it felt good. I proceeded to play one of the best solos I had ever played up to that point. No longer did I care who was listening; I knew that there was at least one person who dug how I sounded and wanted me to explore it further. That was all the encouragement I needed to "go for it" every time from then on.

A band that has everyone as a soloist will be far ahead of those bands that do not, because a soloist requires a much more profound level of instrumental development and skill than simply sitting there and playing a part. But those who can *only* sit there and play a part make a contribution that must not be overlooked. It is they who provide the support a soloist needs.

To demonstrate how wonderful having multiple soloists can be, two recordings come to mind. The first is from *The Great Paris Concert* (recorded in 1963) by the Duke Ellington Orchestra; on "Jam with Sam" (disc 2, track 1), several soloists come down front and Ellington introduces them and mentions their particular place of birth or residence. The other is from the Count Basie Orchestra recording *Chairman of the Board* (Mosaic) on the composition "Easin' It." Every member of the trumpet section—Thad Jones, Clark Terry, Al Aarons, and Sonny Cohn—takes a turn trading fours on a blues. The different personalities are astoundingly clear. To hear this is tantamount to being in a Baptist church when many people stand up to testify. It is simply glorious and further proof of the genius of leaders like Ellington and Basie who used all of the talents in their orchestra, not just a select few.

Teaching jazz trumpet requires understanding that the history of the music must be learned as a part of the process. It is simply not enough to learn scales, chord changes, patterns, and solos, and think that will suffice. Technical skill means nothing without a full understanding of where this music came from and what it is about. I have learned this from conversations with master musicians like Clark Terry, Freddie Hubbard, Nat Adderley,

Sweets Edison, Frank Foster, Lindsey Sarjeant, Pam Laws, Joe Williams, and others, but more importantly from my own personal experiences. Jazz involves creating something as yet unheard by drawing from one's life experiences. As Clark Terry says, "One must imitate, then assimilate, and this will ultimately lead to being able to innovate."

The best example of how a jazz musician learns his craft is Louis Armstrong. He learned by studying King Oliver and playing with him on the bandstand. This might not seem too unusual as it is common among the best musicians, but what is important to realize is that Armstrong did this with only his ears to guide him. No method books of patterns, scales, etc. were available, only practical application and repetition. This type of practice keeps a musician closest to whatever innate or natural ability they already possess. One of the first things I do with a student is to ask them what they are trying to do. If they can answer with a marked degree of clarity, I am able to put together a personalized set of things for them to work on. Then I explain that being a jazz musician is a life-long process and that patience is of the utmost importance. There is so much more music for them to learn and nearly a thousand trumpeters alone they should be familiar with in some way, not to mention the hundreds of saxophonists, pianists, bassists, vocalists, percussionists, and bands worth knowing. Just as I give students particular records to absorb, I recommend books for them to read: *Jazz: America's Classical Music* by Grover Sales; *Early Jazz: Its Roots and Musical Development* and *The Swing Era: The Development of Jazz, 1930–1945*, both by Gunther Schuller; *Good Morning Blues: The Autobiography of Count Basie* and *Stompin' the Blues* by Albert Murray; *Miles: The Autobiography* by Miles Davis; *Jazz Masters of the Twenties* by Richard Hadlock; *Jazz Masters of the Thirties* by cornetist Rex Stewart; *Music Is My Mistress* by Duke Ellington; *The Loudest Trumpet: Buddy Bolden and the Early History of Jazz* by Daniel Hardie; *Treat It Gentle* by Sidney Bechet; *The Music of Black Americans* by Eileen Southern; and *Louis Armstrong: My Life in New Orleans* and *Louis Armstrong: In His Own Words*, both by Armstrong himself. These are but a few of the books that will enlighten anyone interested in the history surrounding the music and the musicians. I would put a premium on those written by actual jazz musicians with a track record of being part of the lineage of their instrument. There is no substitute for experience.

Not long ago, it was forbidden to play and teach jazz on all school campuses the world over. It was even taboo to play it in some households. The great cornetist Nat Adderley once told me that he and his brother, Cannonball Adderley, were not allowed to practice jazz on the campus of Florida A&M University while they were in school there, although it is a historically black university. By the time I arrived there in 1982 some four decades later, however, jazz study was in full swing, thanks in large part to the success of the Adderley brothers. The music and contributions of Louis Armstrong, Charlie Parker, Duke Ellington, Thelonious Monk, and others was acknowledged as sophisticated and profound art, and an attempt was made to understand the music in general from more than just a social standpoint. In other words, the world had to get past the fact that this music was coming from a people who were placed at the bottom of a society and denied rights guaranteed to them by their own constitution. It is interesting what the sound of a powerful trumpet or saxophone or sophisticated jazz orchestra can do.

Today, with the world having the benefit of decades of great jazz music from international tours and recordings, jazz is now beginning to take its rightful place among other art forms worthy of formal study. In fact, much more is required of the musician and student of jazz than of any other type of music. This is because all of the best jazz musicians were and are masters of instrumental technique, rhythm, harmony, melodic invention, and composition. The last three abilities are not necessarily required in most other musical study but are essential for the creative jazz musician—the jazz soloist.

From my experience as a jazz musician and someone who is constantly studying the genre, I have found that it has sharpened all of my natural reflexes as they pertain to music—hearing, recall, flexibility, execution, and reason. I can hear the hum of an airplane's jet engine or a car horn or the chirp of a bird and know what pitch it is and hear chords associated with it, or listen to a Thelonious Monk piano solo and decipher the chords and play it. I could not do this before I began to study jazz seriously. Jazz also requires that I constantly improve my instrumental technique and my knowledge of past musicians on all instruments, and continue to learn the hundreds of compositions that are standard repertory. Just as classical trumpeters are required to know specific and standard repertoire before they are accepted into major symphony orchestras—compositions such as Mahler's Fifth Symphony, Stravinsky's *Petrouchka*, Mussorgsky's *Pictures at an Exhibition*, Bach's Brandenburg Concerto in F—the jazz trumpeter has hundreds of compositions that he or she must be very familiar with that span the entire spectrum of jazz. Some of the compositions we must know are "Indiana," "Struttin' with Some Barbeque," "After You've Gone," "A Night in Tunisia," "Anthropology," "Cherokee," "Joy Spring," "Daahoud," "Birdlike," "I Can't Get Started," "Mack the Knife," "Body and Soul," "What's New," "All Blues," "Up Jumped Spring," "Pinocchio," "Giant Steps," "What Is This Thing Called Love," "Work Song," and perhaps over a thousand more! And know them in all keys if possible! Also, once you consider yourself a jazz musician, you are required to know material that may have become popular and associated with another instrumentalist such as "In a Sentimental Mood" that was originally written for tenor saxophone, or "Misty" which was written for piano. The difference between the two repertoires is that classical repertoires are set in key, tempo, and dynamics, whereas in the jazz repertoire, the performer is required to play in any key and tempo, with varying dynamics. It is a continuous process that will provide a solid foundation of all-around musicianship not attainable elsewhere.

Trumpet section of Florida State University Jazz Ensemble I.
From left: Etienne Charles, Jon Jopling, Pete Carroll, Matt Postle.

Elements of Jazz Trumpet

Embouchure Development and Consistency

Developing a strong and consistent embouchure (the way the lips vibrate together in conjunction with the natural disposition of the oral cavity [mouth/lips] to make a sound on the mouthpiece) is key for playing on all wind instruments. The best way to do this is through private study with an individual who has a proven record of professional accomplishments on his or her instrument. Even at the professional level, however, periodic readjustments may be necessary due to a variety of factors, such as changes in the tooth structure or bite and even things such as fatigue and the normal passage of time.

When I started playing trumpet at the age of nine, my band director at Terry Mill Elementary School in Atlanta, Georgia, Mr. Stanley Gosier, happened to be a trumpeter, which was very good for me. He had us students copy his embouchure, which was perfect, and he didn't believe in pouting the cheeks out and would reprimand those of us who did it. Thus, I had a solid and disciplined foundation on which to build. My next band director, Mr. Gordon Boykin of Gordon High School in Decatur, Georgia, was former U.S. Army Band trombonist, which was

just as good because the only major difference in trumpet and trombone embouchures is the size of the mouthpiece used. Mr. Boykin also had us place a small mirror on our music stands to monitor our embouchure development. I highly recommend this for students today.

All of the greatest technicians (those who have displayed the widest range of flexibility and mastery of finger dexterity and multiple tonguing)—such as Rafael Mendez, Louis Armstrong, Jon Faddis, Freddie Hubbard, Clark Terry, Harry James, Miles Davis, and Wynton Marsalis, to name a few—have nearly identical embouchures. By "identical," I mean the same combination of overall posture and the area between the chin and Adam's apple and the trumpet itself being almost completely parallel to the floor. There are slight variations, due to the differences in the oral cavity from person to person. But generally speaking, they all look the same.

I have found from thirty-one years of study and playing the trumpet that if the chin is flat and not rolled upward and the posture is such so that it allows for a natural flowing of the air stream, and being able to say *foooooo* or *feeeeeeee* (depending on the register you are playing) at any time, then the instrument becomes easier to play, and the sound is enhanced to its fullest potential.

If this is realized, the trumpet then effectively becomes a natural extension of yourself. Further, when warmed up, advanced trumpeters should be able to play tonguing and slurring *and* swinging from the lowest F-sharp or the pedal tones below it to at least the G above high C, with minimal shifting in the embouchure. There are simple steps that can be practiced to achieve this level of proficiency. This is why jazz musicians have to have the most technique: if the mind thinks of something technically outrageous to

The author demonstrates his embouchure while playing the trumpet of Louis Armstrong. Courtesy of the Louis Armstrong Archives, Queens College.

The two most important trumpet teachers I have ever had: Mr. Stanley Gosier, left, and Dr. Kevin Eisensmith, right.

play, the reflexes from the embouchure have to be prepared to execute it through the instrument within a split second.

Circular Breathing

Another playing technique I have found useful is the process of circular breathing. This enables a trumpeter or any other wind instrumentalist to play continuously for however long he desires. This could be two minutes or one hour or more. I think the world record, set by a saxophonist, for this technique is around two and a half hours. (It is much easier to vibrate on a reed than it is on the lips.) Circular breathing is difficult for some at first, but with a little patience and practice, it can be accomplished in one day or less. The key is at the point of the air transfer, when only the cheek muscles are used to push the air through the instrument and the lungs are used to breathe in new air simultaneously. During this second or two, the pitch of the note being played should not waver much. A good area to start is on middle G (second line G).

Circular breathing is best used when the music calls for it or if the trumpeter has breathing problems, and not just to show off. I realized the importance of knowing how to circular breathe while sitting in with Wynton Marsalis in Tampa, Florida, in 1988. During my solo on a minor blues, I found myself on a high C with about two bars left to the top of the form. With the theme I had developed so far, I knew that if I had cut that high C off prematurely, I would sound completely sad to myself and the cats in the band. So, without really thinking about the mechanics of it, I circular breathed on the high C until the back half of beat four in the last measure of the form. This made my solo coherent because the band accented that half of the beat *with* me. The importance of that moment didn't dawn on me until much later.

In the Count Basie Orchestra, I use this technique mainly on ballads if necessary and on the last chord of a number while our lead trumpeter finds a note around double high C or above. With my quintet, I will circular breathe if I am engaged in a dialogue with my saxophonist or drummer that contains long lines as we toss ideas back and forth. I also use circular breathing when there's not enough time to warm up due to travel or some unforeseen circumstance. When flights are canceled or rerouted and you arrive at the concert hall with only twenty minutes to set the stage and get dressed, this comes in handy. I will go into a corner and play chromatically (slurring and tonguing) from lowest F-sharp to high C and do lip flexibility exercises and études memorized from the J. B. Arban, Theo Charlier, or Herbert L. Clarke method books, as well as my own warm-ups, taking the horn away from my lips only for a few seconds at a time. The dynamics are from pianissimo to fortissimo. I do this for intervals of about five to eight minutes with less than a minute between each session. It seems to center my embouchure quickly. I also make sure that I take deep breaths before I begin. Next I will extend the range to G above high C and to the pedal tone C below the F-sharp. I also use an adjustable Denis Wick cup mute as I can put more air through the horn without being too loud backstage. This works for me, and it may take some time for other trumpeters to get used to.

Most technical and endurance problems facing trumpeters start somewhere in the embouchure, posture, or breathing, and there are numerous exercises that have been proven to fix most, if not all of them. Of course, the aid of a teacher who has mastered whatever it is that is plaguing the student is highly recommended.

This section is for those who would like to learn how to play—that is, how to arrive at the point where one can deliver their particular personality and/or thoughts on any given song. What I will say here has worked for me and for those who taught me, and as I understand it, this is the way the masters themselves learned.

A college instructor once asked me, "How did you know when you had arrived at the point at which you knew exactly what you were doing during a solo?" I could not pinpoint the precise moment when I started to truly grasp what I had been after which was constructing a coherent and logical solo. The truth is, I didn't really know what I was after, but I had faith that it would come to me only after hours and hours and maybe months and years of consistent and concentrated practice. The key is what I practiced. Luckily for me, Marcus Roberts and my college professor at Florida A&M University, Lindsey B. Sarjeant, both knew what to tell me to do. Moreover, having someone like Wynton Marsalis play for me over the telephone and pass along information he had gathered directly from Dizzy Gillespie and Art Blakey, among others, was incredibly valuable, although half the time I didn't grasp what he was playing or saying.

Not until I seriously began to dissect recordings and sit down at the piano with Marcus and Lindsey did I begin understand those basic elements that all jazz musicians must have. This, coupled with *constantly* doing gigs, no matter how trivial they seemed, put me on the path to becoming a jazz musician in complete control of whatever I desired to do, whether arranging, composing, or performing.

I was taught that scales, specific patterns, and tunes should be learned proficiently in all keys, which is not easy at all, but when it comes time to step up to the microphone and make music *and* tell a story, those things may or may not help you. When Clifford Brown, Clark Terry, and Charlie Parker were learning how to play, they didn't have all of the books and play-along methods that we have today. Instead they had their ears and the bandstand. Period. Of course, they also had a superior sense of harmony and music history, because most if not all of them studied formally as well as informally "in the woodshed."

As a result of on-the-bandstand training, however, the early musicians were in closer contact with the immediacy of the music and not approaching it from a purely academic standpoint. There is not a book anywhere that will show you how to really play the blues or how to navigate successfully—and with spiritual intensity—through the difficult chord changes of many standards. As a jazz musician, you must listen constantly to those who can play the blues and standards, and your ears should tell you what will be next on your part. This brings me to the all-important task of transcribing. Transcribing solos by many different trumpeters by *ear*, and not from a book, will allow the basic feel of the music to enter one's playing—at least in most cases. The common practice of slowing down solos electronically to half speed is a lazy way of transcribing because it weakens the harmonic and rhythmic reflexes. When you walk onto the bandstand at a jam or recording session, the other performers are not going to slow down the music to make it easier for you to learn. For example, a former student played a Clifford Brown solo that he had transcribed. Brown's inflections and subtle musicianship were missing, and I discovered that he had slowed down the Brown solo to half-speed to learn it. Clifford Brown played at half speed is not Clifford Brown because his

sound disappears and what remains is an electronically distorted imitation.

You should learn as many solos as possible that cover the widest historical perspective your technique will allow. From King Oliver and Louis Armstrong to Bix Beiderbeck, Jabbo Smith, Henry Allen, Roy Eldridge, Harry James, Charlie Shavers, Bunny Berigan, Sweets Edison, Clark Terry, Dizzy Gillespie, Fats Navarro, Miles Davis, Clifford Brown, Nat Adderley, Chet Baker, Kenny Dorham, Cootie Williams, Thad Jones, Lee Morgan, Joe Newman, Freddie Hubbard, Don Cherry, Don Ellis, Snooky Young, Maynard Ferguson, Booker Little, Woody Shaw, and many others up through Wynton Marsalis and Jon Faddis, learning their work will help to provide a foundation for understanding what this music is about. Learn with a desire to eventually be as good as the original artist, although that may seem unrealistic, but having a goal in mind is paramount in achieving anything at all. If just a small percentage of what you are working on is thought about and integrated into your playing, it will enable you to add your own distinct abilities to whatever you play.

A composition you like that has a nice melody at any tempo and that has been recorded by many different players is a good place to begin. At first, play the melody over and over and over again until you have it completely free, meaning you can twist it and turn it however desired without losing its essence. Then practice playing each chord on the piano, holding the sustain pedal down while simultaneously playing the corresponding scale on the trumpet. If you know the scale already, concentrate on getting the overall sound of the chord on the horn rather than continuing to play in a scale-like fashion. I have found that this approach frees me up to explore notes that may not be in the chord technically, but that help me to define its sound depending on my mood.

Next, create a musical idea or motif, no matter how simple, and take it rhythmically through each chord. For me, this allows for the harmony to open itself up; I don't have to chase after it, although all of us are in constant pursuit of deeper harmonic knowledge. However, my study of the piano has helped me understand harmony in such a way as to be able to transmit any emotion that I am feeling on anything I am playing. I now have a greater understanding of what each note brings to each chord and its meaning to me. D minor, for example, doesn't mean the same thing to me now as it did fifteen years ago. Understanding notes and chords revealed some of the secrets of composing and has allowed me to compose original music based on pure experience and emotion. I believe this is what we are all after, regardless of the type of music we play.

No matter what tune one chooses to "learn how to play" on, a major part of the process should be playing the tune completely alone to see if you can hear the bass, piano, and drums in your head, like a professional rhythm section accompanying you. If you can't hear this accompaniment in your head, then many more months of listening must be done. This has worked very well for me and for my students; it may also work for you.

Using the Plunger and Other Mutes

The use of mutes such as the cup, straight, pixie, Harmon, and bucket are a normal part of any jazz trumpeter's routine. These mutes simply fit snugly into or clip onto the bell and may require adjustment of the tuning slide for good intonation. This is especially true of the Harmon mute. There are several versions of the Harmon; some have a more rounded bottom or bubble

Photo by author

The most common trumpet mutes used in jazz today: (above) the metal derby or hat; (below from left) straight mute; Harmon mute; the plunger; cup mute; and bucket mute.

design rather than a flat bottom. The key to finding the right one is for your trumpet is to see if it is possible to play down to a low F-sharp without the notes becoming muddy around low C, when the mute is in place. With my current trumpet, which was built by Dave Monette (AJNA II in B-flat), the Jo-Ral bubble Harmon is the only one that allows for my low F-sharp to come out fully. The other models only allowed me to go to about low C before the notes started to run together and sound muffled. Of course, the optimum range for a good buzz sound with the Harmon is not so much in the lower register as in the middle to upper register. My research tells me that Joseph "King" Oliver practically invented the Harmon mute and was using it when he went to Chicago in 1918. He was playing regularly at the Dreamland Café, which was owned by Paddy Harmon. Harmon had his mute patented and went on to make a fortune selling them while Oliver died broke and destitute less than two decades later. Perhaps the greatest exponent of the Harmon mute was Miles Davis. With his large discography, we are able to hear him use this mute to full advantage on many recordings.

The plunger, however, is much different from all other mutes, and its use is an art form nearly exclusive to jazz that requires above-average dedication. The early cornetists from New Orleans began this practice by experimenting with a half of a coconut, thereby providing a foundation from which the plunger emerged. From as far back as Johnny Dunn who greatly influenced Bubber Miley, Cootie Williams, and Ray Nance with the Duke Ellington Orchestra, and up through Snooky Young, Joe Newman, and Sonny Cohn of the Count Basie Orchestra to Clark Terry, the plunger has been an important part of the vocabulary of jazz trumpet. I used one on my first major recording with Marcus Roberts, *Deep in the Shed* (Novus, 1989), and it is a regular part of my duties with the Count Basie Orchestra on compositions such as Basie's "One O'Clock Jump" and Frank Foster's "Blues in Hoss' Flat." Playing with the plunger is one of my favorite modes of expression.

I have found that use of the plunger only sounds good if the music tells me it is needed. I wait until something lets me know the plunger would be the better vehicle for expression rather than the open horn. I can't really explain what that something is, other than to say it only occurs if there is a certain earthiness to the song being played.

One of the things that I do is study the sound produced by such plunger masters as Cootie Williams, Snooky Young, and Clark Terry, and perhaps the greatest plunger trombonist who ever lived, the late Al Grey, who for many years was with the Count Basie Orchestra. He wrote a book entitled the *Al Grey Plunger Technique*. Only recently have I had the pleasure of performing side by side with Young and Terry, therefore being able to see firsthand how they use the plunger. Clark Terry asked me to do a gig with him at the North

Photo courtesy of Jack Bradley

Thomas Papa "Mutt" Carey of New Orleans, with Kid Ory on trombone. Carey was one of the original masters of using the plunger mute.

Sea Jazz Festival in July 1997, and I was on the plunger while he played flugelhorn. To this day that was one of the highlights of my life.

The preeminent and former lead trumpeter and soloist with the Count Basie Orchestra beginning in 1942, and regular member of the NBC *Tonight Show* orchestra conducted by trumpeter Doc Severinsen for more than twenty years, Eugene "Snooky" Young, even uses his cup mute as a plunger! He also used the metal hat or derby in the plunger style, for example, in his hat/metal mute solo on the Frank Foster composition "Who Me" from a Basie Orchestra recording, *Live in Europe—Olympia 5 May 1962* (RTE 710566). It is one of the most incredible trumpet solos on the blues I have ever heard and is one all jazz trumpeters and especially lead trumpeters should learn. It hammers home my belief that the best-sounding lead players in jazz music are those who can play the blues with absolute authority. Snooky told me that all lead players should be able to solo on the blues and chord changes convincingly and the other players in the section should be able to play some lead. This makes for a well-rounded section and gives confidence to those who may

Jazz trumpet legend Eugene "Snooky" Young soloing with the Clayton-Hamilton Jazz Orchestra in Vienne, France, 2004.

At the North Sea Jazz Festival in 2005, Joe Wilder uses a drinking cup as a mute. The cup mute came from this practice.

need it. This last statement is one high school and college jazz band directors should especially understand.

Cootie Williams—who after Papa Mutt Carey, King Oliver, and Bubber Miley, is among the founding fathers of the consistent use of the plunger—has a plunger solo on the composition the "Intimacy of the Blues" from the Duke Ellington Orchestra recording *And His Mother Called Him Bill*. This is Cootie Williams at his very best. There is also a recording of Cootie with the Ellington orchestra from the *Second Sacred Concert*. He is featured on a composition called "The Shepherd" and it is an absolute must have for anyone serious about the plunger. I also highly recommend learning plunger solos by Clark Terry from the recording *Oscar Peterson Trio + One*.

One of the best lessons I received on the plunger came from a man who is normally not known for his use of it, Harry "Sweets" Edison. However, after thinking about his early career with Basie from the late 1930s, I realized that he used the hat and derby quite often and I am sure the plunger as well. We were in his living room in Los Angeles in 1999 several months before he passed away just talking and playing our trum-

Plunger master Cootie Williams. The epitome of the sound of the plunger.

Bubber Miley, the great plunger specialist with the Duke Ellington Orchestra in the late 1920s. Cootie Williams replaced Miley in 1929.

The author at work using the plunger with Benny Carter and the Count Basie Orchestra in 1997.

pets. I taped the entire two hours I was there and I have included in this book transcripts from that incredible history lesson. The main thing he told me was to squeeze the plunger instead of just using the most common open and close technique. This, he said, would result in better intonation and it would always give that *sound* consistent with that of the better plunger users such as Cootie, Clark, and Snooky.

Using the plunger should be a regular part of practice for all jazz trumpeters, as it is a most important part of the vocabulary of the music. Even beginners will benefit from the use of the plunger, gaining a deeper understanding of a most majestic sound. Choosing a good plunger is pretty easy. Just make sure that its radius is a perfect fit for the radius of your trumpet bell. Then play a middle C open and listen to the intonation. Then put the plunger in the complete closed position on the bell and then play the same middle C. If they are in tune with another, then you have a good plunger.

Necessary Materials

One of the most important pieces of advice I ever got about making serious progress as a jazz trumpeter came from Wynton Marsalis. I was about to go on my first tour with his former pianist-orchestrator Marcus Roberts as a member of his first quintet back in 1989. I asked what tips Marsalis could give, and he said to be sure to pack a lot of underwear and socks! This I know to be very true, having toured the world constantly with the Count Basie Orchestra for some thirteen years at this writing. But the most important thing he told me was to tape myself every night during the gig. I cannot emphasize enough how crucial this is.

When you tape all your performances, whether wedding receptions, rehearsals, or jam sessions, you should be able to hear with greater clarity what sounds good and what doesn't. But the best thing about it is that when you listen to yourself in comparison to the masters of your particular instrument, it becomes crystal clear as to what areas of your playing need greater concentration. For example, when I learn a standard or a blues or a ballad, I have several recordings of the tune by trumpet masters and other instrumentalists to use as a guide. Their versions let me know what level to strive for. After listening to myself play the tune many times and comparing my solos over the chord changes to theirs, I feel more comfortable playing it and can even begin to twist a phrase or two and turn them around for my own use. I have used this method hundreds of times, and it really facilitated my learning. It has also forced me to realize that I had to be patient for progress.

The materials needed would be a stereo recorder such as a minidisc recorder, DAT machine, an iPod that can record or an iRiver, a walkman with built-in microphone, a professional-model Walkman with attachable microphone; or a professional set of headphones; a good stereo system; and as many albums CDs, DVDs, and tapes as your budget allows. Hardly a week goes by that I am not in a record store looking for important recordings. I love to listen! I get the same amount of pleasure from listening to good music as I do from playing it. I am constantly searching for more recordings and not just trumpeters, but vocalists, saxophonists, drummers, trombonists, pianists, bassists, band leaders, and more.

Establishing a Practice Regimen

Aristotle once said, "It is easy to perform a good action, but not easy to acquire a settled habit of performing such actions." To that end, every musician should have a practice routine that is concentrated and consistent, mentally and physically. This routine, with the aid of a teacher when necessary, should cover all of the areas that the musician needs to improve, which could range from articulation to scale studies. For the jazz trumpeter, the skills to be mastered are many. Two of the most crucial are to be able to hear and to swing—to achieve the correct coordination and rhythmic displacement of the eighth-note triplet as mentioned in the introduction. A personal and consistent sound will develop over time, but I believe that one can learn to swing more quickly. By listening analytically and consistently, one can absorb the music naturally and be able to re-create that particular but sometimes elusive bounce that is instantly recognizable to those who swing.

All of the most influential players—Louis Armstrong, Cootie Williams, Clifford Brown, Clark Terry, Miles Davis, Snooky Young, Fats Navarro, Sweets Edison, Lee Morgan, Freddie

Photo from author's collection

Three generations of trumpeters: the author, Harry "Sweets" Edison, Clark Terry, Derek Gardner, Al Hirt, and Mike Williams.

Hubbard, and especially Dizzy Gillespie—had control of the displacement of their eighth-note rhythms to such a degree that whatever they played swung like crazy and with harmonic mastery. An example would be articulating through the mouthpiece and horn something like this: *du-DAH-du-DAH-du-DAH*...as played in quarter-note and eighth-note rhythms over the entire range of the instrument.

A good practice regimen written down might look like this.

1. Warm up with various exercises such as long tones from universal method books, such as those by J. B. Arban, Max Schlossberg, Theo Charlier, Bitch, or Herbert Clarke *Technical* and/or *Characteristic Studies*. The player should be as physically comfortable as possible. Sitting erect toward the edge of a good chair is best, but whatever allows for the *complete relaxation of the body* almost to the point of nonchalance.

2. Work slowly on problem areas such as multiple tonguing, finger dexterity, and lip flexibility (slurred intervals). The first thing that my first private trumpet teacher, Dr. Kevin Eisensmith, formerly first trumpet with the U.S. Army Band in Atlanta and now professor of trumpet at Indiana University of Pennsylvania, ever taught me was that there are basically three areas to playing the trumpet: finger flexibility, lip flexibility, and multiple tonguing. If these are mastered together through various etudes that encompass musicality, then there will nothing that a trumpeter cannot play at least technically. If analyzed, every type of trumpet performance can be broken down into these segments. I must note, however, that the intensity, spirituality, and power inherent in the music of a

great trumpeter, such as Louis Armstrong, cannot be broken down as such.

3. Listen to recordings of trumpeters doing what you would like to be able to do and try to learn their solos. For example, to establish a precise and clear attack, listen to examples of single, double, and triple tonguing by listening to the recordings of the late classical trumpet master Rafael Mendez on "Moto Perpetuo" (*The Trumpet Magic of Rafael Mendez*) and the disc *Carnival* by Wynton Marsalis, which contains most of the greatest solos written for cornet and/or trumpet. For playing in the extreme upper register, check out recordings that feature Cat Anderson (*Cat on a Hot Tin Horn*, Mercury 1962) and with Duke Ellington, Maynard Ferguson, and Jon Faddis (*Legacy*, *Into the Faddisphere*), to name a few. For pure and pretty tones there are many, such as the recordings of Chet Baker, Freddie Hubbard, Bobby Hackett, Clifford Brown, Valaida Snow, Shorty Baker, Miles Davis, Don Goldie, Nicholas Payton, Pete Minger, Art Farmer, and many others. I would even add a recording I did with pianist Marcus Roberts to this list: the composition "As Serenity Approaches" from the CD of the same name by Roberts.

To learn to swing and obtain that elusive bounce, learning the solos of Clifford Brown, Dizzy Gillespie, Louis Armstrong, Freddie Hubbard, Miles Davis, Sweets Edison, and a host of others are recommended. The names listed are the ones on which I spent a considerable amount of time, and they aided in my development of making sure that no matter what I played, it swung. But I always *wanted* to swing. Also helpful were saxophonists such as Dexter Gordon, John Coltrane, Charlie Parker, Cannonball Adderley,

Stan Getz, and Sonny Stitt; pianists Oscar Peterson, Count Basie, Duke Ellington, Wynton Kelly, Red Garland, McCoy Tyner, Thelonious Monk, Herbie Hancock, and Gene Harris; bassists Sam Jones, Ray Brown, Norman Keenan, Cleveland Eaton, Ron Carter, Paul Chambers, Eddie Jones, and many others. There are many ways to learn to swing, and once you've learned the concept behind it, letting the music into your soul, the instrument becomes almost secondary.

I must note, however, that in order to swing effortlessly I still have to think about getting that bounce while I am playing, because each rhythm section is different. Again, listening to every musician I am playing with is crucial. Thousands and thousands of hours of doing gigs, being alone with my trumpet, and listening to and analyzing the recordings of the masters have brought me closer to the ultimate freedom of expression and swing that all jazz musicians are after. It is a lifelong odyssey that is simultaneously a labor of love.

Furthermore, there is nothing like a great trumpet solo in any form of music, but when the solo is improvised over some good and intense swing, for me, it takes on a whole new level of meaning. Someone once said, "There is nothing more beautiful than self-expression." When you hear an improvising jazz band play, you are hearing the collective thought of several individuals in progress or constant motion, whereas in classical music, for example, you are only really hearing what the composer and conductor intended and not what the second violinist, the bassist, or the third trumpeter is thinking. Improvising within a jazz context requires the most thought, the most technique, and the best ears because in essence, the soloist is creating spontaneously while simultaneously interacting with the group in editing and refining his or her statement. For those musicians and laymen who can't fully appreciate jazz and its infinite areas of wonder and who always ask, "Where is the melody?" or "Where is the structure?" the answer is simply this: it is *always* there for you to discover.

The Psychological Factor

Practicing mentally is one of the most important things that musicians can do. Most of us do it even when we don't intend to. Ever have a tune that you just cannot get out of your head? This is your mind at work. But it can be taken further by visualizing and mentally hearing what you want to sound like and/or accomplish on the bandstand. Expressing these ideas on the stage within a group should be one of the goals to strive for.

I remember the first year I learned all of the fingerings for the trumpet. I was nine years old. I can recall mowing the lawn and doing chores around the house, pressing imaginary valves on my thigh while I worked. My passion for learning everything I could about the trumpet had been ignited and I was on my way mentally at an early age. This continued once I began to learn to improvise. I started to map out in my mind ways of connecting chords in an effort to build harmonically cohesive solos. I still do this on a daily basis, whether I am in the mood for it or not, and this allows me to pretty much know what I want to play before I reach the microphone. However, being able to hear what you wish to play is a goal one should always work toward through endless hours of ear-training and practice.

Trumpeter's minds constantly work to solve dilemmas that confront us when we play. My former teacher, Professor Lindsey Sarjeant, who knew the great alto saxophonist Julian "Cannonball" Adderley very well, told me that Adderley often didn't take his horn out of the case when he was home from the road. Instead, he *thought* about what he wanted to play next. Of course, Adderley's situation was unusual and mental practice without a physical foundation on which to build will not produce the desired results. A natural balance between the two should be the goal.

The Importance of Sight-Reading

Sight-reading is an area of musicianship that is extremely important regardless of the level of talent. The ability to read new music while in practice and especially performance can determine the success of a musician. All of the professional musicians I have ever worked with have the ability to sight-read new music as fast as it is put in front of them. When I was in high school, we used to have contests to see who could sight-read the best without making mistakes. This sharpened my ability at a very early age and allowed me to pass every audition I ever went on.

When I got the call to join the Count Basie Orchestra, I knew that I would not have time to look at the music in advance and work out the rhythms of my part. At my first concert, I only had about five or ten minutes to look over about 150 pieces of music that were in the book. Once the concert began, I was not worried because I knew I could sight-read accurately and within the proper style. The time had truly come where my livelihood depended on this facet of my musicianship. I realize how lucky I am to have had a high school instructor who always gave us new music to read and play. However, I did not wait to get to school to sight-read new music. I used to scan the hymnals during church services before I even began to play the trumpet and read every music book I could find.

The conditions in which one may be required to play have broadened tremendously. Gone are the days when there were literally hundreds of bands one could reside in for years and years and not worry about having to play any other style. Today, a trumpeter may be called to do a television commercial, for which the music is by all accounts as straight ahead as an arrow, or to substitute in a jazz orchestra where the rhythms are incredibly diverse and have to be played in the correct style. Simply burying one's head in the music in order to play the correct rhythms is not enough and definitely not professional. Once the conductor gives the downbeat, it is expected that there will be a perfect reading and *interpretation* of the music. This is key—being able to sight-read perfectly any new music and grasp the correct feeling required by its style and/or composer/arranger.

Generally speaking, there are some basic rhythms found in most music. When I am about to play a new piece, I scan the entire part to look for the darker parts of the page. Those usually indicate multiple rhythms or faster passages with sixteenth-note and thirty-second-note rhythms and rests. Sometimes, as with Thad Jones's music, the rests are the problem! The lighter areas of the staff are usually are filled with easier rhythms such as whole notes, half notes, quarter notes, and eighth notes. The tricky places are where different rhythms are tied together across bar lines. This is when private study comes in handy.

In my experience in the world of jazz, whether I am playing the fourth trumpet part with solo fills behind a vocalist or playing the lead trumpet part and trying to swing an entire orchestra, being able to quickly read ledger lines below and above the staff is crucial. For example, when I am home in Los Angeles playing with the Luckman Jazz Orchestra or Pasadena Jazz Orchestra or doing a recording session, I never know what part I am going to play until I arrive at the gig. So I have to

At Diana Krall recording session with Rick Baptist, left, and Sal Cracchiola, right. Capitol Records, Los Angeles, 2005.

Wonderful lead trumpeter Bijon Watson of Los Angeles, CA.

All photos by author

be ready to execute my part perfectly—there are no rehearsals. This is the beauty of these orchestras and being professional because each musician is accomplished and seasoned and can play whatever part is needed on the very first take. One way to work on being able to play any chair in your orchestra is to do just that—pass the parts around. The combined level of professionalism we share is what music is all about and the results are always great.

Finally, developing sight-reading skills is, whether it is reading chord changes in a jazz setting or regular or more common rhythms in a symphony orchestra, an often-overlooked area of private study. The more you have your particular instrument covered, the easier it is to summon the much-needed confidence to jump right on any new piece of music and absolutely nail it the first time. There may not be a second.

The Importance of Studying Piano

The study of the piano is crucial to the understanding of jazz music and music in general. As Dizzy Gillespie told Miles Davis, "You must study the piano so that you can understand the

Veteran jazz trumpet soloist Nolan Shaheed of Pasadena, CA.

complete spectrum of what is possible for you to play." Instead of having only three valves and playing one note at a time on the trumpet, you can have an entire orchestra at your fingertips.

After all, most of the greatest music composed over the last several hundred years was written with the aid and the complete knowledge of the piano. Johann Sebastian Bach, Wolfgang Amadeus Mozart, Ludwig van Beethoven, Samuel Barber, John Coltrane, Charlie Parker, Dizzy, Miles, and Wayne Shorter, not to mention Billy Strayhorn, Duke Ellington, and Thelonious Monk, all used the piano to great advantage and success. When I first played with the great trumpeter Freddie Hubbard in 1990, he played the piano for most of the clinic.

When I first heard my former teacher, Professor Lindsey Sarjeant, playing solo piano and using the "walking bass" figure in his left hand, I was amazed at how he could sound like a band all by himself. I knew I had to learn that particular method of playing the piano. As fate would have it, I suffered serious dental problems as a result of an uncaring orthodontist in Atlanta, Georgia, and could not play my trumpet for nine months. I had to undergo about ten operations to rebuild areas that were damaged by the braces I had worn for over two years. I became the pianist in our college big band for a semester and developed a much more thorough understanding of the functions of harmony.

Later, I studied jazz piano directly with Marcus Roberts and with Professor Sarjeant, who is one of the best teachers, pianists, and most talented musicians in the world. He was also my first college trumpet instructor and once took out his trumpet and flawlessly played one of the difficult exercises in the Theo Charlier Étude book without any warm-up.

Each day I would go to Professor Sarjeant's office and sit down at the piano. He would show me the different ways to voice chords, beginning with the left hand only because this frees the right hand to solo and expand the chord being played with the left. The most important chords were the ii-V-I (two-five-one: D minor/G7/C major 7; A minor/D7/G Major 7) chord progression as they are the most common (albeit in different variations) in jazz standards and blues tunes. Slowly, I would teach myself to play the melodies of tunes all the while playing the corresponding chords. I began to hear with much more clarity and precision what was going on in the rest of the band while I was playing my horn with the rhythm section. This led me to transcribe the bass lines from longtime Count Basie bassist Cleveland Eaton on *Kansas City Shout* (Pablo), as well as Paul Chambers' bass lines from the John Coltrane composition "Mr. P.C." on *Giant Steps*. I could then dissect their lines to see how they connected the chords. The smoothest sound is when each chord is approached from a half-step away.

When I started to work with Marcus Roberts in 1989, I was witness to a true master musician and pianist at work. All of us in the band were amazed at how he could consistently perform at such a high level. Those of us who have had him "comp" (jazz terminology for accompany) behind us while we soloed, have experienced his genius-level ability to quickly adjust to whatever we chose to play which makes the end result harmonically and rhythmically correct. He also told me that if I really wanted to learn how to hear almost anything so that my reflexes would be lightning fast, I should learn some Thelonious Monk piano solos by ear! I thought this was impossible to do, since Monk has a very advanced harmonic knowledge and mastery, not to mention a most difficult technique. However, I somehow managed to learn his introduction to the compositions "Memories of You" and "Just You, Just Me," both from the recording *Standards*. Just this little bit of learning Monk's piano solos transformed my musicianship. I was forever hooked on the piano and can barely walk by one today without sitting down to play. I was just as ecstatic when my new piano arrived at my house, as I was when my mother brought home my first trumpet when I was nine. Using piano is an indispensable part of teaching jazz.

During my early development as a jazz musician, I learned more about harmony and rhythm from Thelonious Monk and Louis Armstrong than from anyone else. From Louis I learned from what he played as well as what he did not play! The space that he left in his perfect solos shouted out to me what was just waiting to be discovered. Henry "Red" Allen, Roy Eldridge, and especially Dizzy Gillespie understood and discovered this all too well. With Monk, after I learned his solos, I wrote them out and studied them closely, and I am forever in awe at his genius. So, with all of this said, find a piano and begin to discover its infinite wonders, and I guarantee you will begin to notice a marked improvement in your overall musicianship.

All photos by author

Piano great Marcus Roberts. New Orleans, 1989.

PART IV
THE CODA
Biographies and Reference

Influential Trumpeters of the Jazz Age (1924–1936)

As described in the previous chapter, Louis Armstrong stands alone in the history of jazz trumpet. He defined an era beginning circa 1924, after he left King Oliver and joined Fletcher Henderson in New York. This period of the 1920s was dubbed the "Jazz Age" by F. Scott Fitzgerald, and it may as well have been called the Armstrong Age.

After Armstrong, there were several other trumpeters who were important from the early 1920s roughly up to the start of the swing era in 1936. Some, like Fletcher Henderson orchestra member Joe Smith, were considered to be the finest in New York until Armstrong arrived and set them all on fire. Leon "Bix" Beiderbeck rose to prominence with the Paul Whiteman orchestra and through his work with Frankie Trumbauer. Bix was an indispensable part of the Jazz Age; he left some 200 recordings and was immortalized in the motion picture *Young Man with a Horn*. There was also the incredible Jabbo Smith, who from my listening and research was the only true rival to Louis Armstrong in terms of technique. Jabbo Smith was so good that Duke Ellington offered him a job. Smith knew how good he was too, and literally laughed at Duke!

This section highlights the trumpeters listed above and several others who deserve special attention. It must remain clear, however, that they are important *after* Louis Armstrong. Whereas they may have added one or two specific things to the lineage of the instrument (Beiderbeck, harmony; Jabbo Smith, speed and dexterity, for example), Armstrong added that and much more and simply was strong in all areas. Therefore he was unique, continually setting precedents for the art.

Henry "Red" Allen (1908–1967)

Henry "Red" Allen Jr. was the son of Henry Allen, leader of the Allen Brass Band of Algiers, Louisiana, with which the legendary Buddy Bolden played his last gig, a parade in the streets of New Orleans in 1907. As a teenager, "Red" played in his father's band, with George Lewis, with the Excelsior Band, and with the Sam Morgan Band. In 1926 he left New Orleans to play with Sidney Desvigne's Southern Syncopaters on the riverboat *Island Queen*, which ran between St. Louis and Cincinnati. In 1927 he joined King Oliver's Dixie Syncopators while they were on tour in St. Louis. When the Oliver band broke up in New York, Allen made his first recordings there with Clarence Williams. After being offered a Victor recording contract and jobs by both Duke

Ellington and Luis Russell, he returned to New York. He made several recordings under his own name in 1929 for Victor, then joined Luis Russell and his orchestra. In 1933, he joined the Fletcher Henderson Orchestra, replacing Rex Stewart as the group's featured soloist. During this period Allen made several popular recordings with Coleman Hawkins, on which Allen sang and played trumpet. Allen's style was a foretaste of modern jazz, as is clear from his amazing solo on a 1934 recording of *Body and Soul*, which places him as perhaps the first precursor to Roy Eldridge and Dizzy Gillespie. In 1937, he rejoined Luis Russell's band, which was then fronted by Louis Armstrong. Allen stayed with them until 1940, when he began leading small groups in New York nightclubs and played on records by Jelly Roll Morton and Sidney Bechet. He continued to record his own albums as well as to tour with Billie Holiday and others throughout the 1940s. In the 1950s and 1960s, Allen continued an active career, recording with his old friends George Lewis and Coleman Hawkins, and with Kid Ory. He continued playing up until his death in 1967 from pancreatic cancer.

Leon "Bix" Beiderbeck (1903–1931)

Bix Beiderbeck's short career, spanning less than ten years, still established him as one of the most influential trumpeters and musicians jazz has produced. Born in Davenport, Iowa, he began picking out tunes on the family piano by the time he was four and astonished his parents by reproducing classical piano works before he had ever had a formal lesson. When he was fifteen, he heard a recording of "Tiger Rag" by the Original Dixieland Jazz Band, featuring cornetist Nic LaRocca. Beiderbeck was fascinated with this new music called jazz and bought a cornet immediately.

Bix Beiderbeck.

In 1921, Beiderbeck attended the Lake Forest Military Academy, about thirty-five miles from Chicago, which was becoming the center of the jazz world. Chicago was where Joseph "King" Oliver, the great cornetist and teacher of Louis Armstrong, was working. Oliver sent for Armstrong to join him a year later, and Beiderbeck would venture regularly to hear these two giants of jazz play on Chicago's South Side. Armstrong recalled in his memoirs when he heard Beiderbeck play, and was quoted as saying, "Ain't none of them play like him yet."

One of Beiderbeck's first important professional associations was with the band called the Wolverines, which based its concept on the very influential New Orleans Rhythm Kings. In February 1924, he made his recording debut with the Wolverines, and it was apparent that a new and unique cornetist was claiming his place in the lineage that had begun a few decades earlier with Buddy Bolden. Beiderbeck played sweetly and with an interesting harmonic awareness on the cornet shown by few other than Armstrong. Later that year, the Wolverines traveled to New York, as their reputation had spread, and Beiderbeck was their main soloist. They made a recording there, "Big Boy," which features Beiderbeck taking a solo on cornet and piano—one of the first in jazz history.

The recordings with the Wolverines made Beiderbeck somewhat of a legend, and he was soon offered a job with the prestigious Jean Goldkette dance orchestra. He promptly accepted and prepared Jimmy McPartland as his successor with the Wolverines. A problem arose with Goldkette, however, because his band was not a spontaneous kind of group like the Wolverines, but rather an ensemble that required strong sight-reading skills, which Beiderbeck did not possess at that time. As a result, he was let go and promised that once he improved his sight-reading abilities, he would be rehired (this did happen, in 1926). Beiderbeck recorded "Davenport Blues" with Tommy Dorsey in 1925, freelanced in the Midwest as well as in New York, and eventually began working with saxophonist Frankie Trumbauer in St. Louis. His association with Trumbauer would turn out to be one of his best connections.

In 1927, Beiderbeck and Trumbauer recorded "Singin' the Blues," which features Beiderbeck's most famous cornet solo. It is bouncy and very melodic, and fit perfectly within the sound of the group. This solo was immensely popular, and other cornetists began to copy it note for note, including Bobby Hackett, who, along with trum-

peter Freddie Webster, was an important influence on Miles Davis. Beiderbeck also began to compose piano pieces influenced by Debussy and Ravel, including the famous "In a Mist." This clearly showed Beiderbeck's talent including all of his experiences in creating his music.

After the Goldkette orchestra disbanded, Beiderbeck joined the Paul Whiteman Orchestra, then considered the most prestigious by the public. Whiteman was erroneously given the title "King of Jazz," which could not have been further from the truth. However, his group consisted of wonderful musicians who were making top dollar and performing a mixture of light jazz pieces augmented by renditions of Gershwin's Concerto in F. Flat-out intense improvisations were not the aim of this orchestra; however Beiderbeck is featured prominently on many recordings with Whiteman, such as "San," "You Took Advantage of Me," and especially "Sweet Sue."

Beiderbeck could have used the Whiteman recordings and his own fame to achieve still greater artistic and commercial success, but he had begun to have a problem with excessive drinking. By late 1928 and into 1929, struggling with the drinking and with the extremely busy schedule with Whiteman, Beiderbeck was unable to fulfill his performing obligations. He collapsed during a recording session on September 13, 1929, and was sent home to Davenport. He recovered briefly, but was never able to fully regain his strength. He had to check into a hospital on more than one occasion due to the effects of severe alcoholism. He eventually contracted pneumonia and died on August 6, 1931. After his death, his legend began to take on nearly mythic proportions.

Bix Beiderbeck was an indispensable part of the era that literally defined jazz and its possibilities. He added to the lineage of jazz trumpet a unique concept of sound and harmonic awareness that was a result of his innate talents and his being influenced by Nic LaRocca, King Oliver, and Louis Armstrong. Beiderbeck was the inspiration for the Hoagy Carmichael classic composition "Stardust" and for the motion picture *Young Man with a Horn*.

Henry Busse (1894–1955)

Born in Magdeburg, Germany, Henry Busse rose to prominence by cofounding the famous Paul Whiteman Orchestra around 1918. By 1924, he was one of the most popular cornetists on Whiteman's touring circuit. He played with the orchestra for ten years and was one of its most famous soloists; he took wonderful solos on the tunes "When Day Is Gone" and "Hot Lips," which can be found on Whiteman's recordings from the early 1920s.

Bill Coleman (1904–1981)

Bill Coleman was born in Paris, Kentucky, but ended up spending the majority of his adult life in Paris, France. He was of the generation of great trumpeters such as Louis Armstrong (by whom he was greatly influenced). Coleman spent some time in New York City playing with Mary Lou Williams, Andy Kirk, Sy Oliver, and Billy Kyle. By 1933 he had moved to Paris, France, where other great jazz musicians were making their living, among them Coleman Hawkins and Benny Carter.

Coleman worked and recorded with jazz-gypsy guitarist Django Rheinhardt and violinist Stephane Grapelli, and toured throughout Europe, Asia, and Africa. He did return to the United States on special occasions when working with Thomas "Fats" Waller (piano), Benny Carter (alto saxophone), and Teddy Wilson (piano). He continued playing in Paris for the rest of his life. He died in 1981 in Toulouse, France.

Lee Collins (1901–1960)

Collins got his early start in professional music by playing in brass bands in New Orleans as a teenager. He was seen as a direct descendent of famous New Orleans jazz pioneers Buddy Bolden and Bunk Johnson. Collins's big breakthrough came in 1924 when he moved to Chicago to replace Louis Armstrong (who had left for Fletcher Henderson's orchestra) in King Oliver's Creole Jazz Band. He even had the same teacher as Armstrong, Peter Davis. Besides his performances with King Oliver, Collins made an important recording as a sideman in Jelly Roll Morton's Kings of Jazz. Morton and Collins were great friends until Morton claimed that Collins stole his tune "Fish Tail Blues."

In 1930, Collins moved to New York City, where he played in Luis Russell's Orchestra for only six months before heading back to Chicago. He stayed there for a year and then went home to New Orleans, where he performed with many blues singers like Lil Johnson and Chippie Hill. Collins had one last burst of popularity in the 1940s when the Dixieland revival occurred.

Sidney DeParis (1905–1967)

Sidney DeParis was born in Crawfordsville, Indiana, in 1905. According to my research and a recording of him with McKinney's Cotton Pickers from 1929 to 1930, he was one of the first trumpeters to use the shake or lip trill within a big band context. This facet of jazz trumpet is now standard practice in big bands and helped to define the sound of the Count Basie Orchestra, among others. DeParis was equally at home playing swing trumpet and New Orleans-style trumpet and was also an expert with many different trumpet mutes. Some of his earliest work was with Charlie Johnson's Paradise Ten, from 1926 to 1931. He moved on to work with Don Redman from 1932 to 1936, returning briefly in 1939. He worked also with Jelly Roll Morton, Sidney Bechet, Art Hodes, and Benny Carter, and recorded the famous Panassie sessions with Sidney Bechet (1938–1939). In the 1940s, he recorded with Blue Note and Commodore. DeParis remained active through the 1950s and worked with his brother, Wilbur DeParis, in his New Orleans Jazz Band. Health issues forced him to retire in the 1960s. DeParis passed away in 1967 while living in New York City.

Natty Dominique (1896–1981)

Natty Dominique studied cornet with Manuel Perez, one of the first five or six important jazz trumpeters in history, and played in Perez's Imperial Band. In 1913, Dominique left New Orleans and played in various bands in Detroit and Chicago. He recorded with Jelly Roll Morton in 1923 and played with Carroll Dickerson's Orchestra, where he was second trumpet to Louis Armstrong. Dominique also recorded with pioneering clarinetists Johnny Dodds and Jimmie Noone, but he is best remembered for his association with Dodds, as they recorded together frequently. In 1940, Dominique's heart condition forced him to retire from jazz, and he went to work as an airport porter. In the early 1950s he started playing again on a part-time basis and released a couple of albums on Bill Russell's American Music label.

Johnny Dunn (1897–1937)

Before Louis Armstrong left Chicago to join Fletcher Henderson's Orchestra in 1924, Johnny Dunn was considered the king of New York's jazz trumpet players. Dunn was discovered in Memphis by W. C. Handy in 1916 and worked for him until he left in 1920 to take over Blues singer Mamie Smith's Jazz Hounds. Dunn then formed his own band, the Original Jazz Hounds, featuring singer Edith Wilson (who later became famous as Aunt Jemima in pancake mix commercials), whom he had met while playing in the Plantation Revue on Broadway.

The show was a great success and even played in London. Upon returning to America, Dunn left the revue and joined Fletcher Henderson's Orchestra. He was always heavily involved in Broadway-style musical productions and played in other shows built around singer Florence Mills.

In 1928, back in New York, Dunn led some memorable sessions with giants of 1920s jazz piano Willie "the Lion" Smith, Fats Waller, and Jelly Roll Morton. Dunn returned to Europe with the Noble Sissle Orchestra and moved to the Netherlands and then Denmark for several years. He died of tuberculosis in Paris in 1937.

Nat Gonella (1908–1998)

I first became aware of Nat Gonella by reading somewhere that he was Britain's answer to Louis Armstrong. This intrigued me immediately and is one heck of a weight to put on anyone's shoulders, but after listening to his work, I know that Gonella truly was the most important jazz trumpeter from England. He came along at a time when jazz was just beginning to become popular in England and other parts of Europe, thanks to Armstrong. His influence on Gonella is obvious; Gonella's recordings from the 1930s show a fire and confidence that definitely was not lost on British trumpeters who came after him, such as the great Humphrey Lyttleton and Kenny Baker. It is also interesting to compare Gonella's version of the song "Jubilee" (on *Nat Gonella and His Georgians*) to that of Armstrong.

Gonella was so popular that he was almost like a professional free agent during the early and mid-

1930s, when all dance bands wanted his services. He also made a great recording of "Georgia on My Mind" that endeared him to an even larger audience and helped him become a major star. He went into the military in 1941 and did not return to his former eminence thereafter. After a long layoff, he came back in the mid-1970s and made some records, but eventually quit playing due to health problems. He lived to the age of ninety and was a national treasure until the end. His legacy is still evident among younger British trumpeters today, including Guy Barker.

Jimmy McPartland (1907–1991)

Another wonderful trumpeter inspired by Louis Armstrong and Bix Beiderbeck, Jimmy McPartland was an original member of the Austin High Gang, a group of high school kids transformed by listening to the music of King Oliver and Louis Armstrong in the mid-1920s in Chicago. McPartland played with the Wolverines, replacing Bix Beiderbeck, and was one of the most important trumpeters after Louis Armstrong, King Oliver, Beiderbeck, and even to an extent Jabbo Smith and Reuben "River" Reeves in Chicago during the Jazz Age. After making a very important record with the McKenzie-Condon Chicagoans, McPartland became an important soloist with Ben Pollack's band, beginning in 1927. This lasted a couple of years, after which he worked in pit orchestras and led his own bands wherever he could during the Great Depression.

McPartland was in the U.S. Army when they landed on the beach at Normandy on D Day. Shortly thereafter, he met a lovely young pianist by the name of Marian Turner, who became his wife and host of NPR's *Piano Jazz* with Marian McPartland. Dividing his time between New York

and Chicago for a few decades, he continued performing good Dixieland jazz until about a year or so before his death.

Bubber Miley (1903–1932)

Bubber Miley is one of the most celebrated and important trumpeters, due to his perfecting the technique of using the plunger mute. Before joining Duke Ellington's band, Miley performed with Willie Gant, Mamie Smith, and Elmer Snowden's Washingtonians, which Ellington took over shortly afterward. Miley is considered Ellington's most impressive early soloist, noted for having begun the practice of using the plunger in conjunction with a straight or pixie mute. The resulting growl effect was adopted by Sidney DeParis, Cootie Williams (Miley's replacement when he left Ellington), Ray Nance, and others. Miley was influenced by King Oliver and Johnny Dunn and also collaborated with Ellington on many early compositions.

Ernest "Punch" Miller (1894–1971)

Punch Miller was a New Orleans legend. Oral interviews he did, now in the Hogan Jazz Archives at Tulane University, are extremely valuable and revealing. Miller played cornet and also with army bands during his stint in the military. He toured with a vaudeville revue before moving to Chicago in 1926, where he played with Al Wynn, Tiny Parham, Freddie Keppard, and Jelly Roll Morton. He was the subject of the documentary film *New Orleans: 'Til the Butcher Cuts Him Down* (1971) and is best remembered for his fast fingering and blues style.

Phil Napolean (1901–1990)

Phil Napolean was one of the most in-demand trumpeters of the 1920s. He was best known as the founder and leader of the Original Memphis Five, which made over one hundred recordings in 1922–1923, and was one of the groups that helped merge jazz with the popular mainstream music of the day. Napolean also recorded with blues singers Alberta Hunter and Leon Williams as well as with the Cotton Pickers and the Charleston Chasers. In the early 1930s, he concentrated on playing with a radio orchestra for RCA. He took some time off and then from 1949 to 1956 led an excellent Dixieland group at Nick's in New York. He made some final recordings for Capitol in 1959, and in 1966 he opened Phil Napolean's Retreat near Miami. He continued to play Dixieland jazz into the 1980s.

Dave Nelson (1905–1946)

Nelson was a protégé and nephew of King Oliver. His first professional work was with the Marie Lucas Orchestra at Lincoln Gardens, and he eventually played with Ma Rainey, Jelly Roll Morton, Edgar Hayes, Jimmie Noone, and Luis Russell. Nelson joined Oliver's band in 1929 and arranged many of the titles recorded in 1930. Through the influence of Oliver, he developed a creative use of muting. Nelson had a big and brassy trumpet tone and was often mistaken Oliver for on recordings that they made together.

Frankie Newton (1906–1954)

Frankie Newton is one of the unsung heroes from the late 1920s and 1930s. He toured the West with drummer Lloyd Scott, then settled in New York. There he worked with Cecil Scott, Chick Webb, Elmer Snowden, Charlie Johnson, Garland Wilson, and Sam Wooding and made famous recordings with blues singer Bessie Smith in the 1930s. In the 1940s he performed with his own groups at Café Society and Kelly's Stable. Newton was an inventive improviser who often used the buzz mute for contrast. He was also an avid painter.

Joe "Wooden" Nicholas (1883–1957)

Nicholas took up cornet and played with King Oliver in 1915. Buddy Bolden and Bunk Johnson were major influences on his style. Nicholas formed the Camelia Band in 1918. His nickname reflects his power and stamina.

Red Nichols (1905–1965)

Similar to Bix Beiderbeck in terms of his approach to rhythm, Red Nichols was a very popular cornetist during the 1920s. Perhaps his most important association was with his group, the Five Pennies. Originally from Utah, he moved to New York in the early 1920s and began working with Sam Lanin and various other orchestras led by the likes of Ross Gorman and Vincent Lopez. Nichols also played briefly with the Paul Whiteman Orchestra, and Beiderbeck was his replacement.

In 1927, the Five Pennies had the biggest hit of Nichols's career, "Ida, Sweet as Apple Cider," which kept him at the top of the sales charts for quite some time. This helped to cement his legend as one of the most popular trumpeters of the decade after Louis Armstrong and Beiderbeck. Some of his sidemen were legends themselves: Benny Goodman, Jack Teagarden, and Glenn Miller, to name a few. Nichols spent considerable time in the studios beginning in the early 1930s and took time off in the mid-'40s to work a day job as a laborer. He was rediscovered on a TV show (*This Is Your Life*) in the late 1950s, and a movie about his remarkable life was made, *The Five Pennies* (1959).

Reuben "River" Reeves (1905–1975)

I read about Reuben "River" Reeves in a book on Chicago jazz that describes his colorful, exciting, wild playing and brief career. That sent me on a hunt for his recordings. They are completely out of print, and I am still waiting to hear this obviously great trumpeter.

Returning to Chicago after studying dentistry in New York, Reeves played in Erskine Tate's orchestra while earning a master's degree from the American Conservatory. In an attempt to counter other record labels' commercial success with other trumpeters, Vocalion signed Reeves to a recording contract, and he recorded 15 selections with the Reuben Reeves River Boys in 1929. He played with Cab Calloway in an army infantry band during World War II, but performed only part-time after that.

Kid Rena (1898–1949)

Kid Rena was highly regarded in New Orleans for his wide range and strong tone. He was also a resident at the Colored Waifs' Home at the same time as Louis Armstrong. When Armstrong left Kid Ory's band, it was Rena who replaced him. Kid Rena stayed primarily in New Orleans, playing with the Tuxedo Brass Band, and led the Pacific Brass Band. He remained active until poor health forced him to retire in 1947.

Jabbo Smith (1908–1991)

Of all of the trumpet players to emerge in the 1920s, Jabbo Smith was the best equipped to challenge Louis Armstrong for supremacy on the instrument. Smith was electrifying and had an incredibly advanced technique that is evident on his introduction to the composition "Jazz Battle" (1929). His colorful and exciting style allowed him to play any which way he wanted. Clark Terry told me that in the 1920s, Smith was already playing with the speed and harmonic dexterity that would be prevalent with Dizzy Gillespie in the 1940s. When most players were playing eighth notes and sticking close to the melody, Smith was

Jabbo Smith.

Photo courtesy of Lorraine Gordon

playing sixteenth- and thirty-second-note rhythms with advanced ideas. No one else other than Louis Armstrong could compete with Jabbo Smith in the 1920s. Smith was a star soloist for Charlie Johnson's Paradise Ten and worked with Eva Taylor, Carroll Dickerson, Sammy Stewart, Earl Hines, Erskine Tate, Charles Elgar, and Tiny Parham. He was so confident in his abilities that when Duke Ellington offered him a job, he literally laughed in Duke's face! Smith played complex ideas way ahead of his time and reached the peak of his career at age 20. Depression and hard drinking led to his decline and he went to work for Avis Rent-a-Car in Milwaukee for many years. Lorraine Gordon, the owner of the Village Vanguard, helped to revive his career in the 1980s with Broadway work in the musical *One Mo' Time*. She also provided the photo of Smith used for this book. Jabbo Smith deserves to be held in high esteem along with all of the other great trumpet soloists from the 1920s and throughout the entire history of jazz.

Francis Joseph "Muggsy" Spanier (1901–1967)

Muggsy Spanier grew up in an orphanage after his parents separated. He studied cornet with players from the Chicago Opera and the Chicago Symphony Orchestra. He had wanted to be a baseball player, and his nickname comes from the Giants manager, Muggsy McGraw. Muggsy began playing cornet professionally with Elmer Schoebel's band in 1921, was inspired by King Oliver's Creole Jazz Band, and recorded with the Bucktown Five, Stomp Six, Charlie Pierce, the Chicago Rhythm Kings, the Jungle Kings, and Ted Lewis's orchestra. His own Ragtime Band contributed substantially to the New Orleans revival of the 1940s. Spanier also played with Sidney Bechet, Bob Crosby, Vernon Brown, Irving Fazola, Art Hodes, PeeWee Russell, and Miff Mole. He had a nice middle register style that was unusual for his generation. He can be seen on the Ralph Gleason Jazz DVD series entitled *Jazz Casual*. In Spanier's segment, he shows and discusses the mute that he got from King Oliver.

Bobby Stark (1906–1945)

Bobby Stark was one of the most important trumpeters of the Jazz Age. He played with Chick Webb, Fletcher Henderson, Elmer Snowden, Charlie Turner, Ella Fitzgerald, Garvin Bushell, and Benny Morton. His style was similar to that of Jabbo Smith. Stark recorded great solos with Henderson in the late 1920s and early 1930s, including a memorable one on "King Porter Stomp," which was Henderson's first head arrangement, a composition is not written down.

Stark's phrasing was also later influenced by Roy Eldridge.

Rex Stewart (1907–1967)

Stewart's claim to fame was his replacing Louis Armstrong after Armstrong left Fletcher Henderson's orchestra in the mid-1920s. Stewart was one of the few very distinct stylists in all of jazz; he also perfected the half-valve technique and developed it to a higher level than nearly any other trumpeter. He worked as a multi-instrumentalist in various New York groups, playing piano, horn, trombone, saxophone, and cornet. His primary cornet work was with Elmer Snowden and Fletcher Henderson. Stewart personified the forceful but good-humored style heavily influenced by Louis Armstrong, Jabbo Smith, and Ellington's Bubber Miley. Perhaps his longest association was with Duke Ellington for eleven years, in which he co-composed several charts. Also, Stewart wrote a very important book, *Jazz Masters of the 1930s* (Da Capo Press, 1972). This book gives wonderful insight into Stewart's deep intellect and reveals his fondness for the English language.

Thomas "Kid" Valentine (1896–1987)

Valentine, born in New Orleans, joined the Pickwick Brass Band at age fourteen and at age eighteen formed a band with clarinetist Edmond Hall, who would later join Louis Armstrong. Valentine also led his own band in New Orleans in the 1930s, '40s, and '50s. He began working at Preservation Hall when it opened in 1961. His style of play was very rhythmic; he used a variety of mutes and with his wide vibrato could play wonderfully melodic lead trumpet.

Arthur "Artie" Whetsol (1905–1940)

Whetsol was one of the first trumpeters in jazz known for a smooth and almost "cool" style of play. He was a childhood friend of Duke Ellington and went with him to New York to join Elmer Snowden's Washingtonians in 1923. Whetsol took a break from the group to obtain his medical degree from Howard University and then returned in 1928 to join the group, which had since become the Duke Ellington Orchestra. However, while Whetsol was away, Ellington replaced him with another outstanding trumpeter, Bubber Miley. With Whetsol's return, the orchestra had two very distinct stylists whose manner of play worked well in contrast that made for an always interesting sound—Miley with the plunger and Whetsol with the lovely open horn or with a cup mute. Whetsol played the melodic trumpet lead on Ellington's first major hit, "Mood Indigo," in 1930. This made Whetsol famous and prompted many other band leaders to look for their own versions of him. When Whetsol had to leave the orchestra for health reasons, Ellington eventually found a suitable replacement, Harold "Shorty" Baker, whose style was directly influenced by Artie Whetsol's work.

Influential Trumpeters of the Swing Era (1936–1944)

2

The swing era produced many wonderful trumpeters, and choosing which to emphasize was a bit difficult. I considered the more influential players who came after the swing era, such as Dizzy Gillespie, Miles Davis, Chet Baker, and Clark Terry, and who were their direct and indirect influences and why. This quickly narrowed the list down to at least thirty, still too many to include here. So this section focuses on those who have distinctly different personal styles.

The vocabulary of jazz trumpet during the swing era—the actual phrasing and overall sound/conception—had a wider range than that of the previous Jazz Age. Players took more chances after Louis Armstrong, Bix Beiderbeck, Henry "Red" Allen, and Jabbo Smith in particular showed them the way. Each trumpeter seems to have been equipped with a wider variety of rhythmic and harmonic devices to use under different musical circumstances. Swing era trumpeters had a smoother delivery of rhythm, compared to the short and staccato rhythms and phrases used by the majority of the trumpeters of the 1920s and early 1930s, largely because players in the swing era were further removed from the influence of the military bands that permeated much of the sound and concept of earlier jazz.

That influence began to fade with the emergence of King Oliver, and even more with Louis Armstrong's emergence as a star soloist with Fletcher Henderson in 1924–1925. Players from the swing era began to play a little more behind the beat rather than right on top of it like the earlier trumpeters did. And the roles of the bass, piano, and especially the drums shifted after they heard Armstrong with Fletcher Henderson. Armstrong was so powerful in his solos that arrangers such as Don Redman, Benny Carter, and eventually Duke Ellington began to write arrangements for their orchestras based on the rhythms he was playing. As a direct result, the rhythm section became freer to interpret rhythms and harmony.

Much can be learned from studying the work of swing era trumpeters because they really prepared the way for the emergence of pioneering modern trumpeters like Dizzy Gillespie, Clifford Brown, Miles Davis, and others. Since the swing era only officially lasted about six or seven years, the great soloists of that era tend to be easily overlooked. The names of men like Buck Clayton, Billy Butterfield, Harry James, Harry "Sweets" Edison, Bunny Berigan, and especially Charlie Shavers are familiar to any serious jazz musician, but not to the average listener. The sole exception is that of Roy Eldridge. I hope that now we can add the following names to the discussion about this most important period of jazz.

Kenny Baker (1921–1999)

Kenny Baker could play the living hell out of the trumpet, according to Humphrey Lyttleton, who along with Baker was a major part of the British jazz scene for many decades beginning in the 1940s. Baker was one of the best soloists in any style and influenced a couple of generations of trumpeters with his unmistakable reverence for the work of Louis Armstrong, Harry James, and even Charlie Shavers.

Baker's career was highlighted by his work with the very popular Ted Heath orchestra for five years beginning in 1944. Perhaps his most famous solo is on the tune "Bakerloo Non-Stop," which features him in a drums and trumpet duet as well as with the rest of the trumpet section. One of my personal favorite Baker solos is on the tune "1-2-3-4 Jump" from the disc *Kenny Baker: Birth of a Legend 1941–46.* He demonstrates his impressive range and accuracy as well as his fresh improvisations that hint at his appreciation for the work of swinging trumpeter Buck Clayton.

Baker was a very busy studio musician during the 1960s and also provided music for a television show, *The Beiderbecke Affair,* during the 1980s. He continued to record up through the 1990s. He is a legend in Britain and deserves more attention here in the United States.

Bunny Berigan (1908–1942)

Bunny Berigan was one of the great stars during the swing era. His playing mirrored his personality, described as gregarious and full of life. Berigan is mostly associated with the compo-

Bunny Berigan.

Photo courtesy of Jack Bradley

sition "I Can't Get Started," which was a major hit in 1937 and was copied by many trumpeters over the years. Arvell Shaw, the late bassist for Louis Armstrong, told me that Armstrong would turn down requests to play this song, saying, "That there belongs to Bunny Berigan."

Rowland Bernard "Bunny" Berigan was born in Hilbert, Wisconsin, and, according to author and critic Scott Yanow, played with college bands, although he never went to college. Around 1930, he was hired to play with Hal Kemp's band and impressed everyone immediately with his control over the instrument and his ability to improvise "hot" solos. From 1931 to 1936, he played mainly in the studios in New York, but also briefly with Paul Whiteman. Another person in those studios of the early '30s was clarinetist Benny Goodman. Goodman formed his band in 1934, and Berigan joined it the following year. This collaboration would soon make Berigan a household name. He soloed wonderfully on Benny Goodman's hit "King Porter Stomp." A nationwide craze was about to begin as a result of one of their performances in Los Angeles's Palomar Ballroom. The version of "King Porter Stomp" they played happened to be broadcast live on the radio, and overnight the swing era was "officially" launched, at least with the public. Everyone wanted to dance and swing to the music of Berigan, Goodman, and of course, Basie, Ellington, and Lunceford, who were already on the scene.

Drinking excessively led to Berigan's decline. He tried to lead his own big band, but it only lasted for about three years. He briefly went back to the band of Tommy Dorsey, but eventually the alcohol overtook him. He passed away in 1942 at the very young age of thirty-three. He was one of a kind, and of course, I recommend everything with his name on it.

Billy Butterfield (1917–1988)

Billy Butterfield was one of the most lyrically powerful trumpeters in jazz. He had a huge sound and a happy disposition that is easily felt when listening to his music. On the reissued CDs that are easily found today, his big sound is often augmented by his use of the all-important plunger.

Born in Middleton, Ohio, Butterfield played several instruments before finally settling on the trumpet. He also studied medicine, but the lure of jazz proved irresistible. Butterfield played in Bob Crosby's band, which was known for a strong New Orleans jazz sound, for four years starting in 1936. With them he made one of the most important recordings in his career, the first version of what later became known as "What's New?" He also played with Artie Shaw, Benny Goodman, and Les Brown. It was in Goodman's band, I believe, that he learned plunger techniques directly from the plunger master himself, Cootie Williams.

Butterfield served in the military during World War II. Afterward, he began to make a lot of recordings in the studio. From 1968 to 1973, he worked with a group calling themselves the World's Greatest Jazz Band and appeared at many jazz festivals. In the 1970s he worked with Joe "Flip" Phillips and toured extensively, usually as a soloist. Butterfield was one of the best of any style.

Buck Clayton (1911–1991)

One of the most beautiful sounds a trumpet can make is when it is played with a cup mute. This is a mute typically made of a soft wood with cork around it that fits snugly into the bell. Of all the trumpeters in jazz history, Buck Clayton best exemplifies the sound of the cup mute. He was a consistently swinging and melodically inventive musician, of whom serious formal study is long overdue.

Born in Parsons, Kansas, Wilbur "Buck" Clayton was raised in a religious and musical household, as his father was a minister. Clayton was able to experiment with several of the instruments kept in storage between church music group rehearsals. He played piano for most of his childhood and switched to trumpet at age eighteen. This is amazing considering his long career and the ease of his executions. Even more impressively, he was self-taught.

Buck Clayton.

Photo courtesy of Doug Lawrence

One of Clayton's earliest important professional jobs was a trip to China in 1934–1935 with his band, originally the band of Earl Dancer. Back in the United States that year, Clayton found himself in Kansas City at the precise time when another powerful trumpeter, Oran "Hot Lips" Page, had left the Count Basie Orchestra. Clayton replaced Page at a perfect time, because Basie was on his way to New York and would soon be the toast of the town. It was great exposure for Clayton and introduced him to a wider audience that included musicians who loved his way of soloing. He remained with Basie for eight years.

Clayton's style remained virtually unchanged, which is an indication of how firmly he was in control. He knew what he wanted to sound like and he proceeded to play that way. His sound is marked by a very sure attack, much like the work of trumpeter Blue Mitchell (who undoubtedly listened to Clayton), as well as a soulful feel for the blues, but he never forgets how to project different moods. Clayton became one of Basie's star soloists and took the first solos on the classic "One O'Clock Jump." He made every note count. Some of his other solos with Basie were on "Jumpin' at the Woodside" and "Swingin' the Blues."

As Clayton's fame and reputation spread, he was soon recording with Billie Holiday, Teddy Wilson, and others. He was also a wonderful composer and arranger and contributed such classics as "Red Bank Boogie" and "Avenue C." One night, Clayton loaned one of his mutes to an up-and-coming trumpeter in New York. This man was working in a club across the street from where Clayton was working and realized that he needed a mute. He went over and asked to borrow Clayton's Harmon mute. Clayton readily agreed to let him use it, and that type of mute became part of this trumpeter's style. His name was Miles Davis.

Although Clayton, like Louis Armstrong, was primarily a swing era trumpeter, he did not let the innovations of the beboppers pass him by. His famous jam session records for Columbia allowed him to learn from the modern players but also to teach them that melodic simplicity was still the essence of what constitutes a great solo. These albums led to his inclusion in the Jazz at the Philharmonic tours and also to many other recordings in the 1950s and 1960s.

During the 1960s, Clayton traveled and recorded extensively. He appeared briefly in the movie *The Benny Goodman Story* and in reunion concerts with Basie. He soloed with great maturity and sophistication, and I am sure that he was the kind of person who always said the perfect thing at the perfect time—just like in his solos.

Harry "Sweets" Edison (1915–2000)

Harry "Sweets" Edison had a trumpet sound that was deeply rooted in the blues as well as the subtle and intense fire of saxophonist Lester Young. It was Young who gave Edison the nickname "Sweets" while they were both in Count Basie's band in the late 1930s.

Born in Columbus, Ohio, Edison began to play the trumpet around the age of twelve, and he landed one of his first jobs with the Jeter-Pillars orchestra in Cleveland. He moved to the great trumpet town of St. Louis and remained there for a couple of years before moving to New York in 1937. In New York, Edison joined the orchestra of Lucky Millinder. Several months later, he made a move that would change his career forever.

The great Count Basie had made it to New York from Kansas City under the care of John Hammond. Edison joined the Count Basie

Orchestra in mid- to late 1937, and soon became one of its most important soloists. His way of soloing, including fanning the derby or metal hat that is used to cover the end of the horn and vary the sounds produced, created a stir among all who heard him.

After leaving Basie for the first of a few sabbaticals in the early 1950s, Edison was in demand as a sideman and toured with Jazz at the Philharmonic on occasion. He moved to Los Angeles in the mid-1950s and lived there until a year or so before his death. Once in Los Angeles, he became one of the most in-demand jazz trumpeter for studio/recording dates. He also began to make recordings with vocalist Frank Sinatra, which brought him even more worldwide acclaim. The Sinatra and Edison vocalist-instrumental collaboration was legendary. Edison's light but definite fills were the perfect complement for Sinatra's phrasing. In 1994 when I worked Sinatra, my parts had "Sweets" on them; fortunately I had studied Edison's techniques and knew how to play behind Sinatra.

Sweets Edison recorded what I consider to be one of the top improvised trumpet solos in jazz history: "Did You Call Her Today?" from the album *Ben and Sweets*. Edison led his own group and even rejoined Basie for a short while in the mid-1960s. In the 1970s, he continued to tour the world and make significant recordings with most of the jazz masters including Count Basie, Oscar Peterson, Eddie "Lockjaw" Davis, and Benny Carter. He also became the musical director for the late comedian Redd Foxx's Las Vegas act. That period was one of Edison's greatest; his recordings showcase his unique style that was ever growing in originality.

Roy Eldridge (1911–1989)

Of all the trumpeters to emerge in the swing era, none had more bravura and influence on other players than Roy "Little Jazz" Eldridge. He had a "bandstand" attitude of complete reckless abandon. His technical command of the trumpet included a range that seemed to go higher and higher, and he believed in always going for the best he could do, even if it meant falling on his face. It is said that he used to go looking for jam sessions in order to "cut" or outplay anyone who might have the audacity to think they could surpass him. One of the reasons Eldridge is so important in the history of jazz trumpet is that he was one the first of the generation after Louis Armstrong to make an impact on *improvisational* trumpet. Of course, there were others, like Jabbo Smith, who was the only real rival for Armstrong, along with Rex Stewart, Charlie Shavers, Harry James, and Oran "Hot Lips" Page, but Eldridge had the greatest impact.

Eldridge made his recording debut in Teddy Hill's band, as Dizzy Gillespie would several years later. Eldridge's direct influence is evident from early recordings of Gillespie with Earl Hines, Billy Eckstine, and Cab Calloway. In 1941, Eldridge became the first black musician to be accepted as a permanent member of a white swing band when he joined the band of drummer Gene Krupa. His renditions of "Rockin' Chair" with Krupa and "Let Me Off Uptown" with vocalist Anita O'Day made him a national celebrity.

From a purely sonic standpoint, Eldridge had a style of tremendous power and fire, further personalized by his addition of a distinct growl beginning around 1940. He also possessed a most intense swing and daring harmonic sense that was a precursor to modern jazz. On most of his recordings, Eldridge displayed his love for the upper register of the trumpet but was never senti-mental. His admiration and respect for Louis Armstrong are easy to hear, but there is also a burgeoning optimism that would soon surface and trigger a whole new movement in jazz itself, the beginning of bebop.

In researching my collection for an example of Roy Eldridge to discuss in this book, I came across his solo on the standard "Body and Soul," with tenor saxophonist Chu Berry. The date was November 11, 1938, one year *before* the ground-breaking solo on the same tune by tenor saxo-phone great Coleman Hawkins! Although Hawkins is credited with steering jazz improvisa-tion in a completely different direction after that 1939 recording, it seems that Eldridge and Berry had already done so a year earlier.

For the remainder of his career, Roy Eldridge played with the same fire, intense swing, and bravura that characterized his most famous work. He was a true giant among jazz trumpeters who provided the solid and crucial bridge between Louis Armstrong and Dizzy Gillespie and left an indelible mark that will never be erased or dimin-ished in any way.

Ziggy Elman (1914–1968)

Ziggy Elman, who was born Harry Finkelman (both names are just flat-out funny), was a fine trumpet soloist who rose to prominence with clarinetist Benny Goodman in 1936. He is most famous for his classic solo on the composition "And the Angels Sing."

Elman was a mainstay with Goodman for a couple of years and enjoyed his role as the main cat on trumpet until Harry James joined the group. James was the more expansive soloist and soon overtook the main solo chair en route to becoming perhaps the most famous musician of the period.

Ziggy remained with Goodman through 1940 and then took a job with Tommy Dorsey. He had many features with Dorsey, but after he was drafted into the military and served his time, the swing era had waned. Upon his return, he had to do a lot of studio work. The beboppers had taken over, and that style was not within the realm of what Ziggy had done. He retired from active playing in the mid-1950s, but his legacy still shines from his work with Goodman.

Bobby Hackett (1915–1976)

Bobby Hackett illustrates the importance of a personal sound, and the lasting influence it can have. Hackett had one of the most beautiful, smooth, and clear trumpet tones I have ever heard. He made an art of stating the melody to standard compositions in a way that seemed simple but was actually quite complex.

I became aware of Bobby Hackett in the early 1990s while playing in a swing band in Tallahassee, Florida, that featured the music of Glenn Miller and Benny Goodman. I had to play the trumpet solo on "A String of Pearls" and was expected to play the classic solo that Hackett made famous. It was a huge hit in the early 1940s and is still played by swing bands everywhere. Bobby Hackett listened to and studied Bix Beiderbeck, which can account for his melodic sense of delivery. But Hackett clearly had his own voice and way of rhythmic interpretation. Hackett played with Louis Armstrong during a 1947 concert and this left him with a stronger overall conception of rhythm; his playing after-ward is markedly different.

Jackie Gleason recorded Hackett in the 1950s and 1960s for a series of mood albums that show-cased his beautiful sound. They were not neces-sarily improvisationally adventurous, but they show what is possible in terms of sound with a cornet. Hackett also recorded several live albums with trombonist Vic Dickenson during the late '60s and was held in high esteem by all of his contemporaries and peers. Everybody loved Bobby Hackett, and his work is instantly recognizable from one or two notes. This is what all musicians strive for during their lifetime; Hackett had it for his entire career.

Harry James (1916–1983)

Much has been written about Harry James, as he was clearly the most famous trumpeter after Louis Armstrong during the 1940s and into the early 1950s. Born in Albany, Georgia, he played in circus bands led by his father in Texas. *Trumpet Blues*, by Peter Levinson, details James's early life

Photo courtesy of Jack Bradley

Harry James.

and entire career. It tells how James developed his prodigious technique at such an early age by playing the demanding circus music. This allowed him to flawlessly execute such demanding but non-jazz pieces as *Flight of the Bumblebee* later. Although playing these types of songs did nothing to further his image as a serious jazz musician, it showed what was possible on the trumpet from the technical side. In other words, Harry James, just as Louis Armstrong had done earlier, made trumpet players go home and practice.

Drummer Ben Pollack discovered James in one of those circus bands around 1935 and signed him up immediately. It was with Pollack that he made his recording debut. In 1937, however, James would begin an association that would truly make him famous, joining the Benny Goodman band at the height of its popularity. The recording of James with Goodman and Basie and others during the 1938 Carnegie Hall Concert makes clear that he had arrived at a high level of projection and clarity. No note is wasted as he confidently improvises his solos. Perhaps this was when James discovered his love for the sound and concept of Count Basie. His records have that unmistakable sound of the Basie rhythm section, especially in the 1950s, and former Basie drummer Gregg Field was one of James's last drummers.

Harry James had his first major break after he left Goodman with the recording "You Made Me Love You" in 1941. The executives at the record label began to understand fully that romance sells, and they soon recorded James playing such compositions as "I Cried for You" and "Cherry." In the 1940s, James also began to appear in movies and became a household name. He married the movie star Betty Grable and became the toast of Hollywood society, which further overshadowed his magnificent trumpet playing.

His handsome looks and seemingly aloof quality made him a perfect choice for the role of a sympathetic musician.

The influence of Harry James was everywhere from the late 1930s on; even Miles Davis admits that he was a fan. He recorded so many albums and music to suit any taste, from light instrumentals to serious jazz, which can be found in his catalogue. Upon hearing Harry James's solo "On Walkin'" (*Verve Jazz Master 55*) I was astounded at his level of improvisational depth. What we have of Harry James is enough to solidly place him among the greatest trumpeters.

Ray Nance (1913–1976)

When I think of versatility on a genius level, I immediately think of Ray Nance. He was mostly known as a quadruple threat with the Duke Ellington Orchestra: one of its star soloists on cornet, violin, vocals, and comic relief. As a cornetist and plunger specialist, however, he clearly understood Louis Armstrong, Cootie Williams, and even Roy Eldridge. Nance rose to stardom after he took Cootie Williams's place in the Ellington orchestra in 1940. Although Nance was originally from Chicago and had worked with the bands of Earl Hines and Horace Henderson (brother of Fletcher), as well as leading his own bands, his association with Ellington placed him among those outstanding musicians who had no weakness.

Nance played with Duke Ellington for more than twenty years. He recorded on such classics as "Black, Brown, and Beige," with the Blanton/Webster Band; *Studio Sessions* from 1956 to 1963; and the 1961 collaboration with the Count Basie Orchestra entitled *The First Time!* He left in 1963 to go out on his own and managed to record a few times with several groups. However, Nance's best work was with Ellington. As a master of versatility, he left a mark that may never be matched. His is that rare breed kind of talent that only seems to deepen upon further study.

Oran "Hot Lips" Page (1908–1954)

It was once said that Hot Lips Page, in the early 1930s, had the entire Midwest sewn up. He was a powerhouse trumpeter who never became as famous as he should have been. Sweets Edition said of Page, "He could take a plunger and kill you. And kill you, and kill you, and kill you!" He was with Count Basie's first orchestra in 1935 or 1936, left and gave his place to Buck Clayton just before the orchestra went to New York and made it big. Page had been convinced by Joe Glaser, the shrewd and smart manager of Louis Armstrong, that he would become a star if he signed on with Glaser. Just like Roy Eldridge, whom Glaser also

Photo courtesy of Jack Bradley

Ray Nance.

Photo courtesy of Jack Bradley

Oran "Hot Lips" Page.

Glaser. As a result of not being an integral part of the new Count Basie Orchestra and being held back by Glaser, Page became the king of the jam session. He developed a reputation like that of Roy Eldridge, an attitude of "come on and get your ass-whipping" to any and every trumpeter who dared get on the stage with him.

Page recorded a hit song with Pearl Bailey, "Baby, It's Cold Outside," in 1949. He was also a wonderful vocalist, as is evident from his rendition of "Take Your Shoes Off, Baby" from his disc *Play the Blues in B*. Page's trumpet solo on the same tune, interestingly enough, is nearly a carbon copy of Louis Armstrong's, complete with half-valved smears, scoops, and solid placement of the fat quarter note right in the heart of the beat. I wish more of Page's work had been recorded, but what we do have is clearly enough to place him in the top category of trumpeters to emerge after 1930.

Charlie Shavers (1917–1971)

Charlie Shavers was one of the most important trumpeters in the entire history of jazz. He was one of the first to improvise long lines consistently in the upper register of the instrument with control. This established his great versatility. He then added other improvisatorial elements to his playing that mirrored those of his contemporaries, such as Dizzy Gillespie. Shavers often practiced with Gillespie, copied some of Roy Eldridge's recorded solos, and played with Gillespie in Frankie Fairfax's band. He also played with Tiny Bradshaw and Lucky Millinder, and then gained recognition in John Kirby's sextet at age nineteen. Shavers played with Raymond Scott's CBS orchestra and was featured with Benny Goodman and with Tommy Dorsey. Like Harry "Sweets" Edison, Shavers toured inter-

had signed, Page never saw the bookings that would have catapulted him to a level economically and artistically commensurate with his immense talents. I believe Glaser was frightened into keeping a lid on Page and Eldridge, so much so that Louis Armstrong never felt their fire breathing down his neck.

Oran "Hot Lips" Page had the perfect nickname, as indeed his chops (lips) were as strong and full of fire as anyone from any era in jazz. He had a strong reverence for the blues and, like Eldridge, believed in going for it even if it meant falling on his face—but Page never did fall. He played with the Bennie Moten Orchestra in Kansas City while Basie was the pianist, from 1931 until Moten's death in 1935. Basie took over the Moten band and Page joined them a year later, but stayed for only a few months before testing the waters as a solo act under the "guidance" of Joe

Cootie Williams, center, flanked by L to R: Freddy Jenkins, trumpet; Lawrence Brown, trombone; Juan Tizol, trombone; and (hidden) Arthur Whetsol, trumpet, all part of the Duke Ellington Orchestra in 1933.

nationally with Frank Sinatra, which placed him in that elite group of trumpeters that understood how to accompany a vocalist. Every lead trumpeter who also has aspirations for being a soloist should know as much of the work of Charlie Shavers as possible.

Gosta Törner (1912–1982)

Gosta Torner was one of Sweden's main swing trumpeters and played with an enthusiasm and fire that was infectious, so much so that Torner was invited to play at the 1949 Paris Jazz Festival, which also featured Miles Davis sounding amazingly like Dizzy Gillespie. The recording of Törner's called *Trumpet Player* is full of his bouncy and playful improvisations. He recorded many standards, including the swing "anthem" in "Indiana." Gosta shows how he internalized the sounds of the greatest players in jazz trumpet history from Louis Armstrong on down. His music does not sound like a foreigner attempting

to play a music that is not in his soul. Törner simply was an outstanding trumpeter whose legacy should be recognized in the United States just as it is in his native Sweden.

Charles Melvin "Cootie" Williams (1911–1985)

Cootie Williams's mastery of the swing style and especially his pioneering use of the plunger mute are of legendary importance. He literally defined the sound of the plunger that was so integral to the success of Duke Ellington. He came to work with Ellington in 1929, when the great plunger specialist Bubber Miley left for personal reasons. Williams perfected his use of the plunger by studying the work of trombonist Tricky Sam Nanton.

Williams was one of Ellington's main soloists and stars in the 1930s, and he also recorded as a leader later in that decade with some of the men from the Ellington orchestra, including Ellington himself. Williams also recorded with Billie

Holiday and Teddy Wilson. At the height of his early fame with Ellington, he accepted an offer to join Benny Goodman. This was a shock but allowed Williams more solo space. When Goodman's band broke up, Williams started his own big band and recorded the first versions of tunes associated with Thelonious Monk, including "Epistrophy" and the classic standard "'Round Midnight." This showed his prescience, for he had in his band the bebop trumpeter Joe Guy and saxophonist Eddie "Lockjaw" Davis, and pioneering bop pianist Bud Powell.

Eventually Williams's big band broke up; he then worked with an R&B group that managed to have a hit called "Gator." After that faded, Williams returned to the Duke Ellington Orchestra after a twenty-two-year holiday. His impact was immediate, and he stayed with the orchestra through the death of Billy Strayhorn in 1967 and the Duke himself in 1974. Upon Strayhorn's death, Ellington wrote an album for him entitled *And His Mother Called Him Bill*. It includes "The Intimacy of the Blues," on which Cootie Williams takes perhaps one of his greatest plunger solos. By this time in his career, 1967, Williams had a certain power and grandeur to his playing that no other trumpeter other than Louis Armstrong could match. Ellington plunger specialist Barrie Lee Hall, who sat next to Williams in the Ellington orchestra, told me that Williams would not even use a microphone, and his sound and volume were astounding. When Williams passed away, he left his trumpet and plunger to Hall.

Influential Trumpeters of the Modern Jazz Era (1943–1970)

The modern jazz era, which began about 1943, produced more distinct and invariably subtle stylists than any earlier period. So much was learned from the master jazz trumpet soloists of the Jazz Age and swing era that it became possible for trumpeters in the modern jazz or bebop (these being pretty much one and the same) period to exploit any and all of what they liked about a particular earlier trumpeter's technique. As an example, Dizzy Gillespie, who is without a doubt the father of this particular era or style, was able to take elements of his idol Roy Eldridge, in particular Eldridge's fondness for the upper register as well as his use of the flat ninth, and explore other sounds in the chord extensions such as the eleventh and the thirteenth. But Gillespie also added elements of the nearly forgotten Jabbo Smith, such as incredible speed and dexterity that enabled him to surpass even Eldridge. Gillespie also inspired a number of trumpeters who arrived around the same time, such as Howard McGhee and Fats Navarro, as well as those after him, such as Clifford Brown, Red Rodney, Nat Adderley, and even Miles Davis.

Bebop is in many ways the most demanding style in which to improvise. This is because the tempos are generally faster than those found in the previous eras, which require a quicker thought process, and the harmonic and rhythmic particulars of this era left many musicians in its dust. A lot of them simply could not keep up with the added demands of instrumental virtuosity and harmonic sophistication. The bebop movement was also a political and social revolution of sorts by musicians such as Gillespie, Charlie Parker, Thelonious Monk, Kenny Clarke, and Bud Powell, who were searching for more challenging and fulfilling means of improvisation. By working on the upper extensions of the chords, i.e., the ninth, the sharped eleventh, and the thirteenth, they found that they were able to create melodies within the already established melodies of whatever they were playing that would fit perfectly harmonically. To play this music called bebop, a trumpeter has to have incredibly sharp harmonic and rhythmic reflexes in order to navigate successfully through the myriad of possibilities that can begin with one simple improvised idea.

Charlie Parker, the alto saxophone genius from Kansas City, is acknowledged without question as the one musician who really gave bebop its characteristics. Dizzy Gillespie said that after he heard Parker, or "Bird," as musicians call him, he knew that this was the way the music was supposed to sound. It is important to remember that at the core of bebop or modern jazz is the sound of the blues. Charlie Parker came out of the blues-based band of Jay McShann. Also, Kansas City was where the great Count Basie got his start with Bennie Moten and went on to establish the Count Basie Orchestra, which was and still is the epitome of the blues sound for a large jazz orchestra. The fact that Parker came from such an environment makes clear that he, Gillespie, Navarro, Clifford Brown, and many other pioneers of bebop were still carrying forth the blues, albeit in an extended and more sophisticated fashion.

The primary stylistic differences between modern jazz trumpeters and their predecessors are: they played much faster while still maintaining melodic invention; they took more chances; and their individual conceptions varied greatly as they were able to develop one or two specific traits and achieve success, although there were exceptions like Clifford Brown, who possessed not one weakness. Further, the harmonic development in bebop was so advanced that it foreshadowed the new avant-garde movement, still some fifteen years away. And the overall requirements placed on the musicians also applied to the audience. This was because although bebop was very danceable, it had another side: it was much more difficult to hear the complex improvisations while trying to relax or dance. So the audience either sat and listened to the musicians create an incredible new extension of an art or danced and somewhat ignored the profundity of the musical moment. To do both is truly amazing.

I cannot list in detail all the names and contributions of every trumpeter who came to maturity in the bebop era or modern jazz era (which includes hard bop), free jazz, and the 1970s. There were literally hundreds of players in these styles, with bebop/hard bop most popular. This is evident in the way that the vast majority of improvising soloists play today. The influence of Dizzy Gillespie, Miles Davis, Freddie Hubbard, Lee Morgan, Don Cherry, and especially Clifford Brown is still very much alive. The following trumpeters, after Dizzy Gillespie demonstrated what was possible, are those whom I consider to be the foundations on which all others began to build.

Nat Adderley (1931–2000)

Nathaniel "Nat" Adderley was born in Tampa, Florida into a musical family. His brother, Julian "Cannonball" Adderley, was one of the greatest alto saxophonists in the history of jazz and would feature Nat in their co-led quintet. Their collabo-

Nat Adderly, left; Author, trumpet.

Photo courtesy of Tracy Horenbein

ration, which lasted until Cannonball's death in 1975, was one of the best ever in jazz, and they helped to usher in what is referred to as "soul-jazz" with compositions like "Mercy, Mercy, Mercy" and "Sack 'O Woe."

Adderley started on trumpet and switched to cornet exclusively sometime after he served in the U.S. Army. He was one of the few jazz musicians to focus exclusively on the cornet, with the exception of Ray Nance, Bill Berry, Wild Bill Davison, and the late Thad Jones. Nat had as much technique as anyone on the trumpet and a wealth of ideas that seemed to flow through his horn. His ability to play solos that were simultaneously funky *and* cerebral was completely original. It is no wonder that his compositions *Work Song* and *Jive Samba* are classics among musicians and fans alike.

Adderley was in the army from 1951 to 1953 and secured a job with the orchestra of Lionel Hampton beginning in 1954. This lasted for a year or so, and in 1956 he joined the band led by his brother, Cannonball. In their work together, Adderley displayed all the essential elements that made him a jazz master. He could play in any number of ways and was as talented a trumpeter as he was a composer and arranger.

Some of the recordings featuring Nat with Cannonball are *Cannonball's Sharpshooters*, *Live in San Francisco*, *Mercy, Mercy, Mercy*, *Radio Nights*, *Live in Japan*, *Country Preacher*, *Nippon Soul*, *Them Dirty Blues*, and *Live at the Lighthouse*. As a leader, some of Nat's recordings include "Work Song," "Naturally," "That's Right," "Hummin'," "That Old Country," "We Remember Cannon," and "Autumn Leaves." Anything with Adderley's name on it is highly recommended.

For about ten years or more, I had the pleasure of knowing Nat Adderley and performing with him several times. I learned many things from him, including the most important: never tell another musician what to play. He was a most gracious, warm, and very funny man, and my admiration and respect for him run deep. His continued encouragement went beyond the trumpet; he always joked that I never made it to his home in Florida to visit him, and his wife even had new carpet put down for my arrival!

Nat Adderley belongs to the top one percent of jazz trumpeters. I believe he was most underrated and hope that with this book, many will begin to appreciate his enormous talent. He comes from the lineage beginning with Roy Eldridge and Dizzy Gillespie, and whoever heard him execute intricate ideas and swing flawlessly on his horn, in the 1950s or since, knew they were listening to a true giant of jazz.

Chet Baker (1929–1988)

Chesney Henry "Chet" Baker was born in Oklahoma and became, in the mid-1950s, a star in the jazz world as both trumpeter and vocalist. He reportedly discovered jazz while in the army, but soon landed a gig with saxophone genius Charlie Parker in 1952. Parker raved about Baker to trumpet master Dizzy Gillespie and others back in New York. After working briefly with Parker, Baker went on to play with the great baritone saxophonist Gerry Mulligan in a pianoless quartet. Working without the aid of a piano is one of the greatest challenges a jazz musician can undertake, but also one of the most liberating because improvisations are not locked into or limited by the chords of the pianist. Doing this in the 1950s brought a freshness to the sound of the jazz small group. It allowed Baker to examine his own sound closely, and I believe helped him to solidify his sound concept. This, of course, was in addition to his close study of Miles Davis.

Photo courtesy of Institute of Jazz Studies, Rutgers University

Chet Baker.

Photo courtesy of Tor Gunnar Lehne

Lester Bowie.

Chet Baker's work with Mulligan, most notably his vocal renditions of "My Funny Valentine," made him famous, and for the rest of his career he would display his unique ability to combine singing with his trumpet playing that never grew sentimental. His trumpet sound was influenced greatly by Miles Davis complete with subtle intensity, clarity, perfect intonation, and controlled vibrato. These characteristics of Baker's playing became synonymous with the West Coast "cool" style of jazz. His recordings with Stan Getz from the early 1950s display his outstanding command of the trumpet. His solos on tunes like "Move" from the Getz *West Coast Sessions* are among his very best.

Baker's singing was an important part of his talent that warrants close listening. *She Was Too Good to Me*, in addition to *Chet Baker Live in Tokyo*, is one of my all-time favorites and further shows Baker's enormous talent that was hindered by drug problems and ended too early with his tragic death in 1988.

Lester Bowie (1941–1999)

Lester Bowie is most associated with the Art Ensemble of Chicago, of which he was one of the founders, but he also recorded some unique albums, particularly *Fast Last* and *Duets* with percussionist Philip Wilson. On *Fast Last*, Bowie gives his version of the Louis Armstrong classic "Hello, Dolly!" It is the most profound version of that piece I have ever heard anywhere. Bowie twists and turns and does everything he wants to the melody, which would seem sacrilegious to those who consider Armstrong's version to be the definitive one. I consider Bowie's to be. That is all he needed to record to show that he completely understood the entire history of jazz music. But more important, Bowie understood how it relates to the history of the United States.

Lester Bowie was born in Maryland, but spent time growing up in St. Louis. He played in some notable R&B bands, including one with Albert King in the early 1960s. He moved to Chicago in the mid-'60s, and that was where he came into his own and further developed his vision. He was a member of the Association for the Advancement of Creative Musicians (AACM) and soon put a group together that would last thirty years—the Art Ensemble of Chicago. This group made major contributions to the avant-garde wing of jazz, but Bowie continued to fully express himself on the trumpet, even if it seemed to some in the mainstream that this music was anything by structured. In some cases, the freer the music is, the more responsibility the musicians have to resolve whatever occurs within the collective. This is evident in the music of Bowie and his group. He could play a great variety of music regardless of what people thought about what he ought to play. Bowie was without question one of the giants of jazz trumpet.

Clifford Brown (1930–1956)

Clifford Brown is perhaps the most emulated trumpeter in all of jazz. The particular style he developed, with elements of Dizzy Gillespie and Fats Navarro in particular, seems to have influenced nearly every jazz trumpeter since the mid-1950s. The fact that "Brownie," as he was known among musicians, only recorded for four years,

but left such a legacy speaks volumes about the level of his talent. He was known as the sweetest human being with a beautiful soul and nobody ever had a bad word to say about him. The warmth of his sound mirrors his personality.

Brown was born and raised in Wilmington, Delaware. He attended college at the University of Delaware and later Maryland State. While at Maryland State, he played and arranged charts for the jazz band. In 1949, when trumpeter Benny Harris was late showing up for a gig with Dizzy Gillespie in Wilmington, young Brown was called to sit in. He greatly impressed Gillespie, who first told Max Roach about him. He also worked with Charlie Parker, who could not believe the level at which Clifford Brown was playing and advised drummer Art Blakey to hire him. Before his tenure with Blakey could begin, however, Brown was in a serious auto accident that left him unable to play his trumpet for a year.

Brown made his recording debut in 1952 with Chris Powell's Blue Flames, although this was pretty much an R&B group. He made his first important records in mid-1953, with the bands of Tadd Dameron and Lou Donaldson. Word of Brown's talent was spreading, and soon he was

Clifford Brown.

asked to join Lionel Hampton's band, at the recommendation of Quincy Jones. Just before going to Europe with Hampton, Brown recorded his first dates as a band leader. While in Europe, he also recorded what are now known as the *Stockholm Sessions* and the *Paris Sessions*. On these, as with all his recordings, Brown displays a depth of natural talent that is refreshing. His solos are full of lyrical beauty and continuity; he possessed an amazing technique.

The most important collaboration in Brown's short career was with the great drummer Max Roach, who hired Brown and made him co-leader. With the Clifford Brown-Max Roach Quintet, Brown made his greatest recordings for the Emarcy label. Brown had it all: a big and beautiful sound, an incredible and natural feel for swinging, an impeccable sense of time, especially double-time, and that "bounce" of optimism inherent in all of the masters, such as Charlie Parker and Louis Armstrong. He also had a very fast single tongue that allowed him to execute the most intricate and complex, yet lyrically satisfying lines of any trumpeter. His solos are textbook examples of how to play and phrase bebop. By 1954, the quintet was steadily becoming one of the hottest groups in jazz. Joe Glaser, who managed Louis Armstrong, began to book them. They went on tour and continued to make recordings with musicians like Harold Land on saxophone (to be replaced later by Sonny Rollins), Richie Powell on piano, and George Morrow on bass. The combination of Brown and Roach in particular was especially rewarding.

Brown was also a wonderful composer and penned such classics as "Sandu," "Gertrude's Bounce," "Daahoud," and the very popular "Joy Spring." All of his compositions have a catchy melody and allow the room to improvise nearly

perfect solos. With his death in an auto accident at the age of twenty-five, the world lost an incredible musician and beautiful person in Clifford Brown. Dizzy Gillespie said, "There can be no replacement for his artistry, and I can only hope jazz will produce in the future some compensation for this great loss to our cause." The legacy of Clifford Brown lives on with jazz festivals and scholarships in his honor.

Donald Byrd (b. 1932)

Donald Byrd is one of the all-around players who can literally play anything and make it sound good. He displays a love for searching for the additional sounds that can be heard after the music stops. This is a rarity, and has allowed him to carve out a unique career perhaps second only to that of Miles Davis in variety of output.

Originally from the great jazz city of Detroit, Michigan, Donald Byrd has played and recorded with a who's who in the jazz world. He played with Art Blakey and the Jazz Messengers briefly in 1956, worked with Max Roach, and also played with Gigi Gryce. Byrd's similarity to Clifford Brown in terms of sound and technique made him one of the most in-demand trumpeters in New York during the mid- to late 1950s. He recorded the magnificent *The Last Trane* with John Coltrane and made dates with Sonny Rollins, Jackie McLean, and Pepper Adams. He and Adams led a band that was one of the finest of the period. They recorded the *Live at the Half Note* gems, which are straight-ahead jazz at its best. Once he signed with Blue Note records in 1958, Byrd became a star, and he used this opportunity to really explore the boundaries of his art.

During the 1960s, Byrd recorded such adventurous albums as *Fancy Free*, *Byrd in Flight*, and *Free Form*, in which he used a choir. Perhaps inspired by not having any obstacles in his musical life, he then began his illustrious career as an educator and lover of knowledge by earning his Ph.D. from Columbia Teachers College, as well as a law degree in addition to his pilot's license! This proves that the mind of a seasoned jazz soloist is able to accomplish anything.

Byrd began to experiment with electronic music and R&B by forming a group at Howard University, where he was teaching. They became known as the Blackbyrds and helped to establish Byrd as one of the major contributors to the jazz-influenced sound of early 1970s R&B and funk. His playing on the recordings from this period (*Places and Spaces* and *Black Byrd*) became a little more sparse than his bebop work, and he tailored it to suit his needs, trying to reflect what was happening in the mainstream of the country as well as in his own community.

During the Wynton Marsalis-led era of the 1980s, when pioneers of jazz like Byrd and Freddie Hubbard were being reexamined, Byrd gathered a group of young musicians, including pianist Mulgrew Miller, and recorded the kind of straight-ahead jazz that he had not done in almost thirty years. The project was significant in itself, and he still was able to deliver his own unique talents. Although he was no longer in his prime, Donald Byrd presented the maturity and clarity that made him one of the all-time greats in the lineage of jazz trumpet.

Don Cherry (1936–1995)

Born in Oklahoma City, Oklahoma, Don Cherry was one of the most important musicians of the post-bop and free jazz periods. He came to prominence when Miles Davis was almost single-handedly reshaping the landscape of small group improvisational jazz. Cherry's work with Ornette Coleman established him as the premier avant-

Don Cherry.

garde or free jazz trumpeter. He also brought credit to the pocket trumpet, on which he usually performed.

Cherry moved to Los Angeles when he was four years old and had begun playing trumpet by the time he entered junior high school. He grew up alongside other jazz greats in his neighborhood, such as Dexter Gordon and Sonny Criss. By the time Cherry started playing professionally, he was making his mark as a bebop player, but this changed quickly after he met alto saxophonist Ornette Coleman. Together, they started experimenting with a new style that would be later called "free jazz." This was a significant period in modern jazz history in which players could explore, free of preset harmonic structure. Cherry's first record was *Something Else* (1958).

His next, *The Shape of Jazz to Come* (1959), unleashed free jazz across the country, especially in New York City, and was the most influential on the jazz community in his lifetime. Cherry's association with Ornette Coleman peaked in 1961 with the album *Free Jazz*, which featured two quartets playing simultaneously with each other. Don Cherry continued pushing the boundaries of jazz until his death in 1995.

Johnny Coles (1926–1997)

Born in Trenton, New Jersey, Coles moved to Philadelphia as a child. He was most influenced by Miles Davis and was even a member of the trumpet section on famous Davis recordings, including *Porgy and Bess* and *Sketches of Spain*. Coles was known for saying a lot without playing many notes. He was a great sideman in many groups, such as the Duke Ellington Orchestra and the Count Basie Orchestra (under the direction of Thad Jones), and he played with Charles Mingus, Herbie Hancock, Ray Charles, the Thad Jones-Mel Lewis Big Band, and Art Blakey, among others. Some of his most famous solos came from *Out of the Cool*, an album led by Gil Evans made in 1960. Coles also recorded under his own name on the Epic and Blue Note labels. His most famous recording as a leader was *Little Johnny C*, which featured musicians like Duke Pearson (piano) and Joe Henderson (tenor saxophone). This album was released in 1963 under the Blue Note label.

In 1997, Coles passed away from stomach cancer. Though he led his own groups and was an important figure in many great ensembles, he did not attain the level of fame he deserved. Among most jazz musicians born before 1970, he is fully known and appreciated.

Conte (Secondo) (1927–2001) and Pete (b. 1923) Condoli

Conte and Pete Condoli were among the greatest brother acts in modern jazz history, and each also had his own list of credentials. Pete was featured in many famous bands led by the likes of Tommy Dorsey, Glen Miller, Woody Herman, Stan Kenton, Less Brown, Count Basie, Freddy Slack, and Charlie Barnet, and was a great lead trumpet player in bands led by Alex Stordahl, Gordon Jenkins, Nelson Riddle, Don Costa, Michel LeGrand, Henry Mancini, and Frank Sinatra. He was also highly regarded as a classical trumpet player, arranger (for Judy Garland, Ella Fitzgerald, and others), and conductor. He won the outstanding trumpeter award from both *Downbeat* and *Metronome* magazines.

Conte Condoli joined his brother Pete in Woody Herman's band in 1945 and continued on the road for the next decade playing with Woody, Stan Kenton, Benny Goodman, and Dizzy Gillespie. Playing with Gillespie was an influential experience, for his own personal trumpet style was similar to Gillespie's bebop style. After his stint with these big bands, Conte formed a small group that played across the country in many top jazz clubs. Later in his life, Conte played in the *Tonight Show* band (during the Johnny Carson years); when Carson retired in 1992, so did Conte from the band.

Both brothers came back together throughout the years and were main acts at events such as the Lionel Hampton International Jazz Festival (Moscow, Idaho).

Miles Davis (1926–1991)

Miles Dewey Davis III was one of the most influential musicians and cult figures of the twentieth century. The fact that he played a powerful and unmistakable trumpet sometimes takes a back seat to his genius of putting together some of the greatest bands in the history of jazz. But this book is a celebration of his trumpet playing as well as his leadership.

Davis's first trumpet teacher in St. Louis was his high school director Elwood Buchanan. Although young Davis was a big fan of trumpeter Harry James, Buchanan suggested that he not try to copy James's shaky vibrato but rather focus on his own natural sound. Freddie Webster was another very important model, as was Clark Terry; the two played jam sessions around St. Louis for a short while. After Davis heard trumpeter Howard McGhee, McGhee replaced Terry as his hero until he heard Dizzy Gillespie.

St. Louis was known for having very good trumpet players such as Levi Maddison, George Hudson, Clark Terry, Leonard "Ham" Davis, and Eddie Randle. It was with Randle's band, the Blue Devils, that Davis began the first, most important phase of his development as a jazz musician. The Blue Devils were the hottest band in town, and Davis soon became their musical director. There were other trumpeters such as Fats Navarro, Howard McGhee, Joe Guy, and Kenny Dorham who were stiff competition; all were direct disciples of Dizzy Gillespie. The specific trumpet style emerging, called bebop and the dominant style for years, had tremendous speed and intricacy on top of the already present attention to detail of melody and space that was inherent in the players associated with the Jazz Age and the swing era. After playing the technically advanced styles of Gillespie, Navarro, and McGhee for a while,

Davis decided to stick to his guns and play how he really felt, and he accomplished this without sacrificing any intensity or spirit. Reports by critics that his limited technique forced him in another direction are completely misguided.

Davis arrived in New York in 1944 to study at the Julliard School of Music, but his primary interest was finding Charlie Parker and Dizzy Gillespie to study with and learn from. Bored with Julliard, he soon dropped out and started his apprenticeship with Parker beginning in 1945. The same year, he made his first recording with saxophonist Herbie Fields. Davis's study of the piano in particular with Dizzy Gillespie provided a foundation upon which he built a tremendous body of work over a period of forty-five years.

Beginning with his legendary *Birth of the Cool* sessions, which were recorded in 1949–1950, Davis began a concentrated and systematic approach to musical discovery and experimentation. He signed with the Prestige label for his first recording dates as a leader in 1951. He also did a recording for Blue Note in 1952, as his deal with Prestige wasn't exclusive. He recorded such classics as *Walkin'*, *Relaxin'*, *Cookin'*, and *Steamin' with the Miles Davis Quintet* for Prestige but moved to the larger label Columbia in 1955. For the Prestige recordings and subsequent Columbia recordings, Davis had a band that included the tenor saxophone giants Sonny Rollins followed by John Coltrane, alto saxophonist Julian "Cannonball" Adderley, pianist Red Garland, drummer Philly Joe Jones, and bassist Paul Chambers. At Columbia, they recorded masterpieces such as 'Round Midnight and Milestones that established this group as one of the very best in jazz during that period. By 1959, Davis, who had earlier replaced pianist Red Garland with Bill Evans, replaced drummer Philly Joe Jones with Jimmy Cobb. With Chambers still on bass and the addition of ridiculously hard swinging pianist Wynton Kelly as a replacement for Evans on one tune, Davis recorded *Kind of Blue*, arguably his most important and popular record. I believe that with this session, Davis went *back* to Louis Armstrong in order to create something new that would propel his vision and jazz music in general forward.

Miles Davis had a beautiful, full, and pretty tone and used a mouthpiece somewhat deeper than preferred by most other trumpeters. This enabled him to produce a sound that was deeply personal and immediately recognizable throughout his entire career. He had a perfect embouchure and precise attack, greatly popularized the use of the Harmon mute without the stem, and during the 1960s in particular, he had mastered his breath control to a degree seldom heard except from Louis Armstrong and Dizzy Gillespie.

There is hardly a jazz musician alive who does not own nearly all of Miles Davis's albums. In the 1950s and 1960s in particular, it became the vogue to have all of his recordings and to be the first to buy tickets for his concerts. He set standards off the bandstand as well, and was once voted one of the best-dressed men in America. As the story goes, after one of his concerts, he asked a colleague, "How was I tonight?" The person said, "Miles, you sounded great as usual." Miles then responded, "I was talking about how did my *suit* look?"

Davis recorded many albums in the 1960s and '70s that were both fresh and innovative in their approach, such as *ESP*, *Miles Smiles*, *Nefertiti*, *The Complete Stockholm Sessions of 1960*, *Friday and Saturday Night at the Blackhawk*, *Cookin' at the Plugged Nickel*, *My Funny Valentine*, *Sketches of Spain*, *Water Babies*, *Porgy and Bess*, *Miles in the Sky*, *Filles de Kilimanjaro*, *Dark Magnus*, and *Live at Filmore West*. He recorded the groundbreaking *Bitches Brew* in 1969, and became the leader in the fusion movement of the early 1970s.

After a few years of electronic exploration in the early 1970s with albums such as *On the Corner* and *Jack Johnson*, Davis disappeared from the scene completely to nurse his health and relax and think. He resurfaced around 1979 and began to record material that was more on the popular side, such as interpretations of songs by pop stars Cyndi Lauper and Michael Jackson. No matter what he chose to do until his death in 1991, he was still making music.

Finally, music mogul and former jazz trumpeter Quincy Jones convinced Davis to do a concert of music he had played years earlier with Gil Evans. In the jazz event of the decade at the 1991 Montreux Jazz Festival, Davis played the scores from *Sketches of Spain*, *Miles Ahead*, and *Porgy and Bess* that had been loved by millions for years. With his failing health evident, and with the aid of his direct trumpet disciple, Wallace Roney, *Miles and Quincy in Montreux* was a smashing success and the very last concert in the career of one of the world's all-time great trumpeters. Miles Dewey Davis III died just three months later in September 1991.

Bill Dixon (b. 1925)

William Robert Dixon was born on Nantucket Island, Massachusetts. He grew up in New York, started playing trumpet at the age of eighteen, studied painting at Boston University, then attended the Hartnott School of Music (1946–1951). In the 1950s he freelanced in the New York area as a trumpeter and arranger, and built friendships with Cecil Taylor and Archie Shepp, with whom he co-led a quartet and helped to found the New York Contemporary Five.

Though he was of the generation that brought bebop to fruition, Dixon did not rise to prominence until the early 1960s, when he emerged as one of the pioneers of the new music. In 1964 he organized the October Revolution – six nights of concerts by young avant-gardists such as Taylor, Shepp, Roswell Rudd, Paul Bley, Milford Graves, and the not-so-young Sun Ra—which is generally acknowledged as the event that gave the New Thing its identity as a movement. Some of his recordings are *The Archie Shepp–Bill Dixon Quartet* (Savoy Jazz 1962), *Archie Shepp & the New York Contemporary 5/The Bill Dixon 7-Tette* (Savoy Jazz 1964), and *Live from the Berlin Jazz Festival* (Soul Note 1997).

Kenny Dorham (1924–1972)

Kenny Dorham is perhaps the most underrated of all jazz trumpeters. He influenced many players who came after him, including Freddie Hubbard, Lee Morgan, and even Clifford Brown. He was a rather quiet type of musician: he simply played and let his ideas do the talking.

After arriving in New York around 1945, Dorham was soon immersed in bebop. He was soon playing with Dizzy Gillespie's big band, Billy Eckstine, and Lionel Hampton. His biggest break came when he replaced Miles Davis in Charlie Parker's band. Everyone realized he was someone to be reckoned with. Dorham's playing reflects his love of the middle register of the instrument as well as his fondness for the meat of the harmony. He had a subtle way of negotiating chord changes that can easily be missed. As Freddie Hubbard told me during our interview, Dorham showed him a smoother way of getting into the bridge of rhythm changes in concert B-flat ("I Got Rhythm," "Oleo," etc.).

Photo courtesy of CTSIMAGES

Kenny Dorham.

Kenny Dorham was quite busy in the 1950s as the original trumpeter with Art Blakey and the Jazz Messengers. He also took Clifford Brown's place with Max Roach in the year following Brown's death. Dorham, who also sang, wrote several jazz standards that are played every night somewhere in the world, such as "Blue Bossa," "Lotus Blossom," and "Prince Albert." By the 1960s, the new trumpet stars Freddie Hubbard and Lee Morgan were garnering all of the attention, and rightfully so; Dorham was performing less and less and even took a job in the post office in the late 1960s. He died in 1972 at age forty-eight.

Don Ellis (1934–1978)

Mainly known for his electric experimentations and odd-meter writing, Don Ellis was a soloist who knew how to take a standard and strip it to its bare essence. Appreciation of his work has increased since his death, and he is now regarded by many as an important figure in jazz. His recordings *Out of Nowhere* and *Live at Monterrey* are absolute jazz classics; in particular, *Out of Nowhere* reveals his advanced harmonic concept.

While in junior high school, Ellis had his own quartet. He attended Boston University, then served in the military. One if his first professional gigs was as a member of Ray McKinley's Glenn Miller Orchestra. Ellis formed a small group, playing coffeehouses in New York's Greenwich Village, and by the late 1950s he was playing with many name bands including those of Woody Herman, Lionel Hampton, Charles Mingus, and Maynard Ferguson. Ellis enjoyed the greater freedom of expression working in small groups allowed. In 1961–1962, he was a member of George Russell's sextet.

Rolf Ericson (1922–1997)

Rolf Ericson was born in Stockholm, Sweden. He had already been playing trumpet for more than two years when, in 1933, he was taken to hear Louis Armstrong during his European tour and was suitably inspired. Ericson played professionally as a young teenager, and during the late 1940s he made a number of recordings. In 1947, he moved to New York and played in several big bands, including those of Charlie Barnet, Woody Herman, and Elliot Lawrence. He was attracted by bebop and also played with Wardell Gray. In the early 1950s, Ericson toured his homeland in company with Charlie Parker and played in numerous big bands, often those assembled for

one-off recording and television dates. Later in the decade and on into the 1960s, he divided his time between the United States and Scandinavia, playing with a wide range of musicians such as Bud Powell, Brew Moore, Kenny Dorham, Stan Kenton, Benny Goodman, Gerry Mulligan, Ernestine Anderson, and Duke Ellington. During the second half of the decade he became deeply involved in studio work in both the States and Germany, but found time to play with visiting American musicians. In the 1980s, he mostly worked from his base in Berlin. In 1990, he was in Los Angeles and joined the Ellingtonian small band led by Bill Berry, which featured Marshal Royal and Buster Cooper. In the mid-1990s, Ericson was forced to leave his home in the United States after his German wife failed to get a green card. He spent his last years residing in Stockholm.

Art Farmer (1928–2000)

Arthur Stewart Farmer influenced a whole generation of trumpeters, and this is evident in the way the ballad is generally approached today. His subtle use of advanced harmony was original and his playing is like that of Dizzy Gillespie, in the sense that it takes many listening sessions to become fully aware of what he is doing. His album *Listen to Art Farmer and His Orchestra* was among one of my first ten jazz records.

Farmer first played professionally in Los Angeles beginning around 1945, and worked in the bands of Benny Carter, Gerald Wilson, and Lionel Hampton, as well as other local jazz greats such as the saxophonist Teddy Edwards, pianist Hampton Hawes, and his own twin brother, bassist Addison Farmer. Art Farmer moved to New York in 1953 and worked with small groups led Horace Silver, George Russell, Gerry Mulligan, and co-led a band with Gigi Grice. However, he became a star after he formed a group with the saxophonist Benny Golson called the Jazztet.

During this time, Farmer began gradually playing more and more flugelhorn, which has a darker and softer sound than the trumpet. With the Jazztet, he recorded a composition by Benny Golson that soon reached cult status, "Killer Joe," which showcased Farmer's abilities as a most lyrical trumpeter who could swing with intensity at any tempo. In the 1960s, he led several groups of his own, including a short stint as a co-leader with guitarist Jim Hall. When Farmer visited Vienna, Austria around 1968, this city had an immediate impact on him. He soon moved there permanently. The European jazz musicians knew they had a gem, and Farmer had his pick of whom to work with. Among these various groups was the Clarke-Boland Big Band.

Farmer continually put bands together and toured the world, and he even re-formed the Jazztet in the early 1980s. This added further fuel to a renaissance of traditional "straight-ahead" concepts, a movement that was being led by trumpeter Wynton Marsalis. Marsalis's emphasis on learning the music of the important jazz composers helped a "rediscovery" of Art Farmer; young trumpeters all over the world began to attend his concerts en masse and ask him for advice.

Since Farmer was known for playing the flugelhorn most of the time and the trumpet only occasionally, he wanted an instrument that would allow him the flexibility of the trumpet but retain the big and soft sound of the flugelhorn. Trumpet maker Dave Monette worked with Farmer and created for him the very first of what is now known as a Flumpet. Farmer played this instrument for the remainder of his career and made several recordings with it.

Maynard Ferguson (b. 1928)

Maynard Ferguson was born in Verdun, Canada. He began his career playing in the bands of Boyd Raeburn and Charlie Barnet in the early to mid-1940s. During his tenure with Charlie Barnet, he made his first solo on record, on the composition "All the Things You Are" by Jerome Kern. It was an advanced arrangement, and with Maynard's upper-register reading of the melody, it became a big hit as well as an outrage to the widow of Jerome Kern. She threatened to sue Capitol Records for three million dollars! This success was followed by one of Ferguson's most important associations, with Stan Kenton, from 1950 to 1953; this made him a star.

Ferguson led bands that ranged in size from a full eighteen to a smaller nine to thirteen pieces. His music ran the gamut of styles from Count Basie to Stan Kenton. This flexibility allowed him to become a major crossover hit in the 1970s. His 1970 recording of "MacArthur Park" made him almost a household name. About seven years later, he scored a huge success with the theme to the movie *Rocky*, "Gonna Fly Now." He was in demand for high school and college appearances as a soloist, and this solidified his position as a most influential trumpeter regardless of idiom. Ferguson is capable of playing several instruments at the professional level, including the soprano saxophone. Maynard Ferguson is still a major force today; at this writing, he continues to lead his band around the world on concert tours.

Freddie Hubbard (b. 1938)

Frederick Dwayne Hubbard was born in Indianapolis, Indiana. It has been reported that he appears on more recordings than any other trumpeter; he told me that it is a little over 300 albums. He comes directly from the lineage of

Clifford Brown and Dizzy Gillespie, and is probably the only one who can consistently make his trumpet sound like the darker-sounding flugelhorn. He has an attitude similar to that of Roy Eldridge: it is better to reach for the stars and fall on your face than not to reach at all.

Hubbard first studied French horn in school, and this could be one of the reasons his sound has always been so smooth and fluid. He played locally in Indianapolis with fellow jazz legends Wes Montgomery, J. J. Johnson, and David Baker. When he ventured to New York, he found himself in the company of Lee Morgan, Dizzy Gillespie, Booker Little, and others—he could hold his own and then some.

Hubbard has recorded with the likes of John Coltrane, Ornette Coleman, and others, and in the early years beginning in the late 1950s and early 1960s he recorded with Sarah Vaughan. He was signed to a contract with Blue Note records that firmly established him as a jazz master. He also replaced trumpeter Lee Morgan with Art Blakey's Jazz Messengers, continuing the band's tradition of having an incredible trumpeter. The album with Art Blakey, *Caravan*, is a perfect example of the level of Hubbard's talent. One of his best recordings as a leader for Blue Note is *Hubtones*. It was made in 1962 and is still considered a classic with his unique blend of sound, technique, and melodic ideas. Freddie Hubbard is one of the most important links in the lineage of jazz trumpeters due to the fact that in his playing one can hear his influences *and* his originality. Hubbard is still performing today in 2005, albeit hampered a little by some recurring lip problems. He is a true jazz legend, and the interview I did with him for this book provides further insight into the world he helped to create.

Thad Jones.

Photo courtesy of Jack Bradley

Thad Jones (1923–1986)

Thad Jones was one of the all-time greatest jazz trumpet soloists. Charles Mingus called him "the Bartók of the trumpet," but Jones's talent goes beyond even that comparison.

Thad Jones was born into a musical family of legendary proportions that includes his brother Hank Jones, one of the very first bebop pianists who is still playing today near the age of eighty, and his late brother Elvin Jones, the master percussionist and drummer who was an integral part of the success of the John Coltrane Quartet. Thad began working professionally in Detroit in the early 1950s, but became famous after he joined the Count Basie Orchestra in 1954, just in time to record one of the most recognizable trumpet solos ever, on the Wild Bill Davis arrangement of "April in Paris." Jones also worked with

Charles Mingus around this time and began to write some incredible compositions and arrangements for Basie and trumpeter Harry James.

Jones co-led a group with baritone saxophonist Pepper Adams in the mid-1960s that produced a great record called *Mean What You Say*; he also formed his famous band with drummer Mel Lewis. The Thad Jones-Mel Lewis Orchestra was on the cutting edge of big band writing and sound. Jones's arrangements and solos are textbook examples of how to combine sophistication of the highest order with an irresistible beat and feel for the blues. Duke Ellington is truly the only other composer who could do this as well as he.

Although Jones continued to play with the orchestra throughout the 1960s, '70s, and early '80s, his compositions seemed to take precedence over his playing. He moved to Denmark in the late 1970s and formed another big band, but in 1984, he was selected to become the leader of the Count Basie Orchestra following Basie's death. Veteran Basie tenor saxophonist Eric Dixon filled in until Jones took over. He led the orchestra until health problems forced him to retire.

Booker Little (1938–1961)

Born in Memphis, Tennessee, Booker Little grew up with and played with other Memphis legends such as pianists Phineas Newborn and Harold Mabern, and saxophonist Charles Lloyd. Little played with Max Roach's group for a year starting in 1958 and eventually moved to New York, where he recorded with John Coltrane and Eric Dolphy. Little was without question the one to completely fulfill the legacy that Clifford Brown was already developing. He was different from Clifford, but they both had that something that made them unique. From 1959 to 1961, Booker

Little was the only one playing trumpet like that, a combination of harmonies being explored by Thad Jones, Dizzy Gillespie, and Miles Davis, and the rhythms of the first two with permutations of his own. He was really a special trumpeter who would have left more incredible work had he not died so young. His work sounds mature, although he only lived to the age of twenty-three. His legacy as one of the greats of jazz is assured.

Humphrey Lyttleton (b. 1921)

Born in Eton, England, Humphrey Lyttleton has carved a place in the history of jazz on an international level, squarely in the lineage that began with Buddy Bolden and E. W. Gravitt and that Louis Armstrong brought across the Atlantic. Lyttleton's playing bears the influence of such musicians as Nat Gonella, that other British trumpet giant who came before him, as well as Buck Clayton, Louis Armstrong, and his good friend, the late Henry "Red" Allen.

Lyttleton recorded with Sidney Bechet in 1949, powerhouse vocalist Jimmy Rushing in the late 1950s, and trumpeter Buck Clayton in the 1960s. One of his most important projects has been to host a jazz program on BBC radio that is still running today. He is still performing with his group as well as running his own Calligraph record label.

Howard McGhee (1918–1987)

Howard McGhee originally played clarinet and tenor saxophone, and switched to trumpet at age seventeen. He played with Lionel Hampton in 1941, then with Charlie Barnet and Andy Kirk, in the trumpet section with Fats Navarro. McGhee also took part in the very important jam sessions at Minton's in Harlem during the early 1940s. He went with Coleman Hawkins when Hawkins ventured to Los Angeles for some concerts.

McGhee stayed out west and was one of the main trumpeters who helped to spread the new sounds of bebop. He was regarded as the "missing link" between Roy Eldridge and Navarro.

As for many musicians of the bebop period during the early 1950s, drugs began to take a toll on McGhee and although he still managed to record, the spotlight shifted to Clifford Brown, Miles Davis, Chet Baker, and others. McGhee seems to have slid into relative obscurity during this time, although he did make some nice records such as *Maggie's Back in Town* and *Dusty Blue*. I think his best recordings, however, are from his complete Savoy and Dial masters, which affirm his huge importance in the very early stages of bebop. Howard McGhee was one of its founding fathers and without him, we might not have some of the work of Fats Navarro and ultimately Clifford Brown.

Richard "Blue" Mitchell (1930–1979)

Born in Miami, Mitchell rose to prominence first with Horace Silver's group beginning in 1958, although he had worked earlier with Earl

Richard "Blue" Mitchell

Photo courtesy of CTSIMAGES

Bostic. Cannonball Adderley recommended Mitchell to the Riverside label, and soon he was recording great material including the classic *Blues Moods*. He also made a great recording with Stanley Turrentine, *A Chip Off the Old Block*. Mitchell toured briefly with Ray Charles in the early 1970s, as well as with blues musician John Mayall, and moved to Los Angeles in 1974. He quickly became everyone's favorite trumpet soloist in L.A. He also recorded material in the mid-'70s that reflected the times: funk and rhythm and blues mixed with a taste of bop. What is most indicative of his talents, however, is that after recording that type of material, he went into the studio and recorded what I consider his greatest jazz album in 1977, *The Last Dance*, a must-have in any jazz collection.

Blue Mitchell was everyone's favorite trumpeter. Without much flash, he simply got better and better and was an inspiration and mentor to a lot of musicians, including Bobby Shew and Wynton Marsalis. He also had much more technique than is evident on his records and was simply concerned with telling a story. This is the essence of what jazz improvisation is about, and Mitchell personified this fully.

Lee Morgan (1938–1972)

In his early career, Lee Morgan played in his hometown of Philadelphia and befriended Clifford Brown and others when they came to the area. In 1956, he joined Dizzy Gillespie's big band and began to make a name for himself. During the mid-1950s, he recorded a landmark album with John Coltrane, *Blue Trane*. On the title track, he displayed the astounding level of maturity and originality and confidence that would mark his entire body of work. He also possessed

Photo courtesy of Barbara Maupin

Lee Morgan.

that quality of trying for the unknown even if it meant falling on his face.

In 1958, Morgan joined Art Blakey and the Jazz Messengers and received worldwide acclaim as one of the new innovative voices on the trumpet. He began to record as a leader for Blue Note records and released such classics as *The Sidewinder*, *Cornbread*, *Candy*, *The Rajah*, *Take Twelve*, and *Peckin' Time*. As a sideman, he recorded the album *Freedom Rider* with Art Blakey and *Dippin'* with tenor saxophonist Hank Mobley, as well as many others. Throughout the 1960s, Morgan was one of the dominant influences on the trumpet. Along with Miles Davis, Donald Byrd, Nat Adderley, and Freddie Hubbard, he was considered among the very best.

As a trumpeter in particular, Morgan had a most unique, almost gospel sound that was anchored by a certain weight seldom heard in others other than Louis Armstrong, Roy Eldridge, Davis, and Gillespie. His use of the half-valve technique became one of his trademarks,

although he was not the first to do this, as is clear from the work of trumpeters as early as King Oliver, Armstrong, Rex Stewart, and Charlie Shavers. Almost every young trumpeter today playing on a funky blues, especially if it is in swinging four-four-time, plays some of what Morgan popularized.

Morgan had a most unusual, that is unconventional, embouchure. This may or may not have limited his technique. The late Emmanuel Boyd, a tenor saxophonist who played with me in my own quintet and recorded with Woody Shaw and the Count Basie Orchestra, who knew Morgan, said that just before the trumpeter's early death, he changed his embouchure to match those who had the perfect "classical" setting, such as Freddie Hubbard, Miles Davis, and even Wynton Marsalis. Undoubtedly, Morgan was seeking to play the instrument better. As with trumpeters Clifford Brown, Bix Beiderbeck, and Booker Little, one can only marvel at what few recordings Lee Morgan left behind and wonder at what might have been had he lived longer. In any event, his work stands as a testament to an incredible talent that was recognized by many.

Fats Navarro (1923–1950)

Theodore "Fats" Navarro was one of the first major links in the evolution of modern jazz trumpet after Dizzy Gillespie. Born in Key West, Florida, he began by playing tenor saxophone and piano and by the age of seventeen had switched permanently to trumpet. In 1943, Navarro began playing with Andy Kirk's band, in which he sat next to another great trumpeter, Howard McGhee, and in 1945 he replaced Dizzy Gillespie in Billy Eckstine's orchestra. That fact alone indicates the level of Navarro's talent. Being one of the main soloists with Eckstine solidified his position as one of bebop's early pioneers. Eventually, for health reasons, Navarro stopped touring with Eckstine and instead focused on the recording studio, where he had more than a hundred sessions between 1946 and 1950.

Navarro was the first-call sideman for many players, including Charlie Parker, Bud Powell, Coleman Hawkins, and most often Tadd Dameron. The recordings he made after leaving Eckstine established him as the only true rival for Gillespie. He too had tremendous control of the trumpet in addition to a sweet and beautiful tone, accented by the natural and infectious quality of his swing.

Fats Navarro influenced generations of trumpet players, starting with the likes of Clifford Brown, Kenny Dorham, and others. Like Brown, he had a brief career, cut short by tuberculosis. Thanks to the reissuing of his recordings on CD, we have the opportunity to further appreciate his talents. Finally, to put his importance into perspective, there would have been no Clifford Brown as we know him, had there not been a Theodore "Fats" Navarro.

Red Rodney (1929–1994)

Red Rodney was a lyrical player who could also play very hot and difficult solos. He was a warm individual and generous in passing on information to young trumpeters. He was truly interested in helping young musicians learn this craft. When he was sixteen, Rodney left home to tour with Benny Goodman; he also worked with Jerry Wald, Jimmy Dorsey, and Les Brown. Originally a swing player influenced by Harry James, he modernized after hearing Dizzy Gillespie and Charlie Parker and went on tour with Parker. He is immortalized in the movie about Parker's life, *Bird*; recognized as one of the finest bop trum-

peters of the 1940s, he also appears in the film *Beat the Band* with Gene Krupa. He played with Georgie Auld, Gerry Mulligan, Claude Thornhill, Charlie Ventura, Buddy Rich, Serge Chaloff, and Dexter Gordon. Rodney took up the flugelhorn in the 1980s, and it was his primary instrument until his death. I had the privilege of playing with him during a clinic in 1985 at Florida State University.

Woody Shaw (1944–1989)

Woody Shaw was simply the last great innovator we have had on jazz trumpet. He was an exceptionally accomplished soloist with oblique, rapid, precise, and subtle melodies with a sweet tone and interesting vibrato. At age fourteen, he played in a YMCA band with tenor saxophone great Wayne Shorter. Shaw later worked with Willie Bobo and Eric Dolphy, and in Europe with Nathan Davis, Bud Powell, Kenny Clarke, Johnny Griffin, and Art Taylor. He played with Max Roach for a time and then with McCoy Tyner, Chick Corea, and Art Blakey's Jazz Messengers. After Freddie Hubbard opened up specific new possibilities in the realm of jazz trumpet improvisation through his collaboration and study with saxophonists John Coltrane, Sonny Rollins, and Eric Dolphy in the mid-1960s, Shaw picked up the torch and ran with it. He recorded landmark albums such as *Song of Songs*, *Rosewood*, *United*, *Stepping Stones*, and the very important *Double Take* and *Down Under*, the latter two with trumpet master Hubbard himself. Shaw's work is still above even the most seasoned veterans on the scene.

Bobby Shew (b. 1941)

Bobby Shew emerged in the mid-1960s, along with Woody Herman and Buddy Rich, as one of the best lead players and soloists in jazz. He was soon in demand for studio dates and gigs with many big bands. Shew is very versatile, able to play everything from studio pieces to any part in a trumpet section. He has a keen interest in jazz education and continues to conduct important trumpet clinics everywhere, and also is on the jazz faculty at the University of Southern California. Shew was very close to trumpet legend Blue Mitchell and soaked up some of his improvisational tendencies, which is no easy feat. Mostly self-taught, he also worked as a soloist with Benny Goodman, Horace Silver, Maynard Ferguson, Louise Bellson, and Art Pepper. Shew also made two great recordings with trumpet masters Chuck Findley and Tom Harrell for the defunct MAMA record label (*Trumpets No End* and *Playing with Fire*). These albums, recorded many years apart, not only demonstrate Shew's superb command of the trumpet as well as his good taste in improvisation but also place him in the lineage of jazz trumpeters that contribute fully to the art. He makes you want to hear more and is at ease in any musical situation.

Clark Terry (b. 1920)

Clark Terry is one of the founding fathers of jazz trumpet because he has always sounded like *no one*. Just before completing the manuscript for this book, I asked him what period he would he consider himself most associated with, and he replied that he had a little of all of the periods of jazz in him. This is obvious to anyone who has truly studied his playing. But I decided to put him here, as he came to prominence during the 1950s, at the height of the bebop movement, even though he spent most of that decade with Duke Ellington. Then as well as now, Terry plays the entire range of the trumpet, complete with his personal sense of swing and style.

Terry was born in St. Louis, Missouri, and at this writing continues to be one of the greatest musicians ever to play jazz. He has influenced hundreds of trumpeters as diverse as Wynton Marsalis, Nicholas Payton, and me, as well as the young Miles Davis and Quincy Jones. Davis and Terry used to go to jam sessions around St. Louis together in the early 1940s.

Terry joined Charlie Barnet's band in 1947 and Count Basie's in 1948. One of his most important associations was with Duke Ellington, beginning around 1951 and lasting for several years. Ellington took advantage of Terry's ability to play in styles ranging from swing to bebop, due to his astounding amount of trumpet technique and finesse. Terry was equally at home playing a plunger solo on the blues just as he was playing bebop at breakneck speed. He also began to develop a style of singing without really enunciating that resulted in a famous song and nickname, *Mumbles*. It is at once hilarious as well as innovative, being not exactly scat in the pure sense of the word. Terry also could use just the mouthpiece of the trumpet to solo, producing the smears and bends he could do with the whole instrument. He was carving out territory that would be solely his own.

After he left Duke Ellington, Terry began free-lancing around New York and secured a spot as a staff musician at NBC. Through this affiliation, he was selected (an easy choice) for NBC's *Tonight Show* orchestra. He told me, incidentally, that he was the one in line to succeed Skitch Henderson as the director of the orchestra, but due to the color of his skin, the position went to another great trumpeter, Doc Severinsen. The rest is history, as far as that is concerned. Maybe due to his not being chosen as leader of the orchestra, Terry made numerous appearances on the show while Johnny Carson was the host.

With valve trombonist Bob Brookmeyer, Terry co-led a group that was very popular in the early 1960s. Another of Terry's collaborations, spanning some forty years, was with the pianist Oscar Peterson. Together they recorded a landmark album, *The Oscar Peterson Trio Plus One*, that is a perfect introduction to Clark Terry and demonstrates his seemingly endless abilities.

By the 1970s, Terry had begun to focus more on the flugelhorn; other than Freddie Hubbard and the late Pete Minger, nobody comes close to playing it the way he can. This makes him a double threat, as he can play a plunger solo on one tune that will scare you to death and on the next play a flugelhorn solo that swings so melodically, you'd think he has a split personality. Also, Terry is known for the unparalleled ability to have "conversations" with himself while playing these instruments simultaneously! There is even video footage of him doing this.

Clark Terry made several landmark recordings in the 1970s, most notably with Dizzy Gillespie, Roy Eldridge, and Freddie Hubbard. On one album in particular, *The Alternate Blues*, Terry's exasperation at the rhythm section (Oscar Peterson on piano, Ray Brown on bass, and Bobby Durham on drums) when they forget to switch to the twelve-bar blues instead of the eight-bar blues on his solo is clearly audible. It is absolutely hilarious.

Honorable Mentions

The following trumpeters, solely due to reasons of space, could not have full biographies and other pertinent information. These musicians are worthy of further study.

Aarons, Al
Aiken, Gus "Rice"
Alcorn, Alvin
Allen, Eddie
Allen, Tex
Allesi, Ralph
Ambrosetti, Franco
Asplund, Peter
Ayler, Don
Bailey, Benny
Bailey, John
Baranger, Louise
Barker, Guy
Barelli, Aime
Barnard, Bob
Barrett, Darren
Basso, Guido
Bayham, Andre
Beaner, Oliver
Beckett, Harry
Belgrave, Marcus
Bergeron, Wayne
Berry, Bill

Berry, Emmit
Best, Ravi
Bocage, Peter
Bolton, Dupree
Boltro, Flavio
Burrowes, Roy
Brashear, Oscar
Bridgewater, Cecil
Bronner, Til
Broo, Magnus
Brown, Ray
Buckner, Teddy
Burns, Dave
Byrd, Winston
Caine, Elliott
Callahan, Anna
Campbell, Roy
Carr, Ian
Carter, Benny
Celestin, Oscar "Papa"
Chase, Bill
Chycoski, Arnie
Childers, Buddy

Chilton, John
Codrington, Ray
Cohen, Paul
Cook, Willie
Coon, Jackie
Copeland, Ray
Culley, Wendell
D'earth, John
Dauber, Jamie
Davenport, Jeremy
Davenport, Wallace
Davidson, Trump
Davis, Spanky
Davis, Stanton
Di Martino, Vincent
Drakes, Jesse
Eardley, Jon
Eckland, Peter
Ehrling, Thore
Elliot, Don
Erwin, George
    "Pee Wee"
Fairweather, Digby

Farras, Josep-Maria
Feza, Mongezi
Findley, Chuck
Franks, Rebecca
    Coupe
Fresu, Paulo
Gale, Eddie
Gardner, Burgess
Gardner, Derrick
Gardner, Earl
Gisbert, Greg
Glow, Bernie
Goe, Gene
Goode, Brad
Gould, Mark
Gordon, Frank
Gordon, Joe
Gozzo, Conrad
Grant, Richard
Guerin, Roger
Hardeman, Bill
Harden, Wilbur
Harold, Keyon

227

Harrell, Tom

Haynes, Graham

Henderson, Eddie

Hill, Freddie

Hillyer, Lonnie

Houghstetter, Steve

Humphrey, Percy

Isham, Mark

Jenkins, Clay

Johnson, Dennis

Johnson, Harold
    "Money"

Jones, Carmel

Jones, Quincy

Jordan, Marlon

Kaminsky, Max

Kerr, Clyde

Killian, Albert

Klein, Manny

Laronga, Barbara

Ladnier, Tommy

Lawson, Yank

Letman, Johnny

Lundgren, Marten

Lynch, Brian

Madison, Louis
    "Kid Shots"

Mahar, Bill

Manone, Wingy

Mares, Paul

Marquez, Sal

Massey, Bill

Maxwell, James K.

May, Billy

Mayfield, Greg
    "Shake"

Mayfield, Irwin

McDade, Steve

McConnell, Jimmy

McCurdy, Ron

McKenzie, Michael

McNeil, John

Meeks, Nat

Metcalf, Louis

Metheny, Mike

Mettome, Douglas

Mikkelborg, Palle

Miles, Ron

Miller, Dan

Minor, Thara

Mitchell, Bob

Mitchell, Ollie

Miyashiro, Eric

Mobley, Bill

Moore, Bobby

Moore, Danny

Morand, Herb

Morris, "Red Mack"
    McClure

Morrison, James

Mossman, Michael

Mullins, Riley

Murillo, William

Mustafa, Melton

Newman, Joe

Nottingham, Jimmy

Ohara, Betty

Okoshi, Tiger

Olu Dara

Osterloh, Klaus

Owens, Jimmy

Padron, Julio

Pelt, Jeremy

Polcer, Ed

Porcino, Al

Price, Mike

Prima, Louis

Rader, Don

Ragin, Hugh

Rampton, Kenny

Randolph, Zilmer T.

Rava, Enrica

Reed, Waymon

Rickman, Patrick

Rodriguez, Bobby

Rotundi, Jim

Royal, Ernie

Ruffins, Kermit

Sandke, Randy

Sandofer, Floyd

Schwartz, Brian

Sharif, Jamil

Shaw, Darrell

Sheldon, Jack

Sickler, Don

Sipiagin, Alex

Smith, John

Smoker, Paul

Soloff, Lew

Spivak, Charlie

Stafford, Terrell

Stahl, Dave

Stamm, Marvin

Stanko, Tomasz

Stokes, Irvin

Stout, Ron

Stripling, Byron

Sudhalter, Dick

Sullivan, Charles

Sullivan, Ira

Summers, Bob

Szabo, Frank

Teagarden, Charlie

Thomas, Joe

Thomas, Michael

Thompson, Malachi

Tinkler, Scott

Tooley, Ron

Tornquist, Lasse

Trottier, Nap

Turner, Sonny

Vache, Warren

Vax, Mike

Vega, Ray

Vitale, Richie

Warwick, William
    "Bama"

Webster, Paul

Wendholt, Scott

Wetzel, Ray

White, Walter

Wilder, Joe

Williams, Herbie

Williams, James

Williams, Tom

Williamson, Stuart
    "Stu"

Wilson, Gerald

Wright, Lamar Jr.

Wright, Lamar Sr.

Young, Webster

Zollar, James

Discography

Jazz recordings are as important to me as my trumpet and piano. They are absolutely indispensable in understanding and appreciation of this great American art. I am always in pursuit of recordings that I have not yet heard that will undoubtedly contain information that will further enhance my musicianship. There is an art to listening. Speaking from the perspective of a jazz musician, one has to be able to hear each piece as a whole as well as its individual parts. Doing so greatly enhances one's understanding and enjoyment of it.

I had the very difficult task of narrowing a list of jazz trumpet recordings from almost 2,000 down to an essential 142 albums. The following recordings will provide you with a base from which to begin to build an important collection of jazz trumpet recordings. The key is to have everything that each one of these trumpeters has recorded. Some of the recordings are out of print or not yet on CD and therefore you may have to search for them through the Internet, private collectors, or record stores that carry hard to find LPs such as Ameoba Records in Los Angeles, California.

Some recordings may also be under the name of another artist rather than the trumpeter, such as with Clark Terry. One of his most important recordings I list here is with pianist Oscar Peterson and is called *The Oscar Peterson Trio + One*. It can only be found under Peterson's name. I have tried to notate this when it occurs.

Find the following recordings if you do not already own them. If you do have them all, then put one on tonight and rediscover a particular trumpeter's gift.

Nat Adderley with Cannonball Adderley. *Sophisticated Swing: The Emarcy Small Group Sessions*. (Verve 3145284082)

Cat Anderson. *Cat on a Hot Tin Horn*. (Mercury Records, 1958)**

Louis Armstrong. *Complete Decca Studio Masters* (1935–39). (Definitive Records, DRCD11171)

Louis Armstrong. *Plays W.C. Handy*. (Columbia, CK 40242)

Louis Armstrong. *The Complete Hot Fives and Sevens*. (Columbia Legacy, CK 6351)

Louis Armstrong. *Louis Armstrong Meets Oscar Peterson*. (Verve, 825-713-2)

Louis Armstrong. *Ella and Louis*. (Verve)

Chet Baker. *The Complete Pacific Jazz Recordings*. (Pacific Jazz)

Count Basie Orchestra. *Swing Shift*. (MAMA) †

Count Basie Orchestra. *Live in Japan 2005*. (Sony). †

Bix Beiderbeck. *The Bix Beiderbeck Story*. (Proper Box UK)

Bunny Berigan. *Introduction to Bunny Berigan, 1935–39*. (Best of Jazz, 4021)

Terence Blanchard. *Flow*. (Blue Note, 78273)

Lester Bowie. *Fast Last!* (Sony Records, SRCS 9408)

Bobby Bradford. *Live at the L.A. County Museum of Art*. (Waterboy Records, 01)

Randy Brecker. *Score*. (Atlantic Records)

Clifford Brown. *With Strings*. (Polygram Records, 1955)

Clifford Brown. *The Complete Emarcy Recordings*. (Emarcy, 838 306-2)

Maurice Brown. *Hip to Bop*. (Brown Records, 2004)

Wendell Brunious. *We'll Meet Again*. (WB, 082896)

Bobby Bryant. *Ain't Doin' Too Bad*. (Cadet, 795, 1967)

Clora Bryant. *Gal with a Horn*. (V.S.O.P. #42)

Billy Butterfield. *The Issued Recordings, 1944–47*. (Compact Classic, EDCD2147-2, 1999)

Donald Byrd. *Freeform*. (Blue Note)

Papa Mutt Carey. *Portrait of a New Orleans Master*. (Upbeat Jazz, URCD 176)

Baikida Carroll. *Marionettes on a High Wire*. (Omnitone, 12101)

Doc Cheatham. *Doc Cheatham & Nicholas Payton*. (Verve, 314 537 062-2)

Don Cherry. *Complete Communion*. (Blue Note, 22673)

Buck Clayton. *The Essential Buck Clayton*. (Vanguard, 103/4-2)

Bill Coleman. *Introduction to Bill Coleman: 1934-1943*. (Stemra, 4043, 1997)

Ornette Coleman, featuring Don Cherry. *The Shape of Jazz to Come*. (Atlantic Records, A2 1317)

Conte Condoli. *Powerhouse Trumpet*. (Avenue Jazz, R2 75826)

Ted Curson. *Traveling On*. (Evidence, ECD 22182-2)

Miles Davis. *Kind of Blue*. (Columbia, CK 40579/64935)

Miles Davis. *The Complete Prestige Recordings*. (CD-012-2)

Miles Davis. *Bitches Brew—Complete*. (Columbia, C2K 65774)

Miles Davis. *The Complete Concert: 1964*. (Columbia, C2K 48821)

Orbert Davis. *Priority* (3Sixteen Records, 31601)

Wild Bill Davison. *The Commodore Master Takes*. (Commodore, CMD-405)

Jimmy Deuchar. *Pal Jimmy*. (Jasmine, JASCD 624)

Bill Dixon. *Bill Dixon/Archie Shepp*. (Savoy, 93008-2)

Kenny Dorham. *Una Mas*. (Blue Note, 7243-5-21228-2-0)

Dave Douglas. *Magic Triangle*. (Arabesque, AJ0139)

Johnny Dunn. *Cornet Blues*. (DGF, 33)

Sweets Edison and Ben Webster. *Ben and Sweets*. (Columbia, CK 408653, 1962)

Roy Eldridge. *The Complete Verve Studio Sessions*. (Mosaic, MD7 222)

Roy Eldridge. *Little Jazz Giant* (Boxed Set). (Columbia, CK 45275)

Roy Eldridge and Dizzy Gillespie. *Roy and Diz*. (Verve, 314-521-647-2)

Don Ellis. *Out of Nowhere*. (Candid, KICJ-8389)

Rolf Ericson. *My Foolish Heart*. (Art Union Records, R340171)

James Reese Europe. *Featuring Noble Sissle*. (IAJRC, CD-1012)

Jon Faddis. *Legacy*. (Concord, CCD 4291)

Don Fagerquist. *Eight by Eight*. (V.S.O.P., #4CD)

Art Farmer with Tom Harrell. *The Company I Keep*. (Arabesque Recordings, 112)

Art Farmer. *Listen to Art Farmer and the Orchestra*. (Polygram Records, #537747)

Maynard Ferguson. *Maynard '61*. (Roulette Records, 1961)

Maynard Ferguson. *Brass Attitude*. (Concord, CCD-4848-2)

Roberto Fats Fernandez. *Tangos and Standards*. (Movieplay Brasil, 5083)

Tony Fruscella. *Tony Fruscella*. (Atlantic Records, 8122 75354-2)

Dizzy Gillespie. *Gillespiana/Carnegie Hall Concert*. (Verve, 314 519 809-2)

Dizzy Gillespie. *Oscar Peterson and Dizzy Gillespie*. (Pablo, PACD 2310-740-2)

Dizzy Gillespie and Stan Getz. *Verve Jazz Masters 25*. (Verve, 521 852-2)

Dizzy Gillespie and Charlie Parker. *The Quintet: Jazz at Massey Hall*. (Debut 044-2)

Dizzy Gillespie, Clark Terry, Freddic Hubbard. *The Alternate Blues*. (Pablo, OJCCD-744-2)

Don Goldie. *Brilliant! The Trumpet of Don Goldie*. (Argo, LPS 4010)

Nat Gonella. *The Young Nat Gonella*. (Retrieval, RTR 79022)

Dusko Goykovich and Stjepko Gut. *Trumpets and Rhythm Unit*. (RTB, BSCP-30074, 1979)

Russell Gunn. *Ethnomusicology, Volume 1*. (Atlantic, 83165-2)

Joe Guy and Hot Lips Page. *Trumpet Battle at Minton's*. (Xanadu Records Ltd., 1941)

Bobby Hackett. *The Complete Capitol Bobby Hackett*. (Mosaic, MD5-210)

W.C. Handy. *W.C. Handy's Memphis Blues Band*. (Memphis Archives, 7006)

Roy Hargrove & the RH Factor. *Strength*. (Verve B0003157-02)

Fletcher Henderson. *Fletcher Henderson 1924-1938*. (Giants of Jazz, CD 53179)

Terumasa Hino. *DNA* (Sony SRCS 2470)

Al Hirt. *Brassman's Holiday*. (Hindsight, HCD-608)

Freddie Hubbard. *Red Clay*. (CBS, ZK 40809)

Freddie Hubbard. *Above & Beyond*. (Metropolitan, 1113)

Freddie Hubbard. *The Body and the Soul*. (Impulse, IMPD-183)

Freddie Hubbard and Woody Shaw. *Double Take*. (Blue Note, CDP 7-462942, 1985)

International Sweethearts of Rhythm. *International Sweethearts of Rhythm*. (Rosetta Records, 1946)

Harry James. *Verve Jazz Masters 55*. (Verve, 314-529-902-2)

Bunk Johnson. *Last Testament*. (Delmark, DD 225)

Carmel Jones. *Jay Hawk Talk*. (Prestige, 1938-2)

Jonah Jones. *I Dig Jonah*. (EMI, CCM 108-2)

Leroy Jones. *Props for Pops*. (Columbia, CK 67643)

Taft Jordan. *Mood Indigo* (Prestige)

Freddie Keppard. *The Complete Set (1923–1926)*. (Retrieval, RTR 79017)

Booker Little. *Out Front*. (Candid, CCD 79027)

Humphrey Lyttleton. *The Best of Humphrey Lyttleton*. (EMI, 83280)

Joe Magnarelli and John Swana. *New York-Philly Junction*. (Criss Cross Jazz, 1246)

Chuck Mangione. *Live at the Hollywood Bowl*. (A&M Records, 1979)

Wynton Marsalis. *Live at the Village Vanguard*. (Sony, 69876)

Hugh Masekela. *Grrr*. (Mercury, B0000605-02)

Howard McGhee. *Complete Savoy & Dial Masters*. (Definitive Records, DRCD11163)

Jimmy McPartland. *That Happy Dixieland Jazz*. (RCA, 07863 50549-2)

Pete Minger. *Minger Painting/Straight From The Source*. (Concord, TJA-10005)

Blue Mitchell. *The Last Dance*. (Jazz America, 1977)**

Blue Mitchell. *Blue's Moods*. (Riverside, VICJ-2226)

Thelonious Monk, featuring Thad Jones. *5 by Monk by 5*. (Riverside Records, OJCCD-362-2, 1959).

Lee Morgan. *Live at the Lighthouse*. (Blue Note, 1957–65)

Fats Navarro. *The Fabulous Fats Navarro, Volumes 1 & 2*. (Blue Note)

Red Nichols. *Red Nichols and His Five Pennies*. (Jazzology, JCD-90)

Joseph "King" Oliver. *1923–1930*. (Jazz Classics, RP2CD607)

Original Dixieland Jazz Band. *Sensation!* (Living Era, AJA-5023)

Hot Lips Page. *Pagin' Mr. Page*. (Living Era, AJA-5347)

Longineau Parsons. *Spaced: Collected Works 1980-1999*. (Luv N' Haight, LHCD032)

Nicholas Payton. *Payton's Place*. (Verve, 314-557-327-2, 1998)

Marvin Hannibal Peterson. *Hannibal Live in Berlin* (MPS, POJC-2554)

Oscar Peterson, with Dizzy Gillespie, Clark Terry, Sweets Edison, Roy Eldridge, & Jon Faddis. *Oscar Peterson & The Trumpet Kings: Jousts*. (Pablo, OJCCD-857-2)

Oscar Peterson, featuring Clark Terry. *Oscar Peterson Trio + One* (Clark Terry). (Verve, 314-558-075-2)

Valery Ponomarev. *Live at Sweet Basil*. (Reservoir, RSRCD-131, 1994)

Enrico Rava, with Ran Blake. *Duo en Noir*. (EFA, 10174-2)

Dizzy Reece. *Blues in Trinity*. (Blue Note, 32093)

Claudio Roditi. *Jazz Turns Samba*. (Groovin' High, 1012-2)

Red Rodney and Sam Noto. *Superboy*. (Muse Records, 1974)

Wallace Roney. *Obsession*. (Muse, MCD 5423)

Arturo Sandoval. *Swingin'*. (GRP, GRD 9846, 1996)

Doc Severinsen. *The Very Best of Doc Severinsen*. (Amherst, AMH 5502-2)

Charlie Shavers. *Horn O' Plenty*. (Lionhill Jazz, 10140)

Woody Shaw. *Stepping Stones*. (Columbia Records, 1978)

Bobby Shew. *Salsa Caliente*. (Mama, MMF 1023)

Don Sleet. *All Members*. (Jazzland, OJCCD-1949-2)

Jabbo Smith. *Hot Jazz in the Twenties Volumes 1 and 2*. (Biograph, BCD 152)

Louis Smith. *Smithville*. (Blue Note, TOCJ-1594)

Wadada Leo Smith. *Kulture Jazz*. (ECM, 1507-519-074)

Valaida Snow. *Queen of Trumpet and Song*. (DRG, 8455)

Muggsy Spanier. *The "Ragtime Band" Sessions*. (Bluebird, 66550-2)

Rex Stewart. *An Introduction to Rex Stewart*. (Best of Jazz, 4005)

Malachi Thompson. *Buddy Bolden's Rag*. (Delmark, DE-481)

Charles Tolliver. *The Ringer*. (Arista Records, 1975)

Gösta Törner. *Trumpet Player*. (Phontastic, CD 9301)

Tommy Turrentine. *Tommy Turrentine*. (Time Records, 1960)

Warren Vache and Derek Watkins. *Warren Vache Meets Derek Watkins*. (Zephyr, ZECD9)

Various Artists (Blue Mitchell, Woody Shaw, etc.). *Trumpet Summit: Live at Club Ruby 1968*. (Fresh Sound Records)

Fats Waller, featuring Herman Autrey. *The Indispensable Fats Waller, Volumes 3 and 4*. (Jazz Tribune No. 32)

Jack Walrath. *I Am the Walrath*. (32 Jazz Records, 32184)

Kenny Wheeler. *Gnu High*. (ECM 1069)

Joe Wilder. *Wilder 'n' Wilder*. (Savoy, SV-0131)

Ernie Wilkins. *Top Brass*. (Savoy, 93007)

Ernie Wilkins (arr.), various artists (Joe Wilder, Charlie Shavers, Shorty Baker, Donald Byrd, Art Farmer, etc.). *The Trumpet Album*. (Savoy Jazz, 2237, 1955–57)**

Cootie Williams. *In Hi-Fi*. (RCA, 09026-63561)

Richard Williams. *New Horn in Town*. (Barnaby Records, 1977)

Snooky Young and Marshal Royal. *Snooky & Marshal's Album*. (Concord, CCD-4055)

**Available only on LPs.

† Features the author.

Bibliography

Armstrong, Louis. *Satchmo: My Life in New Orleans.* New York: Da Capo Press, 1954.

Armstrong, Louis, and Thomas Brothers. *Louis Armstrong: In His Own Words.* New York: Oxford University Press, 1999.

Axelrod, Alan, and Charles Phillips. *What Every American History: 200 Events That Shaped the Nation.* Holbrook, MA: Adams Media Corporation, 1932.

Badger, Reid. *A Life in Ragtime: A Biography of James Reese Europe.* New York: Oxford University Press, 1995.

Baines, Anthony. *Brass Instruments: Their History and Development.* New York: Dover Publications, 1993.

Barker, Danny. *Buddy Bolden and the Last Days of Storyville.* London and New York: Bayou Press, 2001.

Bechet, Sidney. *Treat It Gentle.* New York: Da Capo Press, 1960.

Bergreen, Laurence. *Louis Armstrong: An Extravagant Life.* New York: Broadway Books, 1997.

Berger, Morroe, Edward Berger, James Patrick. *Benny Carter: A Life in American Music, Volumes I & II.* New Jersey: Scarecrow Press, 1982.

Berlin, Edward A. *King of Ragtime: Scott Joplin and His Era.* New York: Oxford University Press, 1994.

Bernadac, Marie-Laure, and Paule Du Bouchet. *Picasso: Master of the New Idea.* New York: Harry N. Abrams, 1986.

Bernotas, Bob. *Top Brass: Interviews and Master Classes with Jazz's Leading Brass Players.* New York: Boptism Music Publishing, 2002.

Berton, Ralph. *Remembering Bix: A Memoir of the Jazz Age.* New York: Da Capo Press, 1974.

Bierley, Paul E. John Philip Sousa: *American Phenomenon.* New York: Warner Brothers Publications, 1973.

Bjorn, Lars, and Jim Gallart. *Before Motown: A History of Jazz in Detroit, 1920–1960.* Ann Arbor, MI: University of Michigan Press, 2001.

Blesh, Rudi. *Shining Trumpets.* London: Cassell & Co., Ltd., 1949.

Blesh, Rudi, and Harriet Janis. *They All Played Ragtime: The True Story of an American Music*. New York: Grove Press, 1959.

Brinkley, Douglas G., and Steven E. Ambrose. *The Mississippi and the Making of a Nation: From the Louisiana Purchase to Today*. Washington, DC: National Geographic Society, 2002.

Brooks, Tim. *Lost Sounds: Blacks and the Birth of the Recording Industry, 1890–1919*. Champaign, IL: University of Illinois Press, 2004.

Bryant, Clora, Buddy Collette, William Green, et al. *Central Avenue Sounds: Jazz in Los Angeles*. Berkley, CA: University of California Press. 1998.

Budds, Michael J. *Jazz in the Sixties: The Expansion of Musical Resources and Techniques*. Iowa City, IA: University of Iowa Press, 1990.

Busch, Jason T., Christopher Monkhouse, Janet L. Whitmore. *Currents of Change: Art and Life Along the Mississippi, 1850–1861*. Minneapolis, MN: Minneapolis Institute of Arts, 2004.

Carr, Roy. *A Century of Jazz*. London: Octopus Publishing Group Ltd., 1997.

Cartledge, Paul. *The Greeks: Crucible of Civilization*. London: BBC Worldwide Ltd., 2001.

Catalano, Nick. *Clifford Brown: The Life and Art of the Legendary Jazz Trumpeter*. New York: Oxford University Press, 2000.

Cheatham, Adolphus "Doc." *I Guess I'll Get The Papers and Go Home: The Life of Doc Cheatham*. London and New York: Cassell Press, 1995.

Chernoff, John Miller. *African Rhythm and African Sensibility: Aesthetics and Social Action in African Musical Idioms*. Chicago, IL: The University of Chicago Press, 1979.

Chilton, John. *Ride Red Ride: The Life of Henry "Red" Allen*. London and New York: Bayou Press, 1999.

Chilton, John. *Roy Eldridge: Little Jazz Giant*. London and New York: Continuum, 2002.

Chilton, John. *Who's Who of British Jazz*. New York: Cassell Press, 1997.

Chilton, John. *Who's Who of Jazz: Storyville to Swing Street*. U.S.: Chilton Book Co., 1978.

Claghorn, Charles Eugene. *Biographical Dictionary of Jazz*. New Jersey: Prentice Hall, Inc., 1982.

Clayton, Buck, and Nancy Elliot. *Buck Clayton's Jazz World*. Oxford, U.K.: Bayou Press, 1986.

Commager, Henry Steele. *Living History: The Civil War*. U.S.: Bobbs-Merrill Co., 1950.

Cone, James H. *The Spirituals and the Blues*. New York: Orbis Books, 1972.

Cook, John. *The Book of Positive Quotations*. Minneapolis, MN: Fairview Press, 1993.

Cooke, Mervyn. *Chronicle of Jazz*. London and New York: Thames & Hudson, 1998.

Dahl, Linda, *Stormy Weather*. New York: Pantheon Books/Limelight Editions, 1984.

Dance, Stanley. *The World of Count Basie*. New York: Da Capo, 1980.

Dance, Stanley. *The World of Duke Ellington*. New York: Da Capo, 1970.

Davis, Burke. *The Civil War*. New York: Barnes and Noble Books, 1960.

Davis, Francis. *The History of the Blues*. New York: Mojo Working Productions, 1995.

Davis, Miles, and Quincy Troupe. *Miles: The Autobiography*. New York: Simon and Schuster, 1990.

Deffa, Chip. *Voices of the Jazz Age*. Champaign, IL: University of Illinois Press, 1990.

Driggs, Frank, and Chuck Haddix. *Kansas City Jazz: From Ragtime to Bebop—A History*. New York: Oxford University Press, 2005.

Drinker, Sophie. *Music & Women*. New York: The Feminist Press, 1995.

Dupuis, Robert. *Bunny Berigan: Elusive Legend of Jazz*. Baton Rouge, LA: Louisiana State University Press, 1993.

Eliason, Robert E. *Keyed Bugles in the United States*. Washington, DC: Smithsonian Institution Press, 1972.

Ellis, Rex M. *With a Banjo on My Knee*. New York: Franklin Watts Library Edition, 2001.

Ehrlich, Eugene, and Marshall De Bruhl. *The International Thesaurus of Quotations*. New York: Harper Collins, 1996.

Erlewine, Michael, Vladimir Bogdanov, Chris Woodstra, et al. *All Music Guide to Jazz*. 3rd Edition. San Francisco: Miller Freeman Books, 1998.

Feather, Leonard, and Ira Gitler. *The Encyclopedia of Jazz in the Seventies*. New York: Da Capo Press, 1976.

Floyd Jr., Samuel A. *The Power of Black Music*. New York: Oxford University Press, 1995.

Foster, Pops, and Tom Stoddard. *The Autobiography of Pops Foster: New Orleans Jazzman*. San Francisco: Backbeat Books, 2005.

Gavin, James. *Deep in a Dream: The Long Night of Chet Baker*. New York: Knopf, 2002.

Giddens, Gary. *Rhythm-a-Ning: Jazz Tradition and Innovation*. New York: Da Capo Press, 1985.

Giddens, Gary. *Satchmo*. New York: Anchor Books, 1988.

Gioia, Ted. *West Coast Jazz: Modern Jazz in California, 1945–1960*. Berkley, CA: University of California Press, 1992.

Gitler, Ira. *The Masters of Bebop*. New York: Da Capo Press, 1966.

Gourse, Leslie. *Madame Jazz: Contemporary Women Instrumentalists*. New York: Oxford University Press, 1995.

Gourse, Leslie. *The Story of Joe Williams*. New York: Da Capo Press, 1985.

Guede, Alain. *Monsieur de Saint-George: Virtuoso Swordsman and Revolutionary— A Legendary Life Rediscovered*. Picador, New York: 2003.

Hadlock, Richard. *Jazz Masters of the '20s*. Cambridge, MA: Da Capo Press, 1988.

Handy, D. Antoinette. *The International Sweethearts of Rhythm: The Ladies Jazz Band from Piney Woods Country Life School*. Lanham, MD: The Scarecrow Press, 1998.

Hardie, Daniel, *The Loudest Trumpet: Buddy Bolden and The Early History of Jazz*, Lincoln, NE: iUniverse, 2000.

Hazeldine, Mike, Barry Martyn. *Bunk Johnson: Son of the Wanderer*. New Orleans: Jazzology Press, 2000.

Hill, Dick. *Sylvester Ahola: The Gloucester Gabriel*. New Jersey and London: The Scarecrow Press, Inc., 1993.

Hillman, Christopher. *Bunk Johnson*. Kent, U.K.: Spellmount Ltd., 1988.

Huyghe, Patrick. *Columbus Was Last*. New York: MJF Books, 1992.

Jason, David A., and Trebor Jay Tichenor. *Rags and Ragtime: A Musical History*. New York: Dover Publications, 1978.

Johnson, James Weldon, and Johnson, J. Rosamond. *The Books of American Negro Spirituals*. New York: Viking Press/Da Capo Press, 1925.

Jones, LeRoi. *Blues People*. New York: Quill/William Morrow, 1963.

Jones, Max, and John Chilton. *Louis: The Louis Armstrong Story*. Boston and Toronto: Little, Brown & Co., 1971.

Kenney, William Howland. *Chicago Jazz: A Cultural History, 1904–1930*. New York: Oxford University Press, 1993.

Kenney, William Howland. *Jazz on the River*. Chicago, IL: University of Chicago Press, 2005.

Kernfeld, Barry. *The New Grove Dictionary of Jazz*. New York: St. Martin's Press, 1994.

Klingaman, William K. *Abraham Lincoln and the Road to Emancipation, 1861–1865*. New York: Viking Penguin, 2001.

Koster, Rick. *Louisiana Music*. New York: Da Capo Press, 2002.

Lees, Gene. *Waiting for Dizzy*. New York: Oxford University Press. 1991.

Lees, Gene. *You Can't Steal a Gift*. New Haven, CT: Yale University Press, 2001.

Levinson, Peter. *Trumpet Blues: The Life of Harry James*. New York: Oxford University Press, 1999.

Lunardini, Christine. *What Every American Should Know About Women's History: 200 Events That Shaped Our Destiny*. Holbrook, MA: Adams Media Corporation, 1997.

Magee, Jefferey. *Fletcher Henderson and Big Band Jazz: The Uncrowned King of Swing*. Oxford University Press: 2005.

Marquis, Donald M. *In Search of Buddy Bolden: First Man of Jazz*. Baton Rouge, LA: Louisiana State University Press, 1978.

Masekela, Hugh, and D. Michael Cheers. *Still Grazing*. New York: Crown Publishers, 2004.

McPherson, James M. *The Negro's Civil War: How American Blacks Felt and Acted During the War for the Union*. New York: Vintage Civil War Library, 2003.

Menuhin, Yehudi, and Curtis W. Davis. *The Music of Man*. New York: Simon and Schuster, 1979.

Menzies. Gavin. *1421: The Year China Discovered America*. London: Transworld Publishers, 2002.

Miller, Marc H. *Louis Armstrong: A Cultural Legacy*. New York: The Queens Museum of Art, 1994.

Oliver, Paul. *The Story of the Blues*. Boston: Northeastern University Press, 1969 and 1997.

Ouaknin, Marc-Alain. *Mysteries of the Alphabet*. New York: Abbeville Press, 1999.

Panassie, Hugues. *Louis Armstrong*. New York: Da Capo, 1971.

Peress, Maurice. *Dvorak to Duke Ellington*. New York: Oxford University Press, 2004.

Reed, Tom. *The Black Music History of Los Angeles, Its Roots: A Classical Pictorial History of Black Music in Los Angeles from the 1920s to 1970.* Los Angeles: Black Accent LA Press, 1992.

Roberts, John Storm. *Latin Jazz: The First of the Fusions, 1880s to Today.* New York: Schirmer Books, 1999.

Roberts, J. M. *A Short History of the World.* New York: Oxford University Press, 1993.

Ramsey Jr., Frederic, and Charles E., Smith. *Jazzmen.* Orlando, FL: Harcourt Brace Jovanovich, 1939.

Rosen, Charles. *Piano Notes.* New York: Free Press, 2002.

Ruhlen, Merritt. *The Origin of Language: Tracing the Evolution of the Mother Tongue.* New York: John Wiley & Sons, 1994.

Sadie, Julie Anne, and Rhian Samuel. *The Norton-Grove Dictionary of Women Composers.* New York: Macmillan Press, 1995.

Sales, Grover. *Jazz: America's Classical Music.* Cambridge, MA: Da Capo Press, 1992.

Santelli, Robert, Holly George-Warren, and Jim Brown. *American Roots Music.* New York: Harry N. Abrams, 2001.

Schelsinger Jr., Arthur M. *The Almanac of American History.* New York: Barnes and Noble, 1993.

Schoenberg, Harold C. *The Great Pianists: From Mozart to the Present.* New York: Simon and Schuster, 1987.

Schuller, Gunther. *Early Jazz: Its Roots and Musical Development.* New York: Oxford University Press, 1968.

Schuller, Gunther. *The Swing Era.* New York: Oxford University Press, 1989.

Schmitt Pantel, Pauline. *A History of Women from Ancient Goddesses to Christian Saints,* London and Boston: Belknap Press/Harvard Press, 1992.

Shipton, Alyn. Fats Waller: *The Cheerful Little Earful.* London and New York: Continuum, 1988.

Shipton, Alyn. *Groovin' High: The Life of Dizzy Gillespie.* New York: Oxford University Press, 1999.

Sidran, Ben, Talking *Jazz: An Oral History.* New York: Da Capo Press, 1995.

Simon, George T. *The Big Bands.* 4th Edition. New York: Simon & Schuster/Macmillan, 1991.

Southern, Eileen. *The Music of Black Americans: A History.* New York: W. W. Norton, 1971.

Stewart, Rex. *Jazz Masters of the '30s,* New York: Da Capo, 1972.

Stone, Merlin. *When God Was a Woman.* New York: Barnes and Noble Books, 1976.

Sudhalter, Richard M. Lost Chords: *White Musicians and Their Contributions to Jazz, 1915 to 1945.* New York: Oxford University Press, 1999.

Tirro, Frank. *Jazz: A History.* New York: W.W. Norton, 1977.

Trotter, James M. *Music and Some Highly Musical People.* New York: Lee and Shepard Publishers, 1878.

Tucker, Sherrie. *Swing Shift: "All Girl" Bands of the 1940s.* Durham, NC: Duke University Press, 2000.

Van Sertima, Ivan. *They Came Before Columbus: The African Presence in Ancient America*. New York: Random House, 1976.

Ward, Geoffrey C., and Ken Burns. *Jazz: A History of America's Music*. New York: Knopf, 2000.

Whyatt, Bert. *Muggsy Spanier: The Lonesome Road*. Jazzology Press, 1995.

Williams, Martin. *Jazz Masters of New Orleans*. London and New York: Macmillan, 1967

Wright, Kai. *Soldiers of Freedom.* New York: Black Dog & Leventhal Publishers, 2002.

Yanow, Scott. *Trumpet Kings*. San Francisco: Backbeat Books, 2001.

Index

taping/studying as, 169, 170,
174-75, 176
transcribing as, 170
Trumpet section, jazz band, 151, 152,
153
components of, 151
cooperation of, 152, 156
flexibility of, 151-52
functions of, 151
intonation of, 152
lead player in, 151, 152, 153
phrases in, 152-53
solos in, 151, 152-53, 156
Trumpet soloists
in big bands, 157, 158, 159
in duets, 158
in small groups, 157-58, 159
in trumpet sections, 151, 152
Turre, Steve, 63
Tutankhamun, Pharaoh (King Tut),
xxiv, xxv
Two-step, xxvi, 15

"Up Jumped Spring," 60

*Valaida Snow: Queen of Trumpet
and Song*, 54
Valentine, Thomas "Kid," 193
Valves
history of, xxiv-xxv
techniques with, 193, 223
Vaughan, Sarah, 119
Vibrato, 155-56
Vocabulary, trumpet
Jazz Age, 195
Swing era, 195
Vocalists, 73-76

Waller, Fats, 113
Waltzes, xxvi
jazz origins and, 17
Washington, Grover, xix
Washingtonians, 194
"The Washington Post," 15
Watson, Bijon, 179
Watts, Jeff, 158
"Weary Blues," 33
Weather Report, xix
West Coast (cool) jazz, 210
"West End Blues," 31, 32, 33, 102,
141
What's Going On?, 65
"What's New," 197
"Wheatleigh Hall," 44
"When You're Smiling," 35
Whetsol, Arthur "Artie," 194
Whiteman, Paul, 29, 187, 188
"Who Me," 172
Wilder, Joe, 173

Williams, Charles Melvin "Cootie,"
xxi, 35, 135, 136, 147, 173, 197,
204, 205
Williams, Joe, 75
Williams, Mike, 151, 155, 175
Williams, Tony, 63, 64, 69
Winding, Kai, 129
Wolverines, 186-87, 190
Women
in early jazz, 50-51
historical contributions of, 49-
50
as historical musicians, 49-50
as jazz trumpeters, 51, 52-55
Woody Herman band, 51, 52
Work songs, xxvi, 16
influences on, 8
jazz origins and, 17, 82
origins of, 9-10
World War II, 46
Wynton Marsalis Quintet, 68

Yamaha trumpet, xv
Youngblood, 64
Young, Eugene "Snooky," 89, 113,
153, 155, 172, 173
Young, Lester, 75, 87, 88, 89, 158,
198
The Young Lions, 75
Young, Trummy, 83, 108